CW00506003

The
TAMING of the CREW

The story of a New Zealand family who
sold up and sailed away into the worst
winter storms for half a century

Michael Brown
&
Sue Neale-Brown

i

THE TAMING OF THE CREW
© Michael Brown & Sue Neale-Brown

First edition 1994
Random House (New Zealand Ltd)

Second edition 2014
Field Finder Publishers (Christchurch)
PO Box 1142, Christchurch, New Zealand
www.michaelbrownbooks.com
Cover and interior design by Renzie Hanham
ISBN: 978-1494918774

OTHER BOOKS BY MICHAEL BROWN:
Finding the Field
The Weaver's Apprentice
The Idiot Played Rachmaninov
The Weaver and the Abbey
Speaking Easy
Media Easy

To Andrew and Sam

Your mother and I believe that our sea journey with you was the most significant single event in our family life. You grew up so very fast.

Reading it again, 20 years after writing it down, has been sobering and astonishing. It's raw. We were not prepared for how it all looks from this older perspective. We had to grow up too.

You were tough little blighters, quick with body, quicker with tongue, and resistant to the rules and disciplines designed to keep you alive. You were also wonderful fun, true companions, and fellow travellers in the biggest sense. We admired you then, as we admire you now.

We hope you'll see this book as something to pass on to your children and grandchildren. Maybe you'll say to them, "Can you believe it? When my brother and I were little kids, we were taken to sea by parents who had romantic notions of cruising, and no idea what was actually going to happen."

May all your days be rich with adventure. Be into life.

With all our love
Mum and Dad

January 2014

Living arrangements on *Alderman*

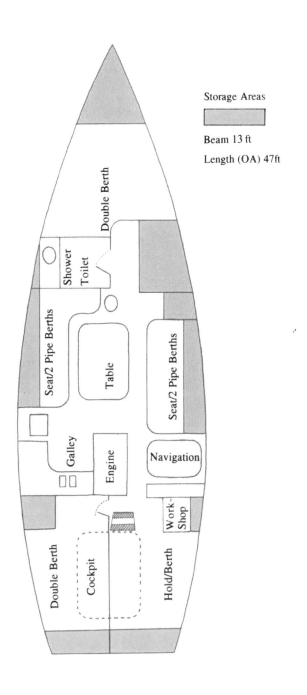

Storage Areas

Beam 13 ft

Length (OA) 47ft

Double Berth

Shower

Toilet

Seat/2 Pipe Berths

Table

Seat/2 Pipe Berths

Galley

Engine

Navigation

Work-Shop

Double Berth

Cockpit

Hold/Berth

Alderman. *A 47 foot, steel, cutter-rigged sloop.*
On Lyttelton Harbour where we began what was
meant to be a dream romantic cruise.

"It might be all right for
families to stick together, but actually
living on top of one another is, well, almost
against the laws of nature."

Columnist Frank Cook

PART ONE

1

There were a lot of people keen to see us leave town. *Alderman's* deck dropped closer to the water with the swarm of friends and family on board. It also dropped with the tide so that the line of faces we knew so well looked down on us.

I felt the pressure of four years of preparation and saw everyone through a tunnel. So I occupied myself checking rigging, lifebuoys, lashings, and a score of obscure objects already looked at so many times they should have been check-worn.

I forgot to hoist the New Zealand flag.

Sue was outwardly calm and collected, but I knew the signs: she was talking slightly too fast and too much as she took a stream of visitors through the living arrangements below.

Alderman is a steel, cutter-rigged sloop, pushing aside fourteen tons of water. She's flush-decked, which means there's nothing substantial above deck level except the mast and the doghouse. She's 14.3 metres long, though 2.1 metres of that is the imposing bowsprit and the seat that curves out over the stern - the so-called Coruba seat. According to the dream, we would sit on it, drifting through balmy days and starry nights, with charged glasses and raised pinkies.

Yeah, right.

From the cockpit, the companionway takes you below, facing forward. Then the aft double cabin is on the left (it doubles as a brig for the boys). On the right is the workshop, behind is the hold. Ahead there's the main cabin living area with table, seats, galley, navigation desk, four bunks and bookshelves. Even further towards the bow is the shower and antique toilet with leather valves. And right up in the bow is the for'd double cabin.

Sue was fielding questions about how we expected to cope with two high-octane boys in such a small space. Not that ten-year-old Andrew looked it at the time. Mr Laid Back Cool was explaining the intricacies of the new fishing rod to friends, comparing the size of expected fish fillets with the length of *Alderman.*

Sam, six years old, was just the opposite - over-cooked, showing off on the free end of the spinnaker halyard. Darwin was on to something when he said we were not long down from the trees. Several people questioned aloud whether Sam would survive the trip.

Yes, funny, but we did not miss the creased foreheads on some friends and relatives as they looked at Andrew and Sam.

The sky darkened slightly, the southwesterly stayed feather-light. A new southerly front was expected and when the worst was past we planned to ride north on its back.

Aileen and Dave McDonald and Dave Vincent, our crew for the first passage to Auckland, stowed their gear. Dave McDonald promptly went into a huddle with the others, trying to persuade them to pretend they'd changed their minds and weren't going.

Well-wishers began to climb up to the landing. My mother got stuck on the way up and had to be pushed. Sam called out jokes to a friend waiting nearby in a trailer sailer, our escort down the harbour. There were hugs, kisses and tears. People passed or threw presents down to us: fruit, chocolate bars, cake and a huge bouquet of fresh herbs for the galley.

It all became unreal. I was overcome by the send-off and found it difficult to talk to anyone. Sue came up and stood beside me, a little pale. Aileen and the two Daves stood ready. I looked at Andrew and Sam, suddenly struck by their fragility. I was certain they knew at some level that they were beginning something that would change their lives. Of course they had little or no idea how. Family conferences had not advanced Sam's expectations much beyond buried treasure, pirates and how to turn Jaws into cat food.

"Boys, it's time to wake up Frankie," I said.

The last streamers break as we pull away from the jetty in Lyttelton
Harbour. As well as the four of us, Dave and Aileen McDonald
and Davey Vincent.

"I will. It's my turn!" they shouted. They crammed into the companionway, pushing and shoving.

"Stop it." My tension jumped to the fore. "Hop into the aft cabin, sort it out and come back."

The boys disappeared while people above us grinned and shook their heads. One or two just shook their heads. They might as well have held up signs that said, "You'll be stir crazy in a week." The boys returned swiftly with a negotiated settlement. Andrew threw on the master switches and the auxiliary generator, Sam turned the key, Frankie stirred and whirred then thumped expectantly under us like a dog wagging its tail.

The lines slid and splashed and coiled. Streamers fell and parted and fell again, then we were sliding away. Sam tried to pass his lungs through the foghorn, but could not drown the shouts of encouragement and farewell.

Alderman suddenly seemed very small.

Just beyond the inner harbour, we raised the main and let out the genoa. A mile down the main harbor, as our escort yacht fell behind, a winch handle fell apart. It was the first of a series of lessons in trust. Before a month was up, we would learn to put our trust in nothing - gear, charts, systems, experts of all persuasions and convictions - nothing except our own immediate senses.

And even those became suspect.

Leaving Lyttleton Harbour. I was suddenly aware that we would be a small vessel in a very large ocean, but still had no idea what that ocean was going to do to us.

3

That night, we cheated. Following the advice of other cruising yachties, we cut round to a quiet, almost deserted bay to anchor and get used to each other in the confined space.

At first, *Alderman* stirred moodily at anchor, as if keen to be getting on with it. Then the southerly died, the anchor chain straightened and stood on end, and the rain came. We dined elegantly on chicken casserole, salad and potatoes, all spiced with suppressed excitement and nervousness.

Andrew seemed impossibly calm. Sam was subdued - a rare condition. Both began diaries, Andrew announcing that no one would be able to look at his because he was, "an individual with rights to privacy". *The Diary of Adrian Mole* had a lot to answer for. He'd already read it four times and it wouldn't be long before he demanded his right to have pimples.

We talked quietly through routines, set cooking rosters, planned watches. We went through safety procedures, the ship's manual and the GPS navigation system. I flourished the elaborate watch log I had drawn up. Watch crew were to make entries every hour on every imaginable subject ranging from oil pressure to wind direction. Aileen looked at it thoughtfully, but mercifully said nothing. It must have seemed like sailing instructions for the sixth fleet. She and Dave were building their own vessel and had been offshore before.

We agreed that to avoid confusion between the Daves, the Vincent version would hereinafter be known as Davey, as in Crocket.

We read aloud some of the letters Sam's classmates had written us, thanking us for a visit to *Alderman*. *Dear Mr and Mrs Brown*, wrote Amelia, *I want to thank you for showing me around Alderman. I hope you have a nice time and catch ten fish.* Also: *I liked the back of Alderman. Yours sincerely, Tara.* And Belinda said: *I hope you have a good time. Have a good Easter. I love you. You are sweet. Have a nice trip. Goodbye.*

The voice of Wellington Radio crackled out of the long range SSB, informing us that the forecast was now for a light southerly. Fifteen knots, Perfect. It would push us up the east coast towards Auckland, 900 nautical miles miles to the north.

So we thought.

As evening closed in, so did the clouds, lying like sodden blankets on the hills. The rain fell in miserly, thin droplets that hardly disturbed the water's sheen and made no sound on the hatch covers over our heads. We slept.

In the morning we would begin the journey up New Zealand's east coast to Auckland, to join the annual yacht regatta to Tonga.

The dream had started five years earlier.

It's not as if we had had nothing to do. I was working as a reporter. Sue ran a toy library. We were making a living and raising the boys. Andrew was six, and even then demanding privacy when he look his girlfriend hand-in-hand down the hall to play in his bedroom. Sam, then two, was only just out of nappies - a detail I remember because it was about the time he crossed his legs and announced, "God help us, I've done a pooh."

Life was busy enough, stretched by endless, demanding trivia. Busy but not full. The days were like a series of different meals smothered in the same dark sauce.

The daily newspaper thumped on the lawn filled with the agonies of spiralling recession. My own items for television news did the same. Whenever possible I made 'good news' feature stories, about initiative and courage and spirit. But mostly my work just poured more lead for the recession. New Zealand's cradle-to-grave social security system seemed to be teetering on its own graveside. There was much talk of saving for the hard times ahead, for security, for retirement. For death. And we had only reached forty.

It was Sue who triggered the dream.

Like me she would have said yes to a bigger house and better car if they had been handed to us on a plate. But they weren't important enough to become an ambition. Even the toy library she ran wasn't enough to fill the niggling ache for something more challenging.

"We've got to do something beyond this," she said.

I agreed and some weeks later, as the boys slept, we took a short walk outside the house. I held Sue's hand, breathed in deeply and felt a delicious surge of anticipation beyond anything I'd had for years. We stopped under a street lamp.

"I keep getting this picture," I said. "I keep seeing us sailing. Overseas, with the boys." Sue stopped and looked at me. I don't recall her exact reply, but her expression boiled down to one word.

Snap.

Two things were immediately obvious. To ship out we would have to sell the house. And being totally ignorant of the sea, we would have to go to classes. I had capsized dinghies as a teenager, Sue had followed power boats on water skis, and that was it.

We had no idea just how steep the learning curve would be. The academic work was just the beginning, and that took two years: boatmaster, coastal yachtmaster, ocean yachtmaster navigation. Then we saw an advertisement in a boating magazine for a steel cutter with a strange name. *Alderman.* A pretentious name, we thought. But when we closed the magazine, her picture wouldn't vanish.

What did vanish, when we finally stepped on board, was our uncertainty. We were still abysmally ignorant of the science of sailing and the technicalities of an ocean-going yacht. But, as we sat below and looked at each other, we both nodded. We touched the fine strong curve of the deck beams above us. We stroked the table made from the oak tree that grew on the property where she was built. One of us, I don't remember who, said, "This is the one."

The following sail and survey rubber-stamped the decision.

With 20-20 hindsight, we now know we were either fantastically lucky or that our gut instincts were in good order. *Alderman* had been built for an expedition to Cape Horn and Patagonia. She was fast, safe and proven, with steel appeal for land lubbers nervous of coral. And she had something more than her materials, design and sailing characteristics - she had personality. Months after we bought her, previous owner Geoff Stone wrote us many pages of advice on how we could make improvements. The last item on the last page was the most eloquent. *Sell her back to me and give me back my soul.*

We moved to a house owned by the bank, began many of Geoff's suggestions and sailed as often as possible. On Lyttelton Harbour we trumpeted our inexperience: throwing an entire mooring line when berthing, changing tack with the boom locked by the gybe preventer, even dropping two anchors on one spot. It doesn't get more basic than that. Even as I write this I can hear the laughter of experienced seafarers.

And, to the annoyance and alarm of experienced racers, I 'barged' the start line. The sight of *Alderman's* huge bowsprit bearing down on them caused strong men to go pale and shriek orders as they reached for the protest flag.

We learned. The boys learned. We could hardly punish them for mistakes, but we heavily discouraged their making the same mistake twice. That policy would save us from disaster more than once. We did the overnight trip to the Marlborough Sounds, cruised there for three weeks and learned some more.

The months counted down towards departure.

We discovered that many people disapproved of taking small children to sea in a yacht. One of those critics was Andrew. He was consistently seasick, classmates accused him of being 'posh' for having a boat, and he took in one too many family discussions about the remote possibility of striking a storm. So he began a campaign.

"You don't know what will happen," he argued.

"No. Of course not."

"No one can know," he persued. "I'm afraid, and it's not right for a child to be afraid of the unknown." Andrew, on a campaign, was not to be taken lightly. On this journey he would hone his tongue as sharply as his sailing skills.

Sue was the one who took the brunt of the criticism.

"How can you do this to young children?" some friends and relatives said. The implication was of manslaughter waiting to happen. "How can you expose them to such a risk with no house and no savings to come back to?" Even our babysitter joined the queue. She said, "I must speak up about this. Andrew is terribly unhappy and he says you're ignoring his feelings."

To Sue's incredulity others said, "Sue, you're not being strong enough. You're not standing up to him (meaning me)." One said, "He's pulling your strings and you're jumping." This to my wife, who once offered to take me out the back and beat the shit out of me (I declined), and who has to my knowledge beaten off three over-heated males with straight rights to the stomach and a knee to the groin.

"It's all very well cruising in the islands with children," we heard, "but you're starting them off in the roaring forties and taking them up one of the worst coasts in the world." A good point. If we had enough money left, we might have considered flying the boys further north.

But one day we met up with a couple who had been cruising with their children. More to the point, they were among the very few who had taken youngsters on the ocean passages.

"How old are your children?" they asked. We told them. And they said, "Perfect. Take them now, before they become teenagers and don't want to be stuck on a crummy boat with their crummy parents."

"But what about the effect on the children?"

"They'll grow up overnight," was the reply. "Take them. They'll come back way ahead of their peers, they'll even do better at school work than if they stayed in class."

A bit optimistic, we thought, but a welcome encouragement.

The months became weeks, then days. We gave the house back to the bank and moved on to *Alderman* with a frenzy of final preparations. The checklist had some 600 items. I was way too intense and obsessively over-organised - and knew it, but didn't know how else to compensate for my inexperience.

The open criticism faded in the last days. Our doubts about the children did not. And yet we knew that right or wrong, on April the twenty-fifth, we would leave for Auckland, Tonga and Fiji. And we would leave as a family.

2

Sunday, 26 April

For years we had imagined it. It should have been blue sky, gentle swells, and dolphins frolicking in the water. Instead it was grey sky, greasy swells and, shortly, the scrambled eggs we'd had for breakfast.

"Up anchor," I ordered with ringing enthusiasm. Then, "Up sail."

"What for?" Davey said. "There's no wind."

So we motored out to the heads where a nor'wester proved me right. Frankie was put to sleep and we gave *Alderman* over to Johnny, the windvane automatic steering system attached to the tiller.

Alderman tilted, tucking up into the breeze under full sail, hissing out into the first of the swells between us and East Cape. We raised the New Zealand flag. The boys and I went forward into the bowsprit, rising and falling over the water. All the work and worry of preparation was fading in the wake, and the exhilaration of the unknown ahead tingled in our spines.

"Yeeeeeeeee ... haaaaaaah!" I yelled at the sea and sky.

"Yeeeeeeeee ... haaaaaaah!" yelled the boys, while down below, Sue put pre-cooked, savoury meatballs out to thaw for the next hearty meal.

Within minutes, Andrew said thoughtfully, "My state of health leaves room for improvement."

In an hour there was a continuous display of backsides large and small at the rail as we recycled our breakfasts into the sea, demonstrating that what goes down must come up, and, in defiance of science, it is possible to get out more than you put in.

The barometer sank. The predicted southerly was still lurking over the horizon, sending a messenger swell ahead. It was going to be anything but light when it arrived. In the meantime, the nor'wester rough-housed the southerly roll, turning what should have been a manageable swell into an unpredictable, plunging, skewing, corkscrewing slop. *Alderman* coped easily, but we didn't. We attached the windsteer to the tiller and lay at odd angles around the cockpit. Only the very first line of my immaculately prepared watch log was filled in correctly. No one was well enough to focus on the attached pen, let alone push it across the page.

Except Sue. She seemed immune to seasickness. While everyone else imitated the crew of the *Marie Celeste*, Sue could easily go below and do a fry up.

Not that she was a sadist. She did it on request, because even those of us with wax complexions had bursts of hunger. In fact, her invulnerable inner ear and willingness to work the galley in a sea had a lot to do with the real pecking order on board. Once, she spent two hours turning out a shepherd's pie. Davey wolfed some down and promptly turned into a frog. He sat there with thin lips and sagging jowls, sucking air through his teeth and looking imminent.

"You can't," Sue said matter-of-factly.

Davey took a deep breath. "OK."

"It's not decent. Not for an hour at least."

An hour later, Davey checked his watch, nodded and had an emphatic word with the sea. Andrew and Sam argued about whether the word was *Biiiill, Beeeert,* or *Huuuuey.*

After throwing up once, Sam was then immune for the entire expedition. He seemed to take the rough seas in his stride. He even had the nerve to enjoy it. And on that first ghastly day, he was bouncy, cheerful and helpful to his stricken elders and betters.

"Need anything, Dad?"

"Noooo..." I moaned. It was like skiing a snow slope on your nose and having a pint-sized ace swish to a stop and ask if you're OK.

The southerly came with albatrosses. From then on they would open the barn doors for every gale, wheeling in on the first gusts. The water colour turned to pinched grey. We took in two reefs on the main, rolled up some of the furling headsail and ploughed on with little change in speed. For an hour, wind speed stayed on 20 to 25 knots. Then it wound up steadily, and by nightfall it was pushing 30 knots out of the freezer.

We took in the last reef on the main, leaving the smallest possible area of sail.

Andrew was continually sick. He asked for a mattress to be brought up into the doghouse, moved in with lifeline still clipped on, and declared that it was impossible for him to go below. Against my better judgement, I let him stay for the night. In the early evening, Sam was there beside him, playing, talking to us, and to my surprise asking Andrew if there was anything he could bring him.

It suddenly occurred to me that neither boy had complained or whined once. I mentioned it to Sue and she nodded and smiled. She had noticed.

We also discovered what a fine choice we had made for crew.

Davey, Dave and Aileen were all sick, but they dragged themselves into the cockpit with bloodless skins and sagging jaws, working their watches, making themselves function. Aileen was the worst hit. Once when she turned up for her watch, Sue offered to take her place. Aileen refused. It took her some time to refuse because she kept breaking off to exercise her stomach.

"No... *Biiill...* I'm going to be... *Berrrrt... Huuueeey...* just fine, thank you." But when she became so ill she couldn't lift her head, there was no choice. She stayed in her berth.

9

The sea built up. The motion became violent. Spray began to slash across the cockpit. We put two crew on for each watch, one lying in the doghouse with Andrew, on standby. I pulled out the hand-held anenometer. Thirty-five knots.

"Sue," I shouted incredulously, "this is a gale!"

Sue gaped at me, then at the boys. Talking about the possibility was one thing, having it happen on the first day was another.

"How could it happen so soon?" she demanded.

I stared at the anemometer. With the reading taken so close to the waves, the figure was probably conservative. And yet part of both of us welcomed the gale. This, I told myself, is what it's all about. And *Alderman*, although battered, was driving strongly and in easy control – she felt safe.

Sue went below and came back with a dish. "Savoury meatballs, anyone?

The cockpit rang with cries of horror.

That long night was the most uncomfortable any of us had faced. On my watch, I heard something strange and back then had no explanation for it - a woman's voice calling to me on the wind. From the port quarter. It was an unfamiliar voice; very clear and close. I peered hard out over the waves, blinking my eyes against the weather, wondering if another vessel was closing on us.

No. So it was impossible. And yet every few minutes I heard it again.

Aileen, on watch with me, clearly wasn't hearing it. I scowled to myself and didn't mention it to anyone. I should have. I would discover later that I wasn't alone in hearing things.

Early in the morning Dave called me urgently up on deck. One glance at the main and I knew we could no longer head for East Cape. A long tear. The reefing outhaul had come loose and all the strain had come onto a single reefing point. In my ignorance I had tied it without enough give – and something had to. There was now a 60 centimetre rip that could only get worse, and since it was on the deepest reefing line, the entire sail was now useless. We had paid a small fortune for a new main just to lessen the odds of this happening.

"Is this a storm, Dad?" Andrew's dark eyes and pale face looked at me from the depths of a sleeping bag in the doghouse. Being sick never affected his hearing.

"No, no," I said. "It's a gale. A small one. Are you worried?"

"No," he said quickly and lightly, and turned away to face for'd. I put a hand on his shoulder.

We dropped the sail completely and ran up the storm trisail. No, not a run, more of a lurching walk; practising the manoeuvre in the harbor hadn't prepared us for hoisting it in heavy seas. Then, regretfully, feeling cheated, we swung the bowsprit west and ran for Cook Strait. Wellington was the closest downwind port and it would take us most of 24 hours to get there.

Yet, here was that feeling again. Part of me felt just fine. A gale, I thought, we're coping with a gale. We're doing OK. I know, experienced sailors would laugh.

Cook Strait itself was merciful - something of a surprise, because wind masses that otherwise run unchecked around the bottom of the planet usually cram through the Strait instead of going over the Southern Alps.

The southerly wound down. We reached Wellington Heads at two in the morning in easy conditions and tiptoed through the light system. We berthed at five. Exhaustion dropped some of us as if we had been mugged, but Sue and Davey were so tired they couldn't sleep and wandered through the streets of Wellington at an hour when only bits of paper blow about.

At eight o'clock I warmed up the SSB and checked in with Ian and Glenys Duff back home. Their voices had already become a lifeline to us, a moment of warmth when all about us was cold and bleak. For now, though, it felt good to be able to say that we had come through a gale safely with only a torn sail to show for it.

The day passed swiftly. We were high on nervous energy, lack of food and the knowledge that we had come through the gale to tell the tale. The sail was mended - the sail maker at Hoods pointed out where we'd gone wrong and I went back to *Alderman* to change the reefing system. My Aunt Francis and Uncle Harry turned up at the wharf, offering refreshments and decontamination in a hot shower. We accepted their hospitality.

Later, we went to a restaurant. Back on board, the savoury meatballs sulked in their sauce.

By five in the evening, we were ready to go back to sea. The forecast could not have been better: a light northerly now to get us out into Cook Strait again and around Cape Palliser, then a 15 knot southerly to carry us north along the Wairarapa coast to East Cape.

Southerly 15 knots. I remember the exact words. I'll never forget them.

Before we left we met Dave, the skipper of *Agio*, a ketch also bound for Cape Palliser. From there they would be going directly to Fiji. They too were delighted with the forecast, expecting perfect sailing conditions. Like us they were in fine, high spirits and we agreed to keep in touch for the first few days. Our Dave spent half an hour on board *Agio* to give last-minute advice about their ham radio.

As ours had done, the families and friends of *Agio*'s crew farewelled them with a chorus of shouts as they bore away from the landing. As they glided past us, the faces of skipper and crew were alight with enthusiasm and anticipation. We added our cheers and Sam sent his with the foghorn.

By the time we slipped away to follow, darkness was falling. *Agio* was out of sight. And, though we didn't know it then, a third vessel, *Navigator*, was already out there, around Cape Palliser and starting to push north along the infamous Wairarapa coast - all of us seduced by the forecast.

3

There was no starter northerly. No wind at all. We slid across a dark mirror from the inner harbour to the Wellington Heads. There, the roll from the south was high and silky black and played tricks with the leading lights. More experienced sailors would have read a lot into that swell and turned back.

The southerly came early, at first light and easy, sliding over the swell. That was no concern, we told ourselves. We could still make Cape Palliser on a tight reach. The long, even swell was predictable and even exhilarating.

When the wind rose to 20 knots, we told ourselves that since we were in Cook Strait, a known wind tunnel, we had to expect it to be a little more brisk than the forecast. Sue and Aileen went forward to reef down, finding the stiff new cloth hard on cold fingers.

By nine o'clock we had 25 knots. Then we all had the same thought. Could it possibly happen again? Another gale? No, surely not. Even with all the ills of an under-manned, under-resourced weather office, a 15 knot forecast could not become a gale twice in a row. Could it? And in any case, once around Cape Palliser we would be going with wind and swell. I called Wellington Radio for an update, but there was no answer. No surprise there; even at the end of scheduled forecasts, when the duty officer signed off saying they would be listening on various frequencies, they never answered.

So. Decision time. On the port bow, Palliser light was beckoning steadily, two white winks every 20 seconds. No sweat, as long as the blow didn't puff its cheeks out any more.

We kept going.

At Palliser it was 30 knots, and then it was too late. If we turned around on a full gale we would have a hungry lee shore waiting for us all the way back to Wellington. No, we were past the point of no return. Even so, we kept going east rather than make an immediate turn to the north. If the southerly dervishes were to hang a little east we would get a lee shore anyway.

The wind speed rose relentlessly. Not gusty – a perfectly steady climb - and somehow that was unnerving.

By midnight, we knew we were in for something serious. Even in the darkness that was obvious. The moaning in the wires made the gale of two days ago seem like a breeze. Under the spreader lights we could see white spume breaking off the wave tops and reaching out to us. Not being able to judge distance in the dark we couldn't tell the height of the swells, but our hearts beat faster looking at them.

Even so, jocular humour increased. Many rude comments were made about the neglected log. Sue, as first-aid officer, got complaints that my red tape requirements were inducing myopia, nausea and paranoid schizophrenia. And did she have a pill for all that?

Davey and Aileen became very ill. Aileen couldn't move her head or even try to talk apart from the occasional murmur that she was afraid she might not die. Dave took over the tiller and stayed there. He seemed exhilarated by the conditions.

Every time Sue passed through the main cabin, she sniffed suspiciously, thinking she could smell vomit. Then she set about tracking down the stench.

The savoury meatballs were given a hasty burial at sea.

I tried to call *Agio*, somewhere out ahead of us. Or maybe they had turned back. There was no answer on VHF or SSB.

Below, Sam was showing the first signs of fear. In the gale off the South Island, he'd not shown a qualm. But he knew this was in a different league, probably by picking up our fear. He didn't say a word or utter even a whimper, but followed Sue like a bright-eyed shadow. She took him into the berth in the hold, and they lay together and murmured to each other. The hold berth became one of the coveted positions on passage; it was low and close to the stern where the motion was easiest.

We angled further north and the violence eased marginally. All of us felt numb. It was hard to act. Something as simple as having a piss took serious contemplation because it was hard even to think. I had mentally rehearsed the procedure for a big blow and even in that state I could have recited the list, but I was slowed down by my own disbelief. I couldn't accept that the faint possibility we had carefully talked over with the boys was becoming a reality. So soon.

We decided, and I still don't know why, that the conditions were too heavy for Johnny windvane. So we continued struggling with the tiller.

I was below when we broached.

It was always a possibility. Going too fast down the waves decreased stability and there was a secondary swell on the starboard quarter continually shoving us off line. One wave skewed us, the second hit full on the side, pushing us over well past the comfort level. With a broach, the danger is that the vessel will dip the mast then barrel roll the full 360 degrees, still side on to the next wave. I scrambled aft and into the cockpit where Davey was struggling with the tiller.

"Sorry, boss," he said. Strange to find time for the courtesies of life, when the life is at risk.

We waited an age for the bow to swing back downwind and for the stays'l to stop flogging like a hundred stock-whips. The main would have to come down completely. That meant crawling forward on a bronco deck under riot-hoses. I considered announcing that it wasn't safe to go forward and the stays'l could bloody well flog to death. But we were going fast, far too fast. Every now and then the bowsprit probed a wave ahead as another tickled the weather cloth at the stern.

That's the first time I became really afraid. It seemed unlikely that a wave could cave us in, but many a strong vessel has been wrecked by pitch-poling - not the sideways barrel roll, but a forward roll, end over mast over end. Worse, some vessels simply sail, bow first, down into Davey Jones' emerald mine and are never seen again.

I turned on the spreader lights, illuminating the nightmare on deck and treating myself to another surge of fear.

"I'll do it," Davey offered.

Personal crisis time. I was skipper, but fear froze my muscles. In my head it boiled down to this: if I let Davey do what I was too afraid to do, then I shouldn't be in charge of other peoples' lives. I would have had to let the whole dream go when we reached Auckland.

Persuading my feet and hands to listen to my instructions was one of the hardest things I've ever done. But soon they did listen, and Davey and I crawled forward, dragging harness clips along the jack stays. I don't know if he ever knew just how afraid I was. He will when he reads this.

We hauled on the cloth with frozen fingers. The wind pressure forced it against the mast but turning *Alderman* into the weather to ease that pressure was begging for a catastrophic roll. Eventually we jerked it down and Davey climbed two metres to secure the halyard. Two metres. Normally, that would be nothing. In these conditions it was like loading himself into a slinghsot. But he had the strength and held on safely.

Abruptly, my fear lifted - even though we were still forward and exposed.

We started laughing. It was beyond bad, as if we were in a nightmare and would soon be tossing off the blankets. We chortled inanely while the spray lashed us like a demented cat-o'-nine-tails. When he came down from the mast I even offered to show him a fast way to tie a bowline – a deliberately absurd piece of timing which reduced both of us to helpless mirth. We crawled back, giggling, arriving at the safetly of the cockpit with a sense of triumph over the elements.

Now we had no sail up. Nothing.

"We're doing eight knots," Dave McDonald shouted.

Hardly believing, we watched the motion and the log.

Fourteen tons of heavy-displacement steel, and she was averaging seven knots with not a stitch of cloth up. Dave held her straight for now, but the seas were rising. No one discussed raising the storm sails. It was quite obvious we couldn't risk any greater speed. She was riding well, but quite fast enough down the grey slopes. So, no storm sails. And no storm drogue. That would be a last card. The slower we went, the more waves we would take over the back.

A delicate balancing act.

After a while one or two went below to rest. I tried calling *Agio* again. But all I heard was the crackling, fizzing, long-range static. I gave it up and returned to the cockpit.

"Dad?" It was Andrew. Still in the doghouse, he hadn't moved or spoken for hours.

"Andrew, you'll have to go below. It's not safe up here any more." Beside me, Dave nodded approval.

"I can't, I'll be sick."

I looked at Andrew closely. He didn't seem too scared. I didn't understand it. If ever a ten-year-old had a right to he scared out of his wits it was now. "You all right?"

"Yes, but I can't go below. I'm just going to keep throwing up."

"It's not safe up here any more. We could get pooped." That was only part of the reason. I didn't want to be distracted by worrying about him. In fact, if I had listened to my own words, I would have looked harder at an uncovered air vent in the doghouse. That oversight was going to cost dearly. I also didn't check that the cockpit hatches were latched. Oversight number two. Maybe my brain was slowed by exhaustion. Maybe I just couldn't contemplate the possibility that the conditions could get any worse.

"Dad? This is a full storm, isn't it?"

"I think so. I can't check the wind speed right now." Officially, 48 knots made it a storm. It was a lot more than that now, but there was too much horizontal water in the air for a check with the hand-held anemometer.

More hindsight - too much chit chat with Andrew. I had yet to learn that in crisis time, I should be giving clear orders, not explaining them, leaving room for argument. But Andrew nodded matter-of-factly, swallowed hard, and manoeuvred himself below. I shook my head. I was more afraid than he was.

Almost immediately, a wave broke over the rail, poured into the cockpit, forced the starb'd hatch and poured through onto the hold berth. Faintly through the noise, I heard a shout of protest from below as Sue and Sam were drenched. They secured the hatch.

I still didn't think about the air vent in the doghouse.

That night I discovered that either we were all raving lunatics or we were all on to a strange phenomenon of the sea. The five adults on board were not usually given to fanciful flights of imagination but we were hearing things that were patently impossible. Between us we heard a voice calling my name, a full male choir in a cathedral, secretive whispers, a high-pitched shrieking as if by a tortured man, a yapping pack of dogs followed by a drawn-out, hair-tingling howl that silenced the dogs. Not all had been heard in bad weather, but now that the storm was building up, our ears were playing more and more tricks. Our heads needed reefing down.

Sometime in the morning, *Alderman* lurched mightily, throwing Aileen head first from the coaming into the cockpit. At first, her face was heading for the sharp iron edges on the gas tanks, but her harness turned her in mid flight, landing her on her back on the tiller. Davey lost control of the tiller as *Alderman* swung sharply to a wave on the starboard quarter. As he struggled to regain control, he yelled for help. Dave manoeuvred Aileen below. She spent the next two days with a big swelling over one kidney, in a lot of pain and quietly frightened of internal damage.

I was angry about the difference between the forecast and the weather. And I wanted someone to know about it. At two in the morning, I went below to try to raise Wellington Radio. To my amazement, I succeeded immediately.

But I never did get to make a complaint.

"Alderman, what is your position?" Wellington Radio demanded. The crisp urgency in the voice stalled everything on my lips. I read the answer off the GPS screen, numbers indicating that we were 30 miles east of the Wairarapa coast.

"Have you activated your EPIRB?"

"No we haven't... " I was flustered. " ... stand by, I'll check it's not been done accidentally." The EPIRB is a floatable radio distress beacon. I came back to reaffirm that we hadn't. Around me, bodies stirred in their berths. Heads up, eyes staring, ears open.

"No, not activated."

"We have an EPIRB activation twenty miles south of your position," Wellington said. *"Do you know of any vessels in your area?"*

I felt a sudden chill round the face and throat and brought the mike slowly back up. "Yes, Wellington. The *Agio* ... the *Agio* ... Alpha, Golf, India, Oscar ... left Wellington 1700 hours last night bound for Fiji."

"Describe her please. Over."

I did, then asked Wellington to confirm that the EPIRB activation was to the south. They did. Which meant that the 20 miles between us and *Agio* might as well have been twenty thousand.

"We can't get there," I told Wellington. "We have fifty knots from the south and at least five metre waves. We wouldn't make it." I was guessing at both the figures. If I had been able to see the real size of the waves, my voice might have carried a note of hysteria.

"No, we're not expecting it," was the curt reply. *"We have an Orion on the way to look for them. You may see green flares."* I thought of the *Agio* crew trying to get into a liferaft in this sea. And if they had succeeded at that, they would now be going through their own personal hell.

I was to discover later that Search and Rescue had already assumed the EPIRB

16

to be *Alderman's* and had contacted our relatives back home. They were expecting bad news about us.

Hours on, we saw flashes of green on the horizon to the south.

At dawn, the full power of the storm slowly revealed itself: great grey mountains that scorned my estimate of five metres. In the half light, it was as if the snow-capped Southern Alps had marched in ranks on to the sea and wheeled northward to grind us under. Albatross with wing spans of four metres shot by like jets while demons shrieked in the rigging. For a while I was too stunned to notice the change in Dave McDonald.

He was still on the tiller. He'd been there all night, refusing to part from it. Now, all the muscles in the upper part of his face seemed to be working to keep his eyes open. But he was on an adrenalin high, steering in perfect control, knowing he'd never had any experience like this and might never again. But now he was desperately tired and agreed reluctantly to give up his shift. I went below to wake Davey. He was still fully dressed - weather gear, harness and boots - in that cold, exhausted, rest-deprived state that is to sleep what permafrost is to the earth.

"Davey, you're on. You've got some big seas out there. Fifteen metres."

"Don't be stupid," Davey mumbled. He struggled off the berth and swung up the companionway.

"Morning," Dave greeted him from the tiller. We watched with anticipation as the sleeper awoke to the scene around him. Davey blinked and screwed up his eyes as he focused. His jaw sagged.

"Christ!" he said and promptly climbed back down below. He went back to his berth, hung on and muttered, "I've gotta psych myself up."

When he had recovered, four of us measured the moving mountains with our eyes, comparing with the size of the mast. That was 15 metres, and some of those wave tops were much higher than that. The wind played the stays like loose violin strings and the pitch was rising.

Sam chose that moment to emerge. We waited, half expecting a cry of terror when he saw the waves, but he was inexplicably calm.

"Wow, fifteen metres," he said in the same tone he used when he watched a news item about execution and declared, "Execution! That's bad luck!"

More waves were breaking over the weather cloth. The seas were more confused, the tiller harder to handle. We decided to try setting the windvane, to see if it would work with no sail up at all. But when we dropped the oar into the violent water, we couldn't slot it home. Either we had to give up or someone would have to go down the back of the stern.

Davey went down. Watching him disappear over the stern between us and the unpredictable combers is not something we'll forget. He was double-harnessed, but there are many stories of sailors being ripped out of their harnesses like parcels out of brown paper. He timed it beautifully, pushed the oar home and emerged, untouched by the water, as calm as if he'd been below for a cup of tea.

Johnny windvane worked superbly. So well that we raised the tiller out of the way to give us more room in the cockpit. Once again the conditions had slowed my brain. Of course the windvane worked well. It didn't depend on sail at all. All Johnny needed was wind and boat speed and there was no shortage of either.

We would hear later that, further north, *Navigator* was reporting waves twice the height of her mast and recording wind at sixty knots, just short of hurricane strength. We estimated the highest waves to be at least five metres higher than our mast. Twenty metres. Well over the heights expected for a hurricane. Which suggested that the water under us was shallow, so I checked our position on the GPS. We were under 30 miles off the coast and closing. Depth 1000 metres. If it was like this here, then we would not survive if we were driven further in where the waves were steeper.

While below, I saw that Sue was showing strain. But I was also worried about checking that the main had been secured properly. First things first: I went away.

But Sue can talk about that:

As Michael clambered back up the steps, muttering into his beard, Andrew spoke in considered tones from the top bunk.

"A child of my age ought to be at home."

My tears, which had been teetering on the verge for hours, spilled over then. I wanted to shout, "I quite agree, I don't want you here, this is murderous and insane!" But I couldn't say a word. I couldn't remember when I'd felt so helpless.

I didn't dare let Andrew see my distress. We managed to squeeze fingers as I ducked my head under his bunk. Sam clamped on to my leg. He thought I was hurt, and of course I was. I felt completely drained by the effort of masking my hacked-about emotions. I longed to lie and tell my children their world would be all better soon but I couldn't do that either.

As I agonised for the hundredth time about our right to force them through such a grisly experience, I remembered one of my father's favourite sayings: "There's always a good time coming, even if it's a good time coming." I made myself latch on to that.

I prayed hard for the first time in years.

It slowly dawned on me that the crew had slipped into traditional gender roles right from the beginning of the storm with barely a discussion between us. We were still in them now. The men, physically stronger, were doing all the heavy work looking after the boat. I, strong in the stomach but frailer over-all, was looking after what life there was below decks. I'd had to become both nurturer and nurse, dealing out soup and sympathy. In any other circumstance, I'd have baulked loudly at being relegated to the kitchen while the men dealt with the real action. But, here, there was no debating the issues. We were plainly in survival mode, and we each had to do the job we were best at. Of course, we were all thoroughly uncomfortable whatever we did, so it made no difference where we did it.

During the afternoon, Dave and I took the comfort level in the saloon down to a new low.

He was on the floor, trying to pull on his storm gear, ready to go on watch. I was fielding flying objects in the galley. The boat wouldn't leave us alone. As it bucked like a demented horse, I crashed on to my tailbone and Dave slid into my lap. I pushed him off, but back he came, both of us wailing as we dented each other's bruises. He thoughtfully put out his booted foot the next time; I was powerless to prevent contact. He skewed off again, then attempted to dry the wet floor with a sodden tea-towel. Within moments, he came back at me, shoulder first. I'd had enough.

"Back off, boyo!'

"Don't think I don't want to!" he shouted.

But now I was forced to pay a visit to his side of the arena. My elbow smacked into his sternum, and we wailed afresh at the impact. It took extraordinary energy to actually roll out of each other's way and quit this absurd double-act before it became a crisis. The previous hours of buffeting had obviously knocked our systems about more savagely than we'd realised.

Later, Michael lurched past the navigation desk, grey and cadaverous. He snarled at me. "I feel positively ... reptilian!"

We argued with thin humour about who most deserved the description. It was an even contest: eyelashes whitened with salt, lips cracked and bleeding, skin flaking, bodies stooped with cold, clothes rank. Right on the spot, we canned our plans to sail around the world.

At home, we're both fairly snappy dressers. Michael wears corporate suits and Rixon Groove ties. My clothes are classical and colour co-ordinated. I couldn't help smiling at our sorry images now. We looked as if we'd strayed on to the wrong planet.

Curiously, I wasn't really frightened for myself during all those hateful hours of turbulence. But exhaustion made me petulant. I let it show to Davey, captive in the cockpit during the next watch.

"Why," I bellowed up at him from the steps, "aren't we like normal people, answering the ads on TV? For just $1000 or so, we could have flown to Fiji and had seven nights of riotous decadence."

The boat sent me crashing into the companionway and I spilled the hot soup I was carrying down the steps. Davey looked thunderous. I'd spent a very long time bent at a 45 degree angle getting it ready for him. There was nothing for it now but to scuttle back to the rock 'n rolling stove and start all over again. I was extremely put out. But, I must have accepted the role in some measure by then because I found myself thanking God it wasn't me who had to be out there on the helm.

Here's Michael:

Soon there was no question of Sue making hot food or drink anyway. The motion of the oven on gimbals was too violent. So she jammed the oven against its housing, then jammed herself into a corner of the cockpit.

"If I'm going to die, I might as well have a cigarette," she said.

Hands shaking with cold, she fumbled through sodden layers and clinging pockets, a long, painfully laborious process. Eventually she produced one dry cigarette and a lighter. The lighter didn't work. Even with Davey's hands cupped with hers the storm wouldn't allow the tiny flame to live. After failures with two lighters, they moved to matches. In all, it took about half an hour, but they succeeded. With a sigh, Sue leaned back, as much as anyone can when they're being thrown around, and closed her eyes. As she began a deep, contented drag, a wave top licked over her shoulder and Davey's and neatly put out the cigarette.

Sue studied the limp corpse. Davey roared with laughter. Eventually they launched into song together.

From time to time we heard snatches of radio traffic from the Orion looking for *Agio*. At 6.20pm Sue kept the sked with Ian and Glenys.

"Oh, thank God for that!" Glenys's voice came back, her relief loud and clear through the atmospherics. *"How wonderful to hear you. It's been a very long day."* That was the first they'd heard back home that we were not the yacht in trouble. Glenys assured us she would contact our families and we arranged a special sked for the morning.

It's said that of all the sailors who go missing at sea, two-thirds of them have their zip down. But in these conditions, even harnessed on, there was just no way to piss over the side. Instead, we had to kneel on the cockpit seats and aim over the after-deck in a pose reminiscent of the Hunchback of Notre Dame. For women bent on modesty, life was much more difficult. Going below was hard enough; going forward to the toilet where the motion was three times as violent was taking modesty too far.

Feeling the urge, I went through the necessary preliminaries. Fingers like frozen chips, lifting the harness, opening up jacket, over-trousers, three layers of pullover and shirt, two pairs of trousers and underpants, finally locating the frightened midget inside. And then it needed encouraging. I was just telling it to produce the goods when a wave dropped in and the cockpit filled with water, creating an instant Eskimo spa pool. Obviously my fault. When the water rolled off and drained out it left a cockpit littered with people, holding their stomachs with hysterical laughter and pointing at me.

Radio Wellington did nothing to quell the comedy. I listened to the crackling forecast with amazement, and went back to the cockpit. "My God, we're in trouble. Wellington says the wind's going up to 40 knots and the seas are going up to 3.5 metres." Momentarily the laughter competed with the howl of the rigging.

But the comic relief vanished when I called Radio Wellington back. The Orion looking for the *Agio* had spotted wreckage. The search was continuing.

Alderman bucked on, stitchless, through the night, rushing further and further from any possibility of helping the crew of *Agio*. If they were still alive.

For the first time, both boys were afraid. For Andrew the only outward sign was a tightening round the mouth and eyes. He admitted being afraid, when asked, but otherwise made no sound. Sam went back to sticking with Sue, cuddling up against her when she was still, keeping a hand on her when she moved. He, too, made no sound. But once, he went to Andrew, four years his elder, and spoke to him with John Wayne bravado.

"Hi ya, kid. How're ya doin'?"

"I'm OK," Andrew replied seriously. And they hugged each other.

4

Midnight, 30 April

The storm peaked as Andrew's eleventh birthday began. He was too sick to appreciate the date, let alone hunt for the loot. He lay in bed worrying a loose tooth between bouts of nausea.

Outside, the waves were only a little bigger, but they were steeper and slopping more unpredictably as we closed on the coastline. It was as if we had been thrown into a giant washing machine overdosed with detergent. Going below was like climbing into a kettle drum. Dave and Davey told us days later of a monster that rolled up behind with a white cap three metres high and 150 metres across. Had it caught us, there would only have been a mast sticking out of the water. That's if it had left us upright. It swept to one side.

The strange noises and voices grew in intensity. And for the first time, two people heard the same thing, hair-raisingly specific. Sue and Aileen agreed that they had heard an African woman wailing in anguish. And Sam - noises being the least of his concerns - said off-handedly, "I heard a machine for making things, a till going off, and chickens in a chicken house."

We began to be seriously pooped. Not pooped as in tired, pooped as in dumped on from a great height, down onto the aft end of *Alderman.*

Dave, on his own in the cockpit for the first time, took it into his head to go below to fetch something. Glorious timing. The moment he closed the perspex hatch after him, the sea thundered down on to the cockpit and he found himself looking up through agitated water. He finished his errand, calmly climbed back out, and clipped on. A quick inspection showed that the weather cloth stanchions had withstood the strain.

Then at one in the morning, the moment that will never fade.

I was alone in the cockpit, as close to the doghouse as I could get, to reduce the buffeting and howling about the ears. The wave served almost no notice of its arrival. The roar seemed only two or three seconds long and then everything was full, even the doghouse.

I was a goldfish, mouthing in a bowl. Then there were only two things above the water: my head and the mast – that's the image burned into my memory. My family was under all that, and my three friends. I thought, *What have I done? What have I done?* It went around and around in my head.

Alderman stayed submerged, though upright, for a ridiculously long time. But she did come up, thrusting aside half the ocean in slow motion.

And now I learned the hard way about the doghouse air vent.

Water poured down through the vent, dividing into two streams. One went through into another vent above the galley, pouring down over the food inside the lockers and out around the locker doors. Bad enough.

The other went down through the electrics cupboard. This was where all the wires were exposed for joining to busbars, fuses, and gauges. Normally an excellent arrangement, because hot air from the engine kept the system dry and free of corrosion. For the next two months, I would be continually taking bits out of the electrics cupboard to scrape them clean.

The bizarre thing was that everyone below was more disturbed by the internal water problems than our time as an unregistered submarine.

The same wave submerged everything left in the doghouse - a mattress, odd bits of clothing, the camera Sue gave me on our tenth wedding anniversary. That died on the spot. So did a Charlie Brown book. That vanished except for a page that showed Lucy and Charlie discussing whether or not to expect rain.

After the 29 April hurricane force storm off the Wairarapa coast,
Michael and Dave up for'd. Swells down to five metres, a tiny
patch of genoa up for the first time, driving us at eight knots.

At four in the morning, when the seas were no longer dropping directly onto us, we sang 'Happy Birthday' to Andrew. We told him that this was one birthday he wouldn't forget and he'd be able to tell his great-grandchildren about it. He summoned a smile thinner than a slice of Chesdale and there was no mention of presents.

Ian answered the morning sked. I had hoped he would. I had a burning desire to throw a spanner into his professional, no-nonsense, unflappable radio manner. A little awe for the magnitude of our sufferings would do nicely. In short, I would impress the hell out of him. Actually, part of me wanted to be as cool as Lady Astor on the Titanic who is said to have complained, 'I ordered ice cubes, but this is ridiculous.' But I wasn't that cool. I laid it on, gabbling about winds of 50 to 60 knots, swells higher than the mast, seas on top of seas, broaching, pooping, skewing, spewing and my God we're taking a pounding out here. Over.

"Roger Roger, Michael," he said, as if I had dictated a laundry list. And he went on to deliver an outlook in exactly the same tone. I should have known better. It was a deliberate policy of course; the last thing a sailor in difficulties needs is an emotional radio operator.

The worst was over by eight in the morning. By ten, we could talk in the cockpit instead of shouting. The sea that would once have frightened us looked manageable. Motion sickness curled up and crept away, colour began to return to cheeks.

For the third and last time I was able to contact Radio Wellington, this time to say that we might soon be able to turn back in case a liferaft from *Agio* had been drifting after us.

"No need thank you, Alderman," the reply came. *"Agio has been spotted, her hull is intact but the mizzen mast is broken. No communication. A rescue vessel is on the way from Wellington."*

No communication.

Within hours we heard what we had been dreading. A wave had broken *Agio*'s mast. She was under tow towards us and Napier. Two crew were seriously injured, and Dave, the skipper, was dead.

Later, in spite of the numb atmosphere, we tried to give Andrew the best birthday we could, But it was without doubt the worst he had ever had and perhaps ever will have. We gathered in the cockpit under the first anaemic sunshine. For those of us eating at all, the birthday feast was instant soup and crackers, and the rich fruit cake given by our families and friends stayed below, still untouched. Dave and Aileen gave Andrew a magnificent book, *The Ocean World of Jacques Cousteau*. But Andrew could only manage a weak thank you. We tried another round of 'Happy Birthday', but the sound shredded in the wild air and produced only a wan smile.

By the time we raised sail, we were off Hawke Bay. We'd travelled half the length of the east coast with no sail and no engine. We were still sobered by the *Agio*, but without saying anything to each other, I know we all felt a quiet elation at having survived the worst physical conditions of our lives.

Inside three hours, the sails were down again. The southerly that battered us for forty hours had stopped dead, leaving a two metre swell. We motored, giving the batteries a long-overdue charge.

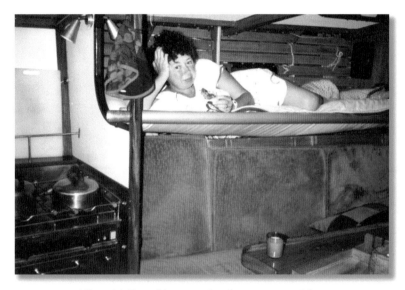

Aileen McDonald recovering from sea seasickness.
This time, it's going to stay down!

Twelve hours later I noticed a temperature rise in the engine and checked the fresh water cooling tank. The level was well down. I topped it up and checked for a leak without success. But inside twenty minutes it happened again. I ended up pouring fresh water into an insatiable tank with no visible leak. It had to be going somewhere.

It was. The sump. We must have blown the head gasket.

We switched off. Once again, we had no sail and no engine. But this time we also had no wind. We were completely helpless, without steering in a two metre swell. Within seconds we were rolling, gunwale to gunwale, the most violent possible motion short of dipping the navigation lights. The only land motion like it is the octopus ride at the fairground. At sea you need eight arms to hold on.

Within minutes, a few were seasick again, groaning more than anything at the dismal unfairness of it. And this time, we didn't have the consolation that we were going in the right direction. I wedged myself in the navigation seat and recorded in the log that we had blown the head gasket. I also recorded that while we had a spare gasket, we didn't have the right tools to make the change safely.

Andrew came to me while I was writing, watching me while clutching the engine cover.

"Dad?"

"Yup?"

"What would you have done if I refused to come on this trip?"

I looked up. The crunch question and only a week out. I looked around for Sue, but she was in the cockpit. In any case, Andrew had that look in the eye that parked the buck squarely with me. *Ask your mother* was not an option.

"It didn't happen. You're here now."

"But what if?"

"You didn't refuse. What's the point of 'if'?"

"I really want to know."

"All right. Yes. I ... We ... would have made you come."

"So I actually had no choice."

I shook my head. "No." *Why do I feel so guilty?*

He nodded and pursed his lips thoughtfully, taking it in. Then he added an extra nod for emphasis and went off up to the cockpit.

It took us four more engineless, mostly windless days to reach Gulf Harbour marina, a few miles north of Auckland.

One way or another, our new furling genoa got little use. We had bought it after enduring an overnight trial with the old system, which meant going out on to the bowsprit to hank or un-hank the sail. On our 1.5 metre bowsprit in a two metre swell, that meant taking a bath up to the neck. Alternatively, it was a toilet with automatic flush.

With no engine to recharge the batteries, we had to limit power to snappy radio links. So with plenty of fresh water and a perfectly functioning plumbing system, we couldn't even shower away the grit and grime of the storm. Only the boys were happy about that. High on the improving weather and high on the nose, they roamed *Alderman* answering to the new nicknames of El Fetid and El Rancid.

We could at least let the oven swing freely on its gimbals again, which meant hot food and drinks. Coffee went back on the menu, though Sue complained that she never seemed to see the bottom of hers.

"Why is it that every time I get halfway through a coffee, someone asks me to do something?"

We had just one patch of strenuous wind. But it was a northerly, sweeping round East Cape against us, keeping water speed below the generator threshold. That breeze went up to 30 knots. Andrew (El Rancid) said in a bored voice, "Is this another storm?" But compared with what we'd had, the near gale was just a tease.

26

When it softened we finally took on real sailing for the first time since Lyttelton. A broad reach, south southeast 20 knots. It gave us enough boat speed for the prop shaft generator to push juice back into the starving batteries.

Sue and I looked at the boxes of correspondence school work. We thought about getting the boys started. No, not on passage, we decided. The boxes stayed put.

We caught a tuna. We brought our sodden clothes and mattresses out again to dry. And a strange new feeling arose in us.

We felt good.

No, we felt great. In spite of *Agio*, we could not and would not suppress the flood of well-being and triumph. We had survived a humdinger of a storm, shaken up deep in the Southern Ocean bottle and allowed to explode over us.

"That storm will make me a hero at school," El Rancid announced confidently. He had a particular girl in mind. He reckoned he could do better than Adrian Mole who tried to impress his beloved by writing to the BBC about his poetry.

Davey Vincent. "Did I volunteer for this?"

5 May, just after dawn

We cleaned up, wanting to arrive like sailors rather than refugees. We turned down the Gulf Harbour marina's offer of a tow boat, dropped the sail at the last moment and used the engine well under overheating time to get us into our allotted berth.

When the lines were tied, we sat there in the warm sun, in the cockpit and on deck, bemused by the peace and stillness. People came and went along the floating pontoons. Aside from them, nothing moved. For a long while, we felt as if we had come from another planet. Just by looking, I could feel the sun-soaked textures of wood and warp and wire, just by breathing I could smell the new surfaces, the varnish and the resins. All around us, fifty vessels were utterly still, painted on to the water along with their lines and their jetties. Like *Alderman,* they were waiting for Saturday when we would head for the open ocean and Tonga.

We popped a bottle of high-quality New Zealand champagne and life was good.

5

The vessels were meditating, but the sailors trod the decks and marina jetties with focus and purpose, preparing for off-shore. And after a day of recovery, we matched their pace. We called a diesel mechanic for the engine. I told him confidently that it was the head gasket. He asked for the symptoms, then just sat there looking at it.

"Go ahead, don't mind us," I said, thinking of his hourly rate.

But he didn't take the hint. He asked more questions and frowned. Finally he took a screwdriver to the freshwater pump and opened it up. There it was. Or rather wasn't. He had somehow deduced that the usual brass plate on the back of the pump was missing and that corrosion had allowed water to get through the chain cover. He fixed it at a fraction of the cost of changing a head gasket.

We made a disconcerting discovery. While the Tonga regatta was billed as a family affair, that didn't apply to the passage itself. Youngsters were usually taken there with kerosene sails at 35,000 feet. We found not a single child of Sam's age who would be sailing with the fleet, though we were told of a lively eight-year-old, Nessa Andersen, on *Chieftain*, already on the way via the Minerva Reef. We looked at Sam who was imitating an Exocet missile along the jetty, decided that a spirited six might play an even hand with a lively eight, and resolved to track Nessa down. Andrew, however, had immediate luck. The only other two boys in the fleet were his age: Hedley from *Astron* and Ian from *Kindred Spirit*. We would get to know those families well. As an obsessed yachtie once said to me in Lyttelton, "I like cruising people. They're into life."

One such couple were in *Mystery Girl*, right alongside us. Jo and Brendan were experienced and tolerant of our fresh-faced inexperience. Jo denied, probably for the thousandth time, that she was the 'mystery' girl. Brendan was an ex-pilot, and he and Dave McDonald recognised each other instantly. Dave promptly reactivated the relationship by giving Brendan a cup of salt-water coffee. We explained to Brendan that there was no holding Dave since we lost his strait-jacket overboard. He explained to Dave that in the years ahead no one would know when or how, but vengeance would surely come. Dave beamed.

Brendan also took to Andrew and Sam, and they to him.

A couple of places down the marina, people swarmed over a new vessel, *Lord Barrington*. With just one short trial in the Gulf, her proving voyage would be offshore with the regatta. That's confidence.

For the first time, we met people with less experience than ourselves. But now that we knew how little we knew, we were reluctant to put it on display. We also noticed that even the most seasoned cruisers didn't jump in with advice unless asked. They were usually the same people who took nothing for granted and prepared their vessels with meticulous care. Unlike the character from previous years who was known for doing the passage in a tiny boat with a sheepskin on the floor for a bunk.

We went back to learning indoors for a couple of days. The regatta organisers, Don and Jenny Mundell, held a series of lectures with invited experts.

An RNZAF pilot made his point by showing a photograph of a liferaft taken from his plane. The fact that he had to use his pointer told us a great deal, considering that the aircraft was only a few hundred feet up and we were looking at half a square mile of water. This was followed by two consecutive facts. One: the motion of a liferaft is the most likely to produce sea-sickness. Two: don't throw up in the sea next to the raft - the sharks get excited and have been known to eat lunch without removing the wrap.

Thank you for that.

The liferaft demonstration was spine-tingling. The instructor came from a local liferaft firm that no doubt wanted to impress the yachties. First he endeared himself to the women by comparing a mechanical function of the raft with the sexual actions of a mistress. But he kept his audience anyway; when you show the safety features of a liferaft to off-shore yachties, they're going to be well focused on what you've got to say. Especially when they've heard stories of whale strikes that can start a yacht on the long drop within 90 seconds. So when he yanked the cord and the liferaft didn't inflate, the laughter in the audience was brittle. The demonstrator's face took on an interesting hue. To be fair, he did show how to overcome the problem. All you have to do is get over the side, grapple with the raft as the waves tenderise you against the hull and then open it up with whatever tools you have to hand.

Thank you for that.

A doctor gave advice on how to administer injections and sew up wounds, urging us to 'have a go' with oranges and pork skin. A customs officer advised how to keep things fast and friendly when we came back. But the really interesting advice on bureaucracy came from other yachties: such as how to expedite arrival formalities in a tropical port. Just before the officials come on board, you hide the cold beer, shut up the portholes reducing ventilation to the minimum, and strip down to just enough clothing to avoid a charge of indecent exposure. Then you wait for the officials from customs, immigration, health and agriculture, in their stiff, hot uniforms. The record, apparently, was four minutes for the lot.

Don Mundell told us about the official who met a fleet at Tongatapu, with no obvious function beyond hopping from boat to boat asking for and sampling the ale. When questioned about this he answered, "I had a course on AIDS. I have to do a check on the yachties." Which, Don said, makes Tonga the world's first country able to detect AIDS by looking you in the eye.

And we heard that the themes of the regatta were fun and safety.

Good. With youngsters on board, that suited us. Rule number four: first boat in gets a bottle of rum. Rule number five: if the first yacht in is more than ninety-six hours ahead of the last yacht it gets penalised a bottle of rum for going too fast. Rule number six: any skipper who lodges a protest has to shout the bar. Rule number seven: any protest will be automatically disallowed. Serious ocean racing was actively discouraged.

Also good.

But the problem is that most cruising men are to racing what Dr Jekyll was to Mr Hyde. Here's a test: look a supposed cruiser directly in the eye and say the word 'race'. Chances are you'll see some lurking thing stir and snarl in there. Some of them are so far gone there's only a thin skin of Jekyll left. They make their crew eat muesli and pump iron on the way to Whitbread worship. And of course they don't know the meaning of fear. They don't know how to reduce sail because they've never done it. They bounce from wave top to wave top to get there three days ahead of the fleet and thereafter drop the fact into conversation.

Women don't seem to suffer from this evil.

Men with families keep Hyde locked in the basements of their souls. They can be recognised by the way they reduce sail for the night, 'just in case' and by the way they cross start lines long after the gun.

Gen Rippingale flew in from Christchurch. She was great company, giving as much cheek as she got, and we were delighted when she agreed to come. It was no easy decision for her. She had to interrupt a degree in resource management and cram in a thesis a year ahead of time. All as a solo mother. If the army ever needs a logistics expert, Gen would qualify. After settling in, she cast about for a good book and settled from a choice of fifty on 'Prince of Tides'. I was reading it at the time. I wouldn't give it up, nor would she, and that started a battle of wits which lasted all the way to Tonga.

We took Davey Vincent to the airport, as reluctant to lose him as he was to go. There couldn't be too many people in the world with the courage to tackle the most dangerous jobs, able to handle *Alderman* in all conditions, always cheerful and even-tempered. And still happy to amuse the boys and keep them occupied.

Two days before the start, a snap southerly front hit the marina. In the middle of the night we heard a thunderous crack and the boat lurched heavily. Three of us reached the deck simultaneously, expecting to see a mast brought down by lightning. But it was nothing like that. Someone had knocked the furling line cleat and the genoa had unrolled. In 40 knots, *Alderman* was trying to climb over the jetty to get at *Ara a Kiwa* on the other side. Half a dozen chaperons came running from other boats, but it took only moments to roll up the furler.

Then for days the southerly whined through the fleet, needling complaints out of those of us who thought we'd served our time in rotten weather. Not that we were too worried. Popular wisdom said that two days was plenty of time for the southerly to blow on through. It said that all we had to do was get 100 miles north of New Zealand, then we could don the shades, drop the hooks, and settle back on the Coruba seat with a rum and a good book.

Yeah, right.

6

Two yachts didn't even make it out of the marina, colliding as they backed out of their berths. In convoy the rest of the fleet pushed into the southerly with flags crackling in 40 knots, out past the crowds huddled in winter coats.

The crew and skipper of *Alderman,* with recent technicolor memories, muttered that this was billed as a fun regatta. Why start today? The gale was so tough at the start line that many vessels didn't turn downwind and raise sail until after the gun. In fact the only way we knew the gun had gone was by listening to the countdown on the VHF.

And yet as we hissed over the line under stays'l and fully reefed main, with sirens wailing and fog horns sounding, Sue and I and the boys were aglow.

"This is it, boys," I said, clapping hands to shoulders. "By morning we'll be in the open ocean with more than a thousand miles to go."

"Waaa ... hooo ... !" Andrew exulted.

Sue and I drew close and found a pleasant way to restrict each other's breathing.

Finally, leaving New Zealand after four years of dreaming, planning and preparation. Yet another gale building, but what could spoil a moment like this?

Sam begged for permission to call *Kindred Spirit* on VHF.

"Ian's *my* friend," Andrew objected, as Sam bounced down the companionway.

Too late. "*Kindred Spirit, Kindred Spirit,* this is *Alderman, Alderman,* your copy?" Sam enunciated carefully, having misheard the usual 'you copy?' Sue and I, heads bent in the companionway to listen, glanced at each other, eyebrows raised. When Ian came to the radio, Sam said, "We want to wish you a good trip and a good time in the tropics." There was a silence as eleven-year-old Ian absorbed this piece of six-year-old formality. But Sam wasn't finished. "Goodbye and farewell until we meet again."

Another silence. We could picture everyone on *Kindred Spirit* staring at the radio.

"Uh, thanks Sam." Ian's voice seemed under strain.

"*Alderman* clear," Sam finished with a flourish. He shot back up the companionway, beaming and demanding due recognition. Andrew glared at him while worrying his now very loose tooth.

Far ahead, some cruising Hydes were in full flight, unreefed mains straining, jibs bulging. Half an hour later two were on their way back for repairs to broken rigging. Around us, others in the fleet struggled to control their sails, regretting their optimistic start. Even in the shelter of the Hauraki Gulf, the waves were up and deepening and we were starting to pitch. Short sharp jolts.

Aileen and Andrew tried out a new theory on seasickness. They both took 'Ginger Calm' tablets that don't contain the normal antihistamines. And, in spite of the slop, they both held out. Gen looked well but cold. Spray was now flying, the wind as biting as any South Island southerly. And our stays'l halyard had loosened, ruining the sail's performance.

"Dad, I'll do it." Andrew was beside me. He wasn't worrying his tooth any more.

"No, I don't-" I stopped. This was the first time on the trip that Andrew had volunteered for a difficult job. Up to this point I had not considered letting him go forward in a gale.

"I can do it," he reassured me.

I doubted it. Which wasn't really the point. On the other hand... what? I didn't know. Sue was below.

"OK. Clip yourself on to the jackstay and let me check it before you go forward."

Andrew, like Sam, is normally an actor. If there is a dramatic moment to be immortalised with cuts of ham, he'll run it through the slicer. Now that he had his first real drama, the actor vanished. He moved forward methodically and carefully, hand always on a support. I was ready to clip on myself and go forward but he didn't seem scared. When he reached the mast and uncleated the halyard he lost tension on the winch. The sail fell into creased bags, but he recovered quickly, cranking on the tension until he got the thumbs up from the cockpit. With the stays'l back to work, Andrew returned the winch handle to its home in the vent cover, and made his way back. I don't recall saying anything, but we did have an arm round each other for a bit.

A few minutes later I heard a cry of alarm and distress behind me.

Andrew was up on the Coruba seat, bent over the rail staring at the water.

"What's the matter?"

"My tooth," he moaned. "The boat bumped me."

"Oh no," I sympathised.

"That's one the tooth fairy's not getting. How much would that be worth in Tongan money?"

The Tongan tooth fairy wasn't sure. But on the bottom of the Hauraki Gulf there's still a boy's tooth, close to the spot where Andrew stepped up a rung on the way to being an adult.

Michael, with Andrew in the doghouse. All right for some.

Dusky dolphins joined us, grinning torpedoes, dipping, dancing, plaiting their timeless ropes under the bowsprit. Two thousand years ago, Roman historian Pliny told of a dolphin that gave a boy rides to school. And even then, the dolphin had woven itself into myth, rescuing the drowning son of Odysseus and bringing him to shore. Now they seemed to nod, commending their omens to us.

After seven hours of successfully beating back the eternal malady of the sea, Andrew and Aileen made the mistake of going below into a hot, stuffy cabin reeking of cooking. Then it was all over for them both.

We discovered why the fleet had not protested at being bowled across the start line in a gale. In spite of customs clearances, one-third of the fleet headed straight for the shelter of Great Barrier Island and Stoneyhouse Bay. There, apparently, they could laugh at the southerly while soaking in heated whale-oil cauldrons on the beach. Of course they may simply have been getting in practice for the Cannibal Islands.

We would have joined them, but didn't have the charts for Great Barrier and didn't fancy negotiating an unknown bay at night in a gale. So, once again, we gritted our teeth at the wind and the sea and tossed on into the night towards the pass between Great Barrier and the Mokohinau Islands.

In the morning, we were alone. The fleet had been swallowed. We had been told it would happen, but somehow still expected that with so many vessels heading in the same direction at the same time, some would be around a few hours later. Not so. From now on, the only contact would be by radio.

Once again, there they were: the great, grey-green combers, the gale-scoured valleys and slop-smothered hills. Not that we were afraid, not this time. We knew *Alderman* would take 40 knots easily. No, it was the certainty that we were in for hour upon hour of hammering, wrenching, grinding discomfort.

Enough is enough, I wrote in the log. The same phrase appears many times.

The berths began to take another round of prone, groaning bodies. Dave and Aileen agreed that they would sell their partially completed yacht when they got back. Asking price three dollars and 50 cents. Aileen gave up the warm lower starboard berth to Gen who had a nasty cough. Dave kept standing on her when he came down from the upper berth, producing groans. To liven things up, he tried standing on some of her softer parts but Gen's tongue became impressively lively, so he desisted.

Once again only Sam and Sue were in good shape. Once again, Sue was the only spare person round to get things done, usually when she was half-way through her coffee.

"Right," she said. "From now on I don't budge from my coffee for anything short of an emergency."

She was asking for trouble, of course. It became a standing joke. Everyone waited for her mug to get to half tide before putting in the boot. They would ask, "You half-way through, yet?" Sue developed a repertoire of replies we didn't repeat in the letters home to Mum.

Another gale. Some vessels were turning back. How could that be possible? On the third consecutive passage? This was incredible. Why? Why? Why? Better still, who to blame?

In fact there was a culprit. We discovered later that it lay more than three thousand miles to the northwest. When Mt Pinatubo blew most of itself out of existence, it sent billions of tons of dust and ash into the atmosphere. The long, slow fall-out combined with the normal El Niño weather phase, generating an endless parade of southerlies and giving New Zealand its worst winter for half a century. In the South Island it became so bad that townies went into the country *en masse* to help the farmers save their stock.

We'll escape the winter, we had vowed. But the winter was following us. And it would keep coming, the southerlies reaching up as far as Tonga and Fiji, pouncing on all our passages except two.

Around midday we found a way to recycle the food back to the sea directly, without passing it through the human stomach. First mend your engine, dropping plenty of diesel oil into the bilges. Next the skipper must forget to get it cleaned up. Now take a fresh gale and stir vigorously, making sure the ingredients are thoroughly mixed, right through into the lower food lockers containing all the vegetables.

But we had enough food left. There was no going back.

One hundred miles out I noticed a round, feathery ball on the doghouse and called to the others. Sam appeared in a flash and the others, in varying states of health, came behind him.

The chaffinch's eyes blinked, the lids slowed by exhaustion. It sat there, about a metre from us, not making a sound. It didn't try to edge away. It didn't move at all, except for feathers beaten about by the wind. We marvelled at the tiny warm-blooded bundle, thrown far from land by the gale. Desperate for a landing place, it had spotted the remote hard speck of *Alderman* in the waves.

Sam swooped on the galley, returning with bread. But the chaffinch showed no interest in the scrap we anchored near it. Half an hour later, it dropped to the deck. I clipped on to the jackstay and went forward, finding the sodden bundle huddled between doghouse and coaming where the water washed about. I was still too ill to make the effort needed now, so I shook my head and left it. When I checked later, it had gone.

That night another southerly front piggybacked on the first, lashing it with lightning, pushing the lustier breezes to fifty knots and over, reducing us from stays'l down to storm jib and a tea-towel of furling genoa.

Late in the evening, Sue gave a startled cry. When I turned to look, she was foraging on the deck near the rail. She came up with a flying fish.

"Hit me in the back," she spluttered.

Another regatta vessel turned back. She had lost a man overboard, then recovered him, but the crew were too shaken to carry on. In these seas, where a bobbing head would be almost invisible, the rescue amounted to what the press so freely calls a miracle.

Another gale. It's annoying that a still photo flattens waves.

Sam, still anxious at night, became cheerful and helpful by day in a way we'd never seen, keen to look after sick adults, clamouring to do whatever was needed. So much so that we awarded him the wear-it-with-pride rank of Rear Admiral. Which encouraged him to thinking that he could do the official sked with Kerikeri Radio.

I resisted at first. The safety sked with Kerikeri was in a different league from a ship-to-ship chat. Some nights, Kerikeri was dealing with scores of vessels around the Pacific, a vast safety net that needed efficient radio work. But Sam had picked up a thing or two in the gales. I wrote down the figures and rehearsed it with him. There's a lot of voice distortion on long-range radio. There's a poetry-like rhythm to reading off a latitude and longitude from the GPS. If the rhythm isn't right, the figures can be misunderstood.

Kerikeri's John Cullen finished with the previous vessel.

"Alderman, go."

"Alderman receiving," Sam replied, frowning with concentration. Only his head was visible over the navigation table. "We are at four three ... no ... " There was a moment of blind panic before he pulled himself together. "I mean three four, three nine, south; one seven seven, zero two, west. Heading is zero two six magnetic, speed seven knots. The wind is 45 knots southeast. The pressure is twenty-nine decimal eight. Over."

"Thank you, Sue," John's voice came back.

There was a hoot of laughter from round the main cabin. Sam's jaw dropped, the mistake impressing him beyond even his own expectations.

John followed with a prediction of westerlies and a comment on our progress. After all I've said about experts and weather forecasts, John Cullen was an outstanding exception. Not only were his forecasts close to the mark, but he managed to provide his scattered flock with a friendly encouraging voice every night, without ever falling into predictable patter.

"*Alderman* out," Sam said when John had finished. Then he milked it. "I was pretty good, wasn't I?" he demanded. Some people need assertiveness training; Sam would need meekness training.

The wind shrugged itself west, dropping a notch or two. Gen and Sue were the only ones well enough to crawl forward to raise the stays'l. They returned with triumphant gleams in their eyes that are not seen by the fireside at home.

More news came in from other yachts. *Kariel* was taking in water and hove-to off East Cape. On *Mystery Girl*, Brendan and Jo had beaten a switchboard fire. And astonishingly, a second vessel had lost - and recovered - a crew member. Aileen told us about two friends who had lost a crew member after he refused to wear a harness. Fifteen years later the couple still found it difficult to talk about. The news made me reaffirm our own rules: in bad weather, harnesses for everyone at all times; in good weather, harnesses on for the night. For the children it was much more restrictive.

That afternoon, Gen noticed Andrew scratching his head with unusual vigour. She examined his scalp.

"Andrew! You've got nits."

In seconds there was a free-for-all discussion about pillow cases - not easily resolved, because in the middle of strenuous weather and rotating berths it wasn't practical to be possessive about pillows. In any case, it was too late. Andrew's head had been everywhere.

Sam thoroughly enjoyed the fuss. He took to being a pest himself, irritating Dave in particular by running up to him and saying, "Ha, ha, you've got nits!"

Dave might have taken a short dose of this treatment, but not a long one when he was dog tired and sore from all the pounding. After the tenth time he spoke with feeling.

"Piss off, Sam."

Silence. Sam was dumbfounded, yet again, by the peculiarities of adults. Later, he was the only one not to brush off pillow cases before sleeping.

Slowly the waves turned from aggressive to listless. The roller furler uncurled and bellied out and we began to push through the water with authority, the bow sending its own spray in horizontal sheets as it sliced down on the grey slopes.

Colour returned to cheeks. Aileen announced that she had discovered a smile that really worked. More of us came up to nod heads weakly to the demands of the motion and to watch flying fish explode from the surface and soar in squadrons. Sometimes, when not chased, they built up speed by sculling like porpoises, then tilted forward for their wings to take over.

We discovered that the seven of us had used only 20 litres of fresh water and very little food in three days.

Four and a half days out, far off to starboard, I saw a light. I waited two minutes before spotting it again and this time there was no doubt. A port light, someone going the same way. We called on VHF, but there was no answer, and after an hour there were no more sightings.

Michael and Sam. Andrew and Sam were able to switch off from discomfort and even fear when listening to a story.

7

14 May

Three weeks after leaving Lyttelton, five days out of Gulf Harbour, we finally caught up with the dream we had nourished for so long. And it allowed us a generous embrace.

Seas, calm.

Wind, five knots and warm on the cheeks.

Cloud cover, none. Instead, a half moon wafting west over a silver evening gown laid out for the night.

We were 40 miles west of Raoul Island, above the thirtieth parallel, with more than half the voyage behind us. We'd been beam-reaching in perfect conditions half the day and making good speed. Now we were slow, down to three knots, and loving every lazy moment.

All of us were well again. We showered away the last of the blues with precious fresh water. We ate our first real meal: chicken nuggets and mashed potato - ordinary at home, but exquisite there - and topped it off with plunger coffee. Then we didn't speak much, but absorbed the sights and sounds that were at last gentle on the senses, taking in the subtle connections between vessel and sea and air.

Except for Sam.

"Sam, hush a minute. Listen to the water. Look at the stars. Isn't that something?"

Sam looked up, surprised. He took it in for all of three seconds. "Yeah. It's great. Can I have a biscuit?"

"OK. Then sit down and don't say a word for a while."

At eight o'clock we inaugurated the *Alderman* branch of the Dead Poets Society, inspired by the movie of the same name. *Carpe Diem*, the movie's theme says: Live for the day. We were also inspired by a growing dislike of recorded entertainment. The rules are simple. First, unplug the stereo. Second, perform (yourself) any song, act, riddle, prose or poetry that appeals to you, especially if it's your own. It doesn't have to appeal to anyone but you.

Out came a guitar and a school recorder, several books, pens and paper. We put a Chinese lantern in the radar stand. Johnny Windvane took care of steering and with the tiller out of the way we slipped on into the evening, creating our own silver wake to join the moon's. Cruising is definitely not cruisy, but there are moments of pure magic and this was the first.

Sue and I sang *Johnny Sands*, about a man with a foolproof way of sending his spouse into a watery grave without laying a finger on her. Aileen read out a poem, *Names*, written by Dave's uncle Donald McDonald, who was killed at the age of thirty-two, in World War II:

> *As I walked the streets of Damascus*
> *A boy said unto me,*
> *'Where is the land from whence you came?'*
> *'It's far away over the sea!'*
>
> *'What is the name of the land?' he said.*
> *'New Zealand's the name,' quoth I.*
> *'And where is your home in that land?' he said.*
> *'Ngaroma,' I said with a sigh.*
>
> *'Ngaroma, Ngaroma,' he softly said.*
> *And in his eyes was a look*
> *That my eyes held when once I read*
> *Of Damascus in a book.*

Ngaroma: it referred to the family farm and the name means many streams, or ocean currents. Dave and Aileen had often thought of Donald McDonald and what he might have become had the war not taken him so early. The steel sloop they were building back in Christchurch would be called *Ngaroma*.

I started to read from *The Prophet*, by Kahlil Gibran, not realising what effect it was having on Andrew till he interrupted.

> *And a woman who held a babe against her bosom said,*
> *Speak to us of Children.*
> *And he said:*
> *Your children are not your children.*
> *They are the sons and daughters of Life's longing for itself.*
> *They come through you but not from you,*
> *And though they are with you they belong not to you.*
> *You may give-*

"Oh no!" Andrew cried out. We all looked at him. His face was screwed up with distress. "I don't want to listen."

"What's the matter?"

"That's a horrible thing to say!"

"What?"

"To say that we're not your children!" His eyes were threatening tears.

"But-" I couldn't think of a quick explanation, so I settled for urging him to listen to the rest of the famous poem, then he would understand. He stayed reluctantly, ready to depart.

> *...You may give them your love but not your thoughts,*
> *For they have their own thoughts.*
> *You may house their bodies but not their souls,*
> *For their souls dwell in the house of tomorrow, which you cannot visit even*
> > *in your dreams.*
> *You may strive to be like them, but seek not to make them like you.*
> *For life goes not backward nor tarries with yesterday.*
> *You are the bows from which your children as living arrows are sent forth.*
> *The archer sees the mark upon the path of the infinite,*
> > *and He bends you with His might that His arrows may go swift and*
> > *far.*
> *Let your bending in the Archer's hand be for gladness; for even as He loves*
> > *the arrow that flies, so He loves also the bow that is stable.*

I looked up from the page at Andrew.

"OK?"

He nodded, biting his lower lip. "Yes. I understand."

Sam was suddenly inspired, went away and put pen to paper while we continued. When he came back he was so eager to read the result that he bounced on his bottom, cheek to cheek.

> *I went to somebody's place and I saw a green pillow.*
> *I felt it and I felt it and I felt it until I felt where you lay*
> > *all the time.*
> *I felt it a wee bit more and I felt it a wee bit more*
> > *until I could feel where you lay*
> > *the very second you were born.*

That was followed by sighs of appreciation, most of them from Sam.

"Did you just make that up?" I asked.

"Yes, Dad!" he said scornfully. He vented hurt feelings by venting his bladder. Into the wind.

"Other side," Dave suggested, protecting his wine glass.

"Oh." Sam up-troued, bounded across the cockpit and re-aimed towards the last

A flying fish. They were blind missiles – fleeing from predators.

glow of day, the fastest little squirt in the west.

On the sked, we heard that a yacht anchored at Raoul had lost a diver. A fifty-four-year-old woman had suffered a heart attack on the way to the surface and never made it.

The same night, at three in the morning, we experienced the most puzzling of the strange sounds and sights following us round the Pacific. I had just woken Andrew to steer for me so that I could go forward to take down the main. The wind had dropped to zero. I just completed that when I heard him call out urgently.

"Dad!"

I scrambled back to the cockpit and found him looking astern.

"What's the matter?" I asked.

"Did you hear that?"

"No? What?"

"Someone called out 'Dad'."

I stared at him. "What are you talking about? You did. You called me. I'm here. What do you want?"

"No I didn't!" He was indignant and mystified at the same time, and flapped his hand at the starlit night out the back. "I didn't say anything. It was out there."

I gaped at him, then checked below. Sam was was fast asleep and it hadn't been his voice anyway. Andrew and I both stared astern for a while. The roll was still deep, but the water surface was so smooth that it reflected the starlight. There was definitely nothing out there.

"That's really weird, Dad," Andrew said, then went to bed.

Most sailors experience strange sights and sounds at sea. Perhaps the background of wind and water acts like electronic 'white' noise, enabling us to hear and see according to the promptings of our subconscious minds. Maybe the sea, the original source of life, holds all possible sights and sounds like all dreams in a bottle, waiting to be uncorked by the imagination.

Now this. No waves, no wind, no background noise except the throb of the engine. And yet we both heard the same specific word at precisely the same moment. That was an interesting new dimension.

The next day was gloriously windless. The only reminder of torment was the long molten-glass roll from the south. The sky was clear and the lightest of blues. Clear even of birds - maybe we had seen our last albatross.

Overnight, the water had changed colour. Gone was the cold green-grey. In its place an exquisite deep blue, like the contents of the old school inkwells exposed to the sun. We dubbed the colour 'Tonga blue'. Its darkness must have been something to do with depth, because when we threw in an empty can we could see the shape flickering for up to a minute after it sank.

Sam liberated his poem in a bottle. Some day the world will open it and know that it was written by Sam Brown aged six.

We thought again about the boys' correspondence lessons and again let the thought go by. The day was too good to waste. We abandoned any urge to keep the race pace going and tried out the *MO* button on the GPS. In theory it goes like this. Whoever sees the unscheduled bath screams, "Man overboard!". The crew nearest the GPS immediately stabs the 'man overboard' button. The machine makes an electronic note of the co-ordinates and then tells which direction to steer to get back there. If it happens in the dead of night and no one notices until morning, pushing the button is optional. That was the theory.

But it didn't work. We cast floating objects forth, then criss-crossed the water, tracing every geometric shape known to man on the surface. The objects are still out there.

Sobering.

We got more serious. We shortened the update time on the GPS.

We lowered the dinghy and Sam and I climbed in. Dave pushed the MO button, then motored *Alderman* away from us. He would attempt to relocate us on electronics alone while the women kept an eye on us. I noticed that Sue and Aileen were looking more than apprehensive.

Quarter of a mile away *Alderman* looked peculiar. When in the valleys between the swells, we could see only her mast. And the surface was so glassy it looked like a mast growing out of the water. Then she started moving about in every direction but the right one. The MO location system still wasn't working.

From that distance, we could hear nothing at all. In fact, apart from our own breathing, we were in total silence. No birds flew, no bug hummed, no breeze or fish disturbed the rolling glass. I persuaded Sam that it might be worth his while to sit totally still and listen very very carefully.

And there it was: as near as possible to absolute silence short of taking a space walk without a suit. The funny thing is that absolute silence isn't silent. It has its own sound that seems like a vibration as long and slow as the roll that moved us up and down. Maybe the human ear and brain are incapable of hearing no sound and create their own.

Not that I discussed it with Sam. He wanted to talk about the possibility of meeting a shark in the very near future. Still, I can testify for the record the unlikely fact that Sam has experienced total silence.

I stood up and waved arms, pulling *Alderman* round towards us within seconds. When we clambered back up the ladder, the women all looked relieved. All three had been spooked by the experience, also imagining a Jaws attack. While we could always see the mast, the roll had often hidden us. In that shining expanse it was as if we had vanished altogether.

That failure didn't spoil a second perfect evening. We put Frankie to sleep again to make the most of it. We held a knot-tying competition - the creator of the fastest bowline to be awarded immunity from dinner dishes. Andrew had it down to three

*Michael, Dave, and pizza. Sue made us cook it, enjoyed the taste,
but didn't appreciate the master-chef boasting.*

46

seconds. We dined on gin and tonics, spaghetti bolognaise and contentment. We sang songs together and in that vast space it seemed important to sing softly, so softly that our voices blended perfectly and 'Greensleeves' seemed part of the pale pastel light.

Dave and Aileen took their three-and-a-half-dollar boat off the market. Andrew noticed how much detail I was writing in the log and asked if I was going to write a book about the trip.

"I don't know. I think so," I added, thinking of the storm off the Wairarapa.

"You can look in my diary, if you like."

"I can?" I looked at him sideways. What had happened to his right to privacy?

"Sure, but I want a cut."

"Oh. How much?"

"Fifty per cent."

"Outrageous! Ten per cent is my last offer."

He nodded. "You got yourself a deal."

As we became sleepy, a breeze of five to seven knots pranced in from the west. We raised sail to catch it, setting Johnny to direct a broad reach.

Just before dark, dolphins joined us to play. They rolled and swayed alongside, eyeing us as we called to them. But our low pace made us poor company and they left us to the night.

Andrew moved his mattress back into the doghouse. And for the first time on passage, Sue and I moved into the forward cabin. In a sea, it's the place of most violent vertical movement, but in good weather it's the most comfortable sleeping pit. We lay listening to the sounds. The forward cabin is a sound box. It transmits not only the creakings and rustlings of the vessel, but also the endless sigh of the bow parting the water and the voices of the sea's inhabitants. Squeaks and squeals and chatterings, and a moan so deep I couldn't imagine what produced it.

We read. Gen had purloined my book again, so I reopened the book that had influenced our anticipated path amongst the islands – 'Friendly Isles' by Patricia Ledyard, an American woman who went to Tonga to teach, loved what she saw, and stayed. She became one of the island' s best-known Europeans. I would try to find her when we reached the Vava'u island group in the far north.

We slept, the best on any passage so far, waking only once when Gen dipped too deeply into my 'Prince of Tides' and allowed *Alderman* to turn ninety degrees into a short chop. Waking from a flying dream in a yo-yo forward cabin is a good way to develop a heart condition.

On the morning of May 18, just after midnight, I turned off the satellite navigation system and pulled the sextant out of its box.

In the previous 24 hours we had done 150 nautical miles, charging through the waves with humming rig and thrumming hull. If a vessel ever enjoys itself, it would be at a time like this. And we had done it effortlessly. Johnny Windvane steered, we slept and read books and yarned. Sam begged to climb the mast and was allowed to go up only on to the spinnaker boom close to the mast. Andrew said that he was an individual and therefore had the right to read 'Penthouse', should there be one on board. Which there wasn't. Instead he hooked a magnificent yellowfin tuna. But it was going to dwarf our freezer, so we swiftly photographed proud hunter and catch to make sure that he need never tell another lie, and gave the tuna back to the deep.

Now, after eight days at sea, we would be sighting land sometime in the afternoon. Ata Island, the most southern in Tonga.

I didn't just turn off the GPS system, I disconnected its supply in the electrics cupboard so no one could do a quiet, faithless check behind my back. Then I fondled the sextant with reverence.

Even back in the planning stages, long before we knew of *Alderman's* existence, I had visualised this day. I had dreamed, literally, in vivid colour, of using a sextant to plot a running fix on the chart and to predict exactly when the first spike of the first land would come up on the horizon.

The sextant is arguably the most powerful, simple and beautiful tool ever invented. Take a beam of starlight and bounce it off two mirrors in succession, rotating one of them until the star appears to lie on the horizon. Attach a scale to measure the angle of that rotation - and therefore the angle of the star above the horizon - and you have a sextant. Now record the time you measured it, run time and angle through tables to work out where you are, and you have navigation.

That's the kind of simplicity that takes genius to bring into existence. When John Hadley did so in 1730, its accuracy consolidated the power of the British Empire at sea. My chart for approaching Ata Island, for example, still used coordinates recorded by Captain Pelham Aldrich on H.M. Surveying Ship *Egeria* on its 1888-90 voyage. One sextant reading puts you somewhere on a line of possible positions. Two readings give you two lines, and where they cross is where you are. It's a science that's also an art, and exponents have drawn the shape of earth and sea in much the same way for two centuries.

But the art of navigation is dying. The science is decaying into technology. Soon, cheap GPS (Global Positioning Systems) will be stacked in redundant threesomes in instrument panels that will look like the bridge of the Starship Enterprise and do all our thinking, seeing, hearing and smelling for us. If we're lucky we may be able to fetch our own mugs of hot soup.

Don't get me wrong. When you're off a stormy coast in the middle of the night, it's handy to punch a button and know exactly where the rocks are and how long you've got before you decorate them. But this was my very first landfall. This day of all days, I wanted to follow in the wake of the likes of James Cook: adjusting the sextant, bracing against the movement of the ship, aiming, luring heavenly body down to earthly horizon, waiting for the kiss, marking the moment, debriefing the sextant, poring over the charts.

I took the first reading from the full moon, just before dawn when the globe was golden and the horizon a razor edge. That became the first line on the chart. There was nothing else to shoot then, so I trod impatiently between navigation desk and cockpit, making bad jokes about the lack of heavenly bodies.

The dawn flared with colour and the moon paled away.

Two hours after dawn I shot the sun, turning it into the second line on the chart and adjusting for the travel between readings. The intersection gave the position, I fiddled with a few more figures, then went up on deck.

"This is it," I announced. "The heading is 347 degrees. Ata Island will appear on the bow at quarter to one. If we keep our present speed," I added to cover myself.

My obsession drew witticisms. Someone suggested that if I got it wrong, I would be honour bound as a gentleman and an officer to dangle myself from the yardarm. They were a scurvy bunch of landlubbers, their ancestors were barnacles, and we didn't have a yardarm.

For one hour, I cultivated an image of relaxed, authoritative assurance. I would have tried a deeper voice, but crew lying about helpless with laughter tends to erode authority. At half past eleven, I couldn't handle the suspense and my cool blew away on the breeze. I climbed the mast.

And there it loomed, a dark, bleak and beautiful triangle of rock, right on the bow. I didn't need to announce anything - a smile that wide is like another sunrise. Such kudos is difficult to lose in a short time.

But I found a way.

Twenty miles out we spotted three yachts close to Ata. No surprise because we knew some of the regatta fleet were intending to fish there before heading in to Nuku'alofa. I called them.

"Vessels at Ata Island, this is *Alderman,* you copy?"

No answer.

Ten miles out. They were barely moving even though their mains were up.

"Dark sails," Dave observed, after looking carefully through the binoculars.

I called up again, loudly and repetitively, coming away puzzled that not one of the three had their VHF on.

"They don't want to know us," I complained.

"Could be because they're triangle-shaped rocks." Dave said helpfully. Dave has an ability to keep a straight face when he's suffering from severe internal combustion.

*Michael with sextant and
Ata Island. There was no satisfaction like using the
device to predict when and where the first land would rise on the
horizon. The sextant is arguably the most beautiful and influential tool
ever invented – without it, the British Empire might
never have existed.*

Ata is part of Tonga, but unlike Tonga.

There were people there once, on the bush-covered eastern saddle. But last century, the 'blackbirders' came, travel agents with pressing arguments about free accommodation and alternative lifestyles in places like the silver mines of Peru. The Peruvians were getting low on Inca Indians and somebody had to do the work. The Tongans were renowned for their fierceness as warriors, but their own empire was dying and on Ata they were vulnerable. Too few, too far from help. In 1860, when the raids had reduced the population to 200, the King of Tonga ordered everyone out to Eua Island, closer to Tongatapu and protection.

The Ata islanders never returned.

On the west side, what looks bleak from a distance is downright unfriendly at close quarters. No harbour, no coral. The sheer faces of the extinct volcano plummet nearly 300 metres into the water and keep right on going as if the sea were only a casual visitor.

We came in close anyway, fascinated by the forbidding atmosphere. Black frigate birds fell on us out of the heights, swirling elbowed wings, screeching round the rigging like lost-valley pterodactyls. When darkness crept over the bastions, we coiled the empty trolling lines and pointed the bow thankfully towards Nuku'alofa, ninety miles away.

PART TWO

8

In 1773 Captain James Cook named Tonga the 'Friendly Islands', an alternative title still inscribed on the navigation charts. If he was looking ahead a couple of centuries, then he was right. But as a description of his hosts of the time, it was blissful ignorance.

He was overwhelmed by the lavish hospitality, the great mounds of food, the dances, the boxing matches - in which his men were soundly trounced – so he got to his feet and offered profuse thanks. He displayed such style and courtesy that the locals, who couldn't agree on the best way to despatch him anyway, shrugged their shoulders and decided to do without the main roast.

Eating the 'long pig' was just one of their friendly ways. They were a fierce warrior nation. At that time, they were strangling babies to appease the gods, using shells to decapitate prisoners, and teaching neighbouring villagers to fly in volcanoes.

They were also astonishingly skilled navigators. As far back as the thirteenth century, they toured western Polynesia in double-hulled canoes that carried 200 warriors, controlling a Pacific empire of a million square kilometres. That's without GPS, without sextant or chronometer, without the mathematics of latitude and longitude.

They were so skilled, they could return to any island, anywhere, when they wanted. That's handy if you're establishing a trading empire. The British certainly needed that ability when they were planting flags around the globe, but they had to have sextant and chronomenter to do it.

Eventually, the Tongan empire shrank to a tenth the size. But still it's as if a giant hand scattered 170 islands like bird seed through vast tracts of water.

Much of the world is still ignorant of the ancient Kingdom of Tonga. For two centuries the kings made use of foreign overtures while avoiding colonisation, a remarkable feat and unique in the Pacific. They successfully kept the modern world at bay. But now, finally, modernity is sifting in through the cracks. The changes are slow, sometimes incongruous. In this kingdom where no one starves, where the monarchy is worshipped and the rulers actually rule, there is discontent and the shocking word 'democracy' is heard in the islands.

Even so, it *is* the last paradise. The dateline kinks east around Tonga, so it's often said that Tonga is where time begins. To most foreigners, it's where time stands still.

James Cook turned out to be a prophet in spite of himself. Just 150 years ago,

Genghis Khan might have used the Tongans as shock troops. Now we were about to find a race transformed from mind-numbing savagery to such warmth, hospitality and spontaneous friendliness as to be beyond the understanding of many of the visiting Europeans. Some change. A seemingly impossible evolutionary gallop.

How could it be? The question dogged our wake through many islands before we found an answer.

Distance plays tricks on the eye in the coral islands. One moment Tongatapu was a courtesy flag under the spreaders and an ache in our starboard bow, the next she was there, just five miles off, a long, dark green belt of palms over a string of surf. As we approached, the light turned another trick, making the end of the island float on the haze.

A sail moved lazily down the outer reef.

"A canoe!" Sam shouted. He bounded to the rail and bellowed across two miles of ocean, *"Malo e lelei! Malo e lelei!"* Hello. Hello. His pronunciation was in the dialect known as 'kiwi schoolboy', but no one was about to nit-pick, certainly no one in the distant yacht. Sam noticed our grins and said cheerfully, "Just practising."

It was too soon for popping corks. We were three miles from the main reef and I felt about coral the way most kiwis feel about scorpions. The steel hull was the best available protection, but a glancing blow could still open us up like a can of chicken stew. And we weren't insured. Offshore insurance is so expensive you either pay the premium or you do the trip.

We hung our eyeballs over the rail and stole northeast, towards the channel, parallel to the outer reef. Dave, who had dived in and flown over coral before, pointed out that colour was our best warning. The very deep blue was probably safe. The lighter blues and greens would be minefields, the browns certain disaster.

We passed a wreck two miles before the channel, an angular patchwork of red-brown rust, warmed by the sun. There are two kinds of vessel in the islands, the saying goes: those that have gone onto the coral and those that are going to.

Once into the channel, desperate to get some kind of feel for the looks of coral, I delegated the steering and climbed into the spreaders. Almost at a glance, coral, colour, depth, danger, safety all jumped into the same picture at the same time to be the beginnings of a working understanding. In the next five months, we would spend a lot of time up the mast, keeping the courtesy flags company.

At the finish line, inside the channel, a police launch swung at anchor. As we crossed, both Andrew and Sam were at the rail calling out the Tongan greeting. Muscular arms waved a reply back. *"Malo e lelei."*

Sam chuckled and expressed his pleasure on the foghorn.

It took another hour to negotiate the coral mazes to the inner harbour of Nuku'alofa. To the boys' delight, Ian from *Kindred Spirit* was standing on the rocks at the entrance waving and calling to us. His father, John, joined him.

"Hello *Alderman*. Well done! Quite an achievement. We did it, too," he added cheerfully, pulling a burst of approving laughter from us as we glided past.

Half the fleet were in already, bows anchored, sterns tied to the shore. Some had been damaged by the gale. One had a blown exhaust system, a patched-up stern gland, and a main torn in exactly the way ours had been. On *Kodiak,* Judy Bach had been catapulted across the main cabin, splitting her forehead open. Laurie had successfully tackled stitching her up in a gale and was said to be considering a career in brain surgery.

Chocolate children ran along the wharf and gazed down at us with shy, shiny-black eyes. Jenny Mundell from regatta headquarters passed down a welcome basket woven from strands of palm leaf, loaded with bread, coconuts, pawpaw, oranges, and *vines* (pronounced veenays) - a small fruit with a hard skin and delicious centre. We held the basket and stared at it. Quite a gift for people out of the roaring forties.

Three officials tromped on board with set faces and spotless uniforms. I greeted them with a nervous smile. It was, after all, my first clearance into a foreign port. And I got three stiff smiles in return. This was not the Tongan warmth I had heard about. They sat, handing out documents, asking for passports. I remembered that I had forgotten to set up the fast-turnaround hothouse treatment.

But then Sam appeared.

"Malo e lelei," he said to them, as if conjuring a rabbit out of a hat.

Huge melting smiles spread over their features. They returned the greeting with such delight and enthusiasm that I looked at Sam with new respect. He lapped it up, standing there with his blonde hair and blatantly false modesty. It's often said that the best passport you can take with you is a child.

Suddenly it was clear that the ice had only been born of Tongan shyness. The friendliness of the three expanded like a sphere to include the rest of us.

"Have a beer," Sue offered. "Cheers," I said.

"*'Ofa atu.*" Cheers.

They rattled through the documentation efficiently, sipping appreciatively, then settled back for a yarn. About New Zealand and Tonga, about children and church choirs that sang like angels, about the law against male toplessness. And about busted yachties who get thrown in tiny cells, many years, many fleas.

"Have another beer," I said.

But we ran out of cool beer and gave the man from agriculture and health a frozen beer.

"Take it with you. Don't open it now, it'll hit the roof," I said, with hand actions to avoid translation difficulties. But he waved aside the advice and pulled the tab. It didn't hit the roof. It exploded over him, from hair to waist, dripping down on to his pants.

"He told you! He told you!" The immigration man bounced to his feet and denounced his sodden, sheepish colleague before turning to me. "He is very sorry."

We parted on excellent terms, good wishes and shaken hands.

All three found twinkling smiles for Andrew and Sam. What was left of the exploded frozen beer left with the man from the ministry. And as the customs man stepped over the rail he said, "You can take down your Q flag now."

We did. We had arrived.

Tongatapu means 'Sacred land' or 'Sacred south'. Two out of every three Tongans live there. Which is a problem.

Within an hour of starting to explore the island, we learned three things. The Tongans really are that friendly, they really do like children that much, and they liked Sam even more. They were drawn to his fair skin, blonde hair, blue eyes, his small build and cheeky grin. The boy had everything going for him. They never touched him without implicit permission, they were too polite for that. But they openly adored him - which would turn out to be both a blessing and a problem.

Everywhere we walked we saw natural abundance. When Mount Pinatubo blew up two years ago, it gave us months of gales. When Tofua Island blew up 20,000 years ago it gave Tongatapu, centre of the empire to come, a layer of ash that turned to rich soil.

The boys were mute as they absorbed their first full-on cultural immersion: the luxuriant growths of shrubs and frangipanis and palms, the smells of pungent earth, the tin and wood shacks and fast, ragged chickens, the horse-drawn carts and rusting vans. The gracious and amiable adults wearing sulus or wearing the more formal *ta'ovala* mats, finely woven from leaves of pandanus or hibiscus. Old women in mourning wore their grief in tattered *ta'ovala* handed down through the generations.

Children watched us shyly for a word or glance that would allow them to break into glowing smiles. Andrew and Sam smiled back, but didn't speak and made no comment to us about men and boys wearing 'dresses'.

Tongans understand *carpe diem.* For them, seizing the day means appreciating what you have when you have it. They go by a philosophy known as *nofo fiefia,* living happily. They're experts at extracting fun from the juice of life and they tease more out of each other with good-natured, ribald jibes. With strangers, including their own, the code is *nofo fakalata,* making others feel at home.

And these were the descendants of the warrior empire.

They treasure children. At the same time, they're disciplinarians, instructing with the stick at school and at least the hand at home. But you seldom see displays of anger, they don't often get impatient or gesticulate or shout at each other.

Nuku'alofa is the capital, hardly more than a town. The name means 'abode of love', which may once have fitted the original array of villages, but now the town looked like a prop for a spaghetti western. The dust was heaped in the comers and under the peanut sellers' tables, the buildings tatty with punishment from the sun. Even so, Nuku'alofa wasn't really dirty, it still managed a suprising look of freshness. And there were few outward signs of the modem west: one fast-food outlet, a disco, and very few tourist stalls.

The boys were a tourist entrepreneur's dream. They dragged us to the stalls and to beaming attendants who showed us carved dolphins - grotesque parodies. But we told the boys that they had the real thing visiting them in sunsets, dawns, calms and storms. In other words, No.

"OK, could we spend our own pocket money on them?"

"It's your money."

"We haven't got enough."

"Tough."

Most contacts, even for trivial transactions, were personal. We had animated conversations with people who genuinely wanted to know. With Louisa, for example, who ran a bone and black coral jewellery shop. When she learned that we were planning to sail to the Vava'u group she clapped her hands in delight.

"I live there when I am young! Why do you go there?"

"Because people say it's very beautiful," Sue said.

"It is! Yes. Most beautiful in Tonga."

"I'm looking for a woman called Patricia Ledyard. All I know is she lives in a village called 'Utelei."

"I know it. I will show you." In a moment, Louisa was outside with a stick in her hand, drawing outlines in the dust, relating 'Utelei to Neiafu, capital of the Vava'us.

We came across an enormous parade of school children for the opening of parliament. A vividly coloured, multi-scaled snake of children marched to the bands in their spotless uniforms, chests out, stomachs in, heads high, out-performing anything we had ever seen from children at home. They were good. They knew they were good and took themselves seriously. But Tongans are also good at teasing. While parents, uncles and aunts watched proudly from the pavement, cackling crones called out jibes aimed at cracking the youngsters' stiff-faced self-importance. They rarely succeeded.

The parade flowed on towards the palace of His Majesty King Taufa'ahau Tupou IV, a fine Victorian mansion in grounds by the sea. But no spectators would lean on or even touch the fences, for that would be disrespectful to the king.

As we prepared for travelling into the more remote regions, we noticed a change in Andrew. He'd not had an easy school life, with all our shifting. One school in

A typical dust-filled sunrise in a cloudless sky. The dust and ash were from the explosion of Mount Pinatubo in the Phillipines, responsible for the worst winter gales in nearly half a century.

particular had been dominated by bullies, children made vicious by indifferent parenting. We took him to another school, but he'd only had three months there when we sailed from Lyttelton.

Now, we had never seen him so happy, so focused and confident, partly through his friendship with Ian Peacock on *Kindred Spirit.* The two of them carved out their territory, which took in several yachts, three dinghies, the inner harbour water, the fishing wharf, the fish market. They made it their home, exploring, fishing, visiting yachts, staging water wars worthy of Cecil B. de Mille.

Brendan from *Mystery Girl,* who still had an eleven-year-old boy alive and well inside him, gave them a word new to the English language. The verb 'hoon'. When Andrew and Ian went hooning, the entire inner harbor knew about it. In general it meant the feeling you get from full-on macho action. For example, it included climbing into *Kindred Spirit's* dinghy, winding the throttle up to full, and simulating a maddened bumble bee amongst the yachts. It usually happened in *Kindred Spirit's* dinghy because our outboard motor was "Disgustingly Underpowered, Dad" (Get it, Dad? DUDley). There were complaints from the fish market and requests from regatta HQ to be more considerate of the locals' no doubt unreasonable desire to stay sane. So hooning died, briefly.

Only two flies struggled in Andrew's ointment. The first was his parents' heartless insistence that he wear a lifejacket whenever he was in a dinghy. It cramped his style. It wasn't cool.

"Then learn to swim."

"I can swim, Mum. You know that."

"I don't know it. The sea is not a swimming pool."

"All right, I'll prove it right now. You'll be happy if I can swim right round *Alderman,* right?

"It'll be a good start."

"OK. Right. Actually it's a bit cold right now. I'll do it straight after lunch."

The other fly was Sam. Andrew had coped well with the fact that Sam was immune to seasickness. He was even coping with his little brother's immense appeal to the locals, limiting his reaction to a resigned, wry shrug. But he balked at Sam muscling in on the friendship with Ian.

Sam used every cannon on his deck. Back home, keeping up with Andrew's activities was something he eased into when he eased out of nappies. Now, with Andrew having cool macho fun, he zeroed in like a pigeon turning for home. He begged, wheedled, bribed and corrupted, he appealed to justice and fair play, and when all else failed he folded arms in the centre of the action and refused to budge. And most of the time, he won.

Andrew asked if it was legal to strangle little brothers, but to the best of our knowledge the law took a dim view of it.

Sometimes Sam managed to lose the war right after winning the battle. Like the time the three of them were in full flight across the harbour in the dinghy and Sam decided it was a good time to wash the anchor.

But then eight-year-old Nessa came into Sam's life.

She came in on a magnificent 23 metre ketch. When *Chieftain* scribed a stately arc into the inner harbour, Nessa of the long light-brown hair was standing at the rail. There had already been some radio contact, so on each vessel a parent bent over, spoke to a child and pointed. The two youngsters raised half an arm and gave each other a tentative wave. Until now, Sam had considered girls a lower species of pest. Why? Apparently they're not like boys.

There were a couple of parent-conducted inter-yacht visits, one each way. The two circled each other warily. Then it was on. We knew it was on when they started telling each other secrets through a snorkel. Sam liked to affect nonchalance, but Nessa had no time for such nonsense. When she saw him come rowing towards her she would rush away to her cabin to put on a good dress and brush her hair. The fact that Sam looked like a castaway didn't seem to make a difference.

It wasn't an arranged marriage. More like a relationship of convenience for the parents. The quality of life for everyone on both vessels picked up immediately.

While the two of them played below, we settled into *Chieftain's* luxurious aft deck seats and got to know Nessa's parents. Steen and Geraldine Andersen were a

Scandinavian and Irish combination running an Australian vessel on international charter. They'd been sailing, with Nessa, for six years. They had a reputation for sea know-how, sailing skills, and for helping sailors in distress.

"We like the life," we said. "We like the people."

They smiled.

"They always help each other out," I gushed.

There was a silence. Steen and Geraldine glanced at each other.

"Sure, they'll help," Geraldine said in her rich Irish brogue. "as long as there's no danger to them or their boats."

They told us about an Australian who went up on a reef and called frantically for help. No less than fourteen vessels in the area could not provide that help.

I heard the sound of my illusions breaking up on the rocks.

"When you're out there you have to count on being self-sufficient," Steen said. "It's dangerous to think any other way."

"Oh great, correspondence school, now my day is perfect."

Note the yacht up on a coral 'bombie' in the background. It refloated safely on the next high tide.

9

We attended every regatta function as if our lives depended on them. Because they did. A room full of international cruising yachties is a collection of experience precious beyond description. We never knew when someone would drop a pearl that would make us blink and say, "My God, how come we got here alive without knowing that?"

One such function was the dance. I remember loud food, tasteless music and the discovery that there is more to a *snub* than being turned down for a foxtrot. You snub an anchor chain by taking up the tension at the top with a rope, which has 'give' that the chain doesn't. That little pearl has kept many a stranger from the lee shore.

Sam snubbed Nessa - original meaning – when she wanted to dance. Dancing was going too far. However, holding hands was acceptable as long as no one saw and no one told.

Andrew appeared at my side, frowning and clearing his throat. "Dad, I notice that Annabel isn't here." Annabel was a blonde French girl from *Hibiscus* with an accent to set a boy's heart floating towards the sunrise.

"No, I don't think they came. You want to dance with her?"

"No, no." His face was an instant radiator. "I just noticed she isn't here."

"Well, what about Lisa?" Ian's big sister.

"No, Dad! She's much older."

"Not too much. And she's nice. If she says no, she won't be cruel about it."

"No. I couldn't."

"I'm out of suggestions."

"I didn't ask you for suggestions, Dad."

Travelling down the anchor chain from the snub, we come to the anchor. Steen discovered that we were using a 45 pound CQR and kept a ninety pound version under the for'd cabin for storms. He looked incredulous.

"Your spare is bigger and you keep it *below?"*

"Yep." I was proud of the big one. It took a winch to get it up on deck.

"So when the storm comes you will change them over?"

"Yes," I said with only a slight quaver.

"How much time do you think you will have?"

It didn't take a yacht to fall on us. We swapped the anchors over the next morning. Even in perfect conditions it took an hour.

By now we were itching to leave. And not just because we wanted to continue the voyage. We wanted to move out from the frustrating travel trivia found in any city. And somehow just being attached to a city brought its own irritations on board.

On passage, five adults and two boys was no problem, we got on well. In port, the number was close to critical mass. Naturally, Gen, Dave and Aileen stayed on for a few days to enjoy Tonga. But one experienced cruiser, noticing the number of bodies had not been reduced after the passage, said simply, "You'll learn."

The boys became ratty with each other and with us. Ashore one night, Sam threw fizzy drink at another child. Rather than face parental wrath he ran across the road and, to the huge delight of the Tongans present, would only allow Nessa to approach. His sob story to her?

No one ever listened to him.

Why?

Because he was the family reject.

Had a hug and a kiss followed, he would have won a Tongan standing ovation. No, the hugs and kisses came later, in the conciliation talks. Sam pointed out that in spite of us all living on top of each other, I was so busy preparing I actually spent less time with him and Andrew than I did back home. I swallowed a retort that I was busy preparing to keep them alive.

"All right. Fair enough. I'll spend some more time with you."

"Neat," Sam said, "let's play Memory." It's a game that involves turning a heap of cards face down and torturing the brain into remembering where they all are. Sam won hands down, fingers dripping with cake mix that he scooped from the bowl between turns.

I began to read them stories, and did it through calm and storm for the rest of the voyage. They had the ability to forget being battered and thrown when we were cuddled up with a book on a berth or curled in a corner of the cockpit. To my amazement, Enid Blyton went straight to number one slot. Nothing went down better in a gale than hearing what the Famous Five and Pongo did to Tiger Dan.

Andrew lost another tooth. At five Tongan dollars (five *pa'anga)*, he pronounced the tooth fairy exchange rate favourable. We agreed. Andrew didn't believe in the tooth fairy until he lost a tooth.

Some irritations came straight from city dependence.

"Dad, how can I earn more money? I'll tidy the ropes."

"You earn enough, Sam. Listen, think about this. You've got to do most of your jobs because you *want to help out."*

Incomprehension. "But I don't."

"You don't? Not even a wee bit?"

"No. But ... Look, it's all right. I'm charging Dave fifty cents Tongan to row him ashore in the dinghy."

Andrew saw the direction of the wind. "I've dropped my price to free."

"Oh no!"

"Look." I waved my arms indignantly. "Get this. Where you two are going you won't be *able* to spend money."

"What! What do you mean?"

"No shops."

"That's silly! You can't live without shops!"

After a few days, Moses came to Sam's rescue. Tall, handsome, magnificent physique, vibrating with good humour and health. He was on the supply run to a holiday resort and had already been giving the boys free rides in the inner harbour. Could he take Sam on his bicycle to church?

Sam was willing.

The open preference for one child was difficult for us, but in Tonga that indicated nothing unusual about Moses. To me that is. I let Sam wobble away on the bicycle bar, white dwarfed by black. When Sue returned, she was horrified and angry, and let me know in no uncertain terms. So I was left with very mixed feelings. Yes, we should have discussed it first. Yes, maybe I had been naïve. Yes, I was sad at our own culture of suspicion and distrust when we were in a culture that treasures children.

Sam returned, waving happily from the handlebars of Moses' bike.

Christianity has a lot to answer for in the islands. But it can at least take a bow for giving wings to great musical talent. The singing in the churches soars with vibrancy and exultation. For the cruisers there is no need to go to church to enjoy it, the sounds ring out across the water even in the most distant and obscure islands.

It's easy to imagine how it began.

You wake up in your woven coconut-leaf hut one morning in 1643 to find a full-sized sailing ship in your harbour. Stunning. No one has ever seen such a thing.

But you're a warrior, and you're expected to overcome paralytic terror, so you mutter an incantation, grab your spear and canoe and paddle out. Slowly. The sides of the monster rise to awesome heights. The vines and dead trees in the centre rise to the sky. Its warriors have skin that is unnaturally pale and some of them have yellow hair like the *siola'a* flower. These are surely warriors of the gods. You give them the name *papalangi,* which means 'from heaven'. There are hardwoods that turn without moving, gleaming stones shaped by master sculptors, *tapa* cloths bigger than a *fale* yet so fine you cannot see the weave of the leaf. And on the shoulders of the great chief there's a cloth that glows with the light of the sun.

At the command of the chief, a mouth in the side of the canoe belches fire and smoke louder than a volcano, so loud that branches fall from a *fao* tree above the beach. And yet before you can flee, the *papalangi* warriors (*palangi* for short) beckon you in a friendly manner.

The great white chief now orders three of his warriors forward, each holding up a different fantastic object. The first object shines like the moon on the water and coils like a sea snake under a rock. When the warrior blows into it, it makes a sound like many conch shells, so piercing that you cannot have thoughts. The second is the carving of a god. When its warrior strokes it with hairs on a stick it bursts out laughing at three other warriors who link hands and dance the tale of that god. And the third, perhaps the most wondrous of all, is a cold shining stick with a mouth in its side. When the mouth feels the touch of its warrior's lips it wails like the passing of souls to Pulotu.

The great chief points to his own chest, says, "Abel Tasman". He signals for much water and food, so you bring it to him.

And much later, when more great canoes come with tongues that speak to ears that hear, tongues that tell you the white man's god is more powerful than all other gods, you don't just believe it - you already knew it. And then comes the clincher: Tongan gods say that only chiefs have souls. The white man's God says all people have souls.

So you buy the whole package.

It takes time, of course. Particularly when you discover that some of the *palangi* are far from heavenly but taste good anyway. And of course there are inconveniences, like the white man's diseases that wipe out your family, the new laws that punish you for keeping graven images and for doing a hundred things your ancestors have done for centuries. And there are the Methodist ministers who tell you that while God loves all men equally, some - the hewers of wood and the drawers of water - are a little less equal than others. Namely, you. Immortality may have been democratised, but don't start counting your wings until you've earned them.

So you gladly fetch and carry for His Methodist ministers.

By the time the Tongans noticed all the cracked beads in the basket, too many fine necklaces of quite real beauty had been made. Many island nations became more Christian than the Christians. In Tonga the constitution declares the Sabbath sacred forever: you don't work, trade, or hold sporting events. Sign a contract on Sunday and it is void. Drive a car without police permission and you're in trouble. Methodist-based Christianity is such a force that even the Seventh Day Adventists observe Sunday, pointing to the bend in the dateline as their excuse for the bend in the rules.

The graveyards are open hearts on the sleeve of Christianity. Grief and joy at the passing of a loved one to better things is permanently displayed over the mound and round the stone: vividly coloured banners and flags and rugs, artificial flowers, sea shells, black stones from the volcanoes. And around it all there are often borders of inverted beer bottles stuck in the coral sand. That last may simply reflect the drinking habits of the first ministers.

Tonga has the world's lowest death rate.

And you can be sure that the family planning clinic is doing its best with the other end of life. So said an article in the daily *Matangi Tonga,* with the glorious headline 'What You Need To Know About Sex, Baby'. It reported an outlying village with a problem. It was a time of national condom shortage and the village had discovered a long-forgotten stockpile. Which might have led to some unrestrained celebrations, except that the rubbers were ten years old and came with a guaranteed life of only two years. What should the amorous villagers do? The elders went to the family planning clinic for advice, and duly brought the answer back to the village: Use five.

One morning, Brendan and Jo appeared.

"Take a break. Come with us. We'll show you what it's all about." And we went with them in *Mystery Girl* to Pangaimotu Island. It was just one hour from the inner harbour. But it was enough.

Pangaimotu had the sort of coconut palm, white sand, outrigger canoe combination that causes sadists to send home a postcard with the words, 'It's hell here'. On top of that there was a another wreck to explore.

Within seconds of switching off, Brendan was on deck stripped down to a swimsuit and a grin. He pointed back towards the inner harbour and the city.

"You see that? That's not what it's all about." His hand changed direction, taking in the island beside us, his own yacht, and water so clear we seemed to be floating on air above the sand. "This is what it's about. You anchor by an island, you get up in the morning, you dive in the water." And he put his last words into action.

We followed him. The wreck, with much of its wood still in place, was a multi-level apartment for fish straight out of the rainbow. On one rail was a growth of brain coral, an exposed brain with thoughts composed of a hundred luminous blue fish, surrounding it in a perfect sphere. When we swam near, the sphere imploded maintaining its shape and the fish re-entered the corrugations.

"Incredible," I gasped on the surface.

"It's nothing," Brendan grinned. "You've just begun."

In the dinghy with me, Andrew renewed his demands to be rid of the lifejacket.

"No. You have to be confident enough to fall in without panicking."

"I am, I am."

I grabbed his ankles without warning, tipped him out the back and got ready to dive. He came to the surface wide-eyed, dog-paddled to the dinghy, climbed in, and burst into tears. Meaningful dialogue followed. Andrew began serious work on his swimming.

I had no sooner returned to *Mystery Girl* than Sam was on my back. Literally.

"Can I take my lifejacket off now? I only want to jump off the boat and climb back up. Can I? All the others are doing it. Can I? It's not fair. I ... "

Encouraged by the success with Andrew, I grabbed Sam and dangled him over the edge. He developed instantaneous respect for deep water and panicked, gouging me in the neck with a talon that hadn't seen scissors for weeks. Meaningful dialogue followed. Sam announced that he hated me.

While fixing my neck, I looked at myself in *Mystery Girl's* mirror, My hair hadn't seen scissors for months. A Christchurch newspaper had once called me the Rasputin of broadcasting, which was fine when there was hair on top. Now it was downright ridiculous. Gen, who had always said she could cut hair, took me ashore and had her way with my locks while I sat on the dinghy transom and dangled my feet in the water.

"How do you usually have it done?" she asked me. Which was an interesting question because she had already finished.

When I saw myself in *Mystery Girl's* mirror I knew my hair wouldn't see scissors for months: it was the Yul Brunner look. Sue's tan disappeared when she saw my head. Brendan said - after he and half the fleet had stopped sniggering - that he had once had a haircut like that. Gen said it really suited me.

The others left to beachcomb the circumference of Pangaimotu, insisting on taking the boys and pointedly leaving Sue and me alone. Thinking, of course, that having seven on board *Alderman* must have led to severe abstinence. Fools.

"How do you get time?" I asked Brendan later. "Today's been fantastic, but there's so much to do. Sue and I are so busy keeping the boat going we don't get enough time to enjoy it."

"How long since you started?" he asked, the condensation on his beer can tipping gently over a finger. I subtracted.

"Nearly four weeks."

"Ah." He nodded. *Mystery Girl* stirred to a puff from the southeast. "It'll take maybe six weeks to two months. Then you'll take time off to relax. It's a state of mind."

One of the last things I saw of Pangaimotu was John, from *Lord Barrington,* walking the beach. I didn't know John well and would not normally have noticed except that he was walking oddly. Stumbling and with drooping shoulders. It wasn't drunk weaving, so I decided he must be over-tired. But the same afternoon, he lost all sense of balance and was rushed to Nukualofa hospital. Within a few days he was back in New Zealand being investigated for a rare condition that had lodged a blood clot in his brain stem.

He was in his fifties, a grandparent. To most it would have been the end of offshore adventuring. But much later, his wife Barbara told me what happened after he was discharged. She found him in front of the mirror, looking at himself, not realising that she was standing behind him. He had lost control of the muscles on one side of his face - eyelid, cheek and lip - and the flesh was sagging.

"Look you old bastard," he said to himself in the glass. "If you don't do something about this face of yours, your sailing days are fucked."

Barbara came further into the room, crying silently. "Honey," she said, "we'll bloody well do it."

"Yes, we'll do it," he said. And with immense effort, he visibly firmed up some of the sagging muscles, regaining a little of the lost control.

The specialists told him that he could not go ocean sailing again. But we would see John again inside six weeks.

Gen found a place on *Dawn Treader* heading directly for the Vava'u Group. She only had a few days left before returning to New Zealand and we were going the slow way. I assured her that the sight of my scalp was causing Tongan women to faint with desire and promised to return the favour when we met again.

Dave and Aileen McDonald came to the end of their time. We ferried their bags to the breakwater and a waiting taxi and made regretful farewells. They had *Ngaroma* to finish building back home. Some landlubbers asked Aileen how she could even think about it when she suffered so much from seasickness. But she had no doubts. "The joys outweigh the temporary discomfort. It's important to think positive." Some people decay when they retire. Dave and Aileen couldn't get enough hours in the day or days in the year.

There were regrets on both sides at the partings, but it was time to reduce the pressure on *Alderman's* social bulkheads and everyone knew it.

Now we were alone as a family for the first time.

We took another trip to Pangaimotu Island. Andrew swam, unaided, between *Alderman* and the wreck. Sam climbed into the spreaders, clipped on and gazed out. I brought Sue a coffee. When the level of her coffee was exactly half way down the mug, she studied the black surface carefully then looked up at me with a wry smile.

"Must be time to go," she said.

10

On the map, Atata Island looks like a tadpole with ambition to be a frog. It's a short hop from Nuku'alofa, on the edge of the Egeria Channel a mile inside the outer reef. From there we started our first family solo passage.

Just getting to Atata had been a hurdle for family confidence.

Both boys got hurried lessons in reading from the depth sounder, an old Marlin with a scale. Both were placed in the bow at times to look for coral heads, or 'bombies'. An apt name for any yacht hitting one at more than a crawl.

On the east side, to our heartfelt relief, we were met by one of the narrow island longboats to be led through a maze of bombies.

"Follow close," the guide ordered and turned under our bow.

The relief lasted half a minute. About then, the guide did something important. He looked in front of him. What he saw plugged his hair into ten thousand volts.

"Stop!" he screamed. An interesting concept for fourteen tons of steel right on his transom.

Sue threw the tiller hard over, slamming into full reverse. "Don't follow!" he added helpfully above the labours of our abused engine.

We missed by three metres and the four of us gazed down at the coral fronds, Medusa's hair, rippling beside us.

When we anchored, a New Zealand yacht, there already, was busy hatching a bombie, balanced on top with a receding tide – probably parked there by the same guide. With high tide, he would get off lightly, only his pride punctured. After the VHF links established that all he could do was wait, we heard an unknown voice poking fun at his problem. And then Steen's heavily accented voice came through, saying what we all knew.

"You don't want to laugh at them. It can happen to anyone. It can happen to you."

We took to snorkels and flippers to inspect the nearest bombie, Sam in a lifejacket, Andrew now comfortable without. Sue and I kept glancing towards the reef entrance looking for sharks. They're partial to anything thrashing about on the surface, preferring to eat first and consider the taste afterwards. Sue was especially nervous with the snorkel gear over deep water and refused to dive.

The bombie made the coral at the wreck look like a cheap imitation. This was a submerged pillar eighteen metres tall, three metres across: a complete, nearly self-contained ecosystem and a living tapestry. Think of a garden that always moves, that contains more colours, shapes and textures, more varieties of attendant fish than you could list in a month. Then think of those fish folding in and out and around the garden and around you when you dive, some peering curiously through your mask. That's the coral bombie. The breathtaking drop-off to the sand far below left us with the feeling that we were in orbit looking at a massive tower rising from the earth. Beautiful, the way a boa constrictor is beautiful.

We had a night start ahead of us and this was no place to begin, so we tip-toed round to the western side of Atata, to the edge of the Egeria Channel.

29 May

The anchor clanked up just after midnight in pitch blackness. Not the easiest start for a family on their own at sea for the first time. The Nomuka Island Group was sixty miles away. Not having a death wish, we didn't want to arrive at a strange destination after four when the sun reflects off the water. Even coming in from the west, it would be too difficult to see the deadly coral. *The moral for sailors of yore: take coral from ten to four.* Five yachts would be leaving with us. The rest of the fleet had broken up, scattering to all points, following their own hunt for interesting people and places.

I had hoped at least for starlight, but there was none. And yet following the lights of another yacht hoping they've got it right is like tagging along with the Light Brigade. We had to put trust in our homework the night before: 252 degrees magnetic for 0.8 miles, turn starboard on the leading lights, 307 magnetic for 1.6 miles, turn on to 015.

Around us the navigation lights of the other vessels were on and moving. *Kindred Spirit* and *Mystery Girl* would be amongst them, but in the overcast night, it was impossible to tell who was who. The four pinpoints of red or green were the only visible objects outside our own universe. We motored. Arguing with coral under motor is one thing, insisting with a sail is quite another.

To our alarm we found we were first on to the leading lights. The other four vessels swung in behind us, leaving us to lead the convoy out to sea. Ahead, Stygian black. Beside us, nothing to indicate even water let alone coral. Behind, the other four were so precisely in line with the leading lights, they often obscured them. The blind leading the not so blind.

When the depth sounder gave us a healthy sixty metres, we were safely beyond the outer reef. We drew deep breaths, let them out slowly, then turned on to 015 degrees, heading for a GPS way point just off Nomuka Island.

Just once on a previous passage, I had set a way point directly on a destination chunk of land and aimed *Alderman* right at it. A change of watch, a moment's thought, and the folly of it gave me beads of cold sweat. It was the sort of mistake you never make twice. And it doesn't just apply to satellite navigation. One yachtie told me of a landlubber friend who took over the tiller on a night trip.

"Just aim for that light in the distance," the yachtie said and went below. Two hours later there was a jolt and a crash and the yachtie raced up on deck.

"Got the light," said the friend.

Around us, the other yachts turned on spreader lights to raise their sails. In that darkness, each yacht became a self-contained island under spotlight before a vast black curtain. The sails up, the spotlights winked out. But soon the conductor raised the baton, the curtain drew back and the night filled with stars. Sue and I stayed together side by side while the boys slept below.

Come breakfast, the crew and skipper of *Alderman* were riding high. The other yachts had vanished. We were truly alone as a family, masters of our world and romping through it at nine knots.

And no one was seasick.

Under the new regime, the boys made a discovery that would transform their behaviour on deck: the jobs we gave them were no longer created to keep them educated, quiet, or punished. There were no other adults around to do the essential jobs. For the first time in their lives their actions influenced our safety, even our survival. They didn't need it explained. They knew.

Andrew went forward on to the bowsprit to soar over the waves, yelling and shaking his fist triumphantly at spray and sky. Sam demanded to climb the mast, but accepted the refusal without a murmur. He remembered it was his birthday the next day, took sunglasses and lay reading on a sail bag, legs crossed nonchalantly. Tomorrow he would be seven, and there would be a cool image to keep up. Sue, determined that Sam was going to have the finest birthday possible, set about making two chocolate cakes. Two cakes! The news was shouted the length of the deck, making three males howl and hang their tongues out. We felt fine.

Alderman hummed across a quartering swell of three metres. I tried not to ask myself why we had a three metre swell for a mere fifteen knot trade wind. Turning back was already too tricky.

Sam began shivering and the spray got to his book. Andrew began to take a gratuitous shower. Both of them came back to the cockpit. Below, the gimbaled oven went into rock and roll and Sue issued a dismal forecast for the health of the chocolate cakes.

By mid-morning, we had one horizontal chocolate cake, one with horizon difficulties, and 35 knots from the southeast. Heavy cloud came over the horizon, spreading its wings, then engulfing us. The rain began.

"This is another storm, isn't it?" Andrew said in disgust.

"No." Sue shook her head slowly. "Just a gale."

But, if anything, our mood improved. Sue and I went forward together in rough conditions, reefing down, with the boys watching wide-eyed from the cockpit. In a sea, the cockpit and the deck are two very different places. Sue felt that separation from the boys keenly, even though it was only a few paces. But we returned with idiot grins. The boys didn't ask us why we were grinning. They knew.

Very, very carefully, we tucked in close to the prison island, Nomuka Iki.

Even when we were as close as we dared, the shelter was almost non-existent. The gale blew straight across the low coral and the sea rolled round it, searching us out.

Anchoring demanded our first real family team-work. Sue steered, Sam went on depth sounder, Andrew prepared the anchor winch. I went up the mast for bombie spotting, where I discovered, the hard way, the value of rehearsed signals.

We were in position, Andrew hovered over the winch, staring eagerly at me.

"Drop it!" I yelled.

He released all friction on the winch and the anchor took off as if gravity was about to be cancelled. When the eighty-seven pound CQR reached the bottom, the chain kept right on going, developing more momentum. and drowning my screams. I came down the mast like a chimp on fire, reaching Andrew just as he sussed the problem and stopped it.

We locked it off, made our way back to the cockpit and indulged in a lot of back-slapping and family hugging.

That was followed by a debrief, another institution that stuck.

Several problems were resolved on the spot. Example: if you know the vessel's draft is two metres, and the boy on the depth sounder calls out, "Seven" it's nice to know if he's working from the metric scale or the imperial. Example: when the look-out is screaming at you, eyeballs bulging with terror, stabbing the air frantically to starboard, it's nice to know if he's indicating a patch of coral or which way to go to avoid one.

Three other yachts, including *Kindred Spirit* and *Mystery Girl,* had chosen the same dubious shelter. There was a bit of radio chit-chat, but little physical contact as we rode out the gale. Each vessel was working its chain hard, each chain snubbed.

In the late afternoon, the gale scaled back to a stiff breeze, 25 knots. A longboat set out from the main island of Nomuka, splashing precariously towards us. It proved to be the dirtiest longboat ever to touch *Alderman.* Vea climbed aboard, introducing himself as the postmaster, and his assistant as Ese. Ese never opened his mouth.

There are four main island groups in Tonga. Each has its own capital and in theory its own customs service. Vea was one of those outpost officials with one head and many hat pegs. He wanted to see our passports and clearance papers from Nuku'alofa.

No problem. But we were surprised. Our information was that if the weather permitted it was considered a courtesy to call ashore on Nomuka to present people and papers. For Vea to cross rough waters to see the yachts late on Saturday indicated something unusual.

He recorded a few facts in his exercise book, we yarned about this and that to do with regulations, slipping into the point sideways: a yacht had been busted for marijuana smuggling. A New Zealand yacht.

"Very bad. Small cells. Many years. Many fleas."

There was a silence.

"Would you like a sweet?" Sam asked.

Vea took one, his face breaking into a Sambeam. Ese took one but still didn't find it necessary to open his mouth. He threw it overboard, putting the wrapper in his pocket. All without a smile. Sam's face contorted with the effort to adjust to a universe that could allow a lolly to get the heave-ho. But neither man's expression offered any clues.

Vea seemed to forget about busting international drug runners. He kept on talking happily. Then he and Ese went to the rail and hauled their boat back alongside. Just before climbing down he pointed across the water to the nearby prison island.

"You are permitted to go ashore."

"Malo." Thank you.

After they went, we eyed the island. The wind still flailed the palm leaves and rasped the empty beach. There was no movement around the two prison buildings, which looked from our distance to be made of some light material like coconut leaf. Around us, the sea was dark and fretful. This was where Captain William Bligh anchored *Bounty,* taking on water. The legendary harsh treatment of his men would come to an end a few miles north.

30 May, Sam's birthday

His feet thumped on the boards at seven in the morning, and continued to thump to the bathroom where he readied himself, emerging with slicked-down hair and his best clothes. Best clothes meant his freshly washed Ninja Turtle T-shirt.

We raised our heads blearily. Outside, the breeze was still whining in the rigging. That didn't penetrate to Sam, who bounced on us while we did our best with 'Happy Birthday'. Andrew watched him sourly, remembering his own birthday in the Wairarapa storm.

"It won't be a very big party," he gloomed and went back to sleep soothed by Sam's cries of anguish.

But, Sam told us later, it turned out to be the best birthday he ever had. Balloons were run up the mast, one immediately taking off for the prison island. Jo and Brendan came from *Mystery Girl,* with gifts prepared back in New Zealand for just such an occasion. Ian, Lisa, Sarah and John came from *Kindred Spirit.* Lisa had made a card complete with bar code and personal logo. And although Sam was expecting only a few presents, a cache was found, long hidden in the inner recesses of *Alderman.* There was an inflatable canoe, modelling clay, a book of masks and, to cries of delight from both boys, a box of felt pens which had been sorely missed.

"Someone must be psychopathic," Andrew said.

Chuckling evilly, Sam divided the masks according to character. I got the clown, Sue the spacewoman, Andrew became Sir Lancelot. Sam retained the cowboy and put aside the Raggedy Ann mask for when he met up again with Nessa. Andrew climbed the mast in his, but the wind ripped it off and Sir Lancelot set off after the balloon.

Sam glowed with the attention. The horizontal chocolate cake had his name on it. The tilted cake had the word 'seven'. This time the rendition of 'Happy Birthday" seemed to make him expand. He didn't know it, but his parents were happier than he was. Being able to provide such a party far from civilisation meant a great deal.

A pillow fight raged from one end of the deck to the other, giving the nits a fright and beginning the end of many pillows. Weapons were upgraded for an

Sam's seventh birthday. Note the cake with the horizon problem – produced in a gale. On passage, Alderman *could be tilted on one tack for days.*

intergalactic war on the deck of the starship *Alderman:*

"OK, Pork Chops, it's dying time."

"Pow! Acid shot!"

"Blurp! Plastic acid immobiliser to immobilise the acid!"

For hide and seek I immobilised Andrew under the port berth in the for'd cabin, telling him it was a perfect hiding place.

"I wish *my* birthday had been like this," he said mournfully as I closed him up.

No one came to look for him.

So, when the visitors left, it was as if one of them lit a fuse on the way out. Mix one very happy seven-year-old with one very unhappy eleven-year-old inside a boat and it's like what happened when my brother sprinkled ammonium tri-iodide all over the science lab. Where'er you walk - explosions.

Of course we intervened. It was that or unhinge entirely and stand on top of the mast on four legs making donkey imitations. Several severe and arbitrary punishments later the boys went into a huddle and decided not only that the blame lay with their parents but that a great opportunity existed.

"Would you guys like a break from us?" Sam asked me.

"Could be," I growled suspiciously.

"Well, what's that island group we're going to?"

"The Ha'apais."

"No, no, you've got it all wrong. After that!"

"The Vava'us."

"Yes. OK, well when we get there we could go sailing on *Kindred Spirit* and get a break from you."

"I think you mean we get a break from *you."*

"Yes! Yes! That's right. That's what it is."

Sue and I put our headaches to bed. Andrew crawled, appropriately, into the doghouse. Sam slept in his yellow inflatable canoe which was shorter than he was.

But in the morning we found them sleeping together, lying close. When they got out, they were sheepish and contrite. They worked together to bring Sue breakfast in bed and they made cards saying, *I love you.* To both of us. The cards stayed on the mast base in the main cabin for months.

11

31 May – Prison island

Next morning we stayed to look over the prison island. The other yachts departed to look for better shelter, except for a new arrival, *Boozewater*, flying the Australian flag.

I had to row against a stubborn 25 knots because twenty-one-year-old Dudley was on a go-slow, farting feebly under water. While I broke my back rowing for the gap in the reef, the boys lectured us about the relative merits of Yamaha, Mariner and Tohatsu, tossing out horsepower figures as if they'd been born at sea. Andrew, getting wiser in the ways of adults, made an offer.

"If I do a proper survey of outboards, would you look at it and consider a new one?"

"No dice," I panted. "Dudley just needs TLC."

They sighed. I rowed. Then we hauled the dinghy ashore and planted the anchor high up the sand.

The prison was deserted, except for a savage dog. It allowed us to look out over the extensive vegetable garden, even to glance inside the two open-plan huts where personal items lay about. But it went berserk when we tried to inspect a terminally split canoe. Even so, behaving like the Hound of the Baskervilles just doesn't work if you're length and height of a bratwurst sausage.

This was no Alcatraz. The birdman wouldn't even have to breathe hard on the coconut leaves. Not only were there no locks, no doors, no windows, no bars. Just window spaces and doorways for the breeze to blow on through. Outside were the coconut trees, hibiscus, frangipanis, golden sand and the fish-laden reef: the sort of self-contained paradise that makes squillionaires reach for fat cheque books.

Still no sign of prisoners or guards.

We wandered along the beach, Sam paddling his yellow blow-up canoe. Andrew asked where the girl trees were because he wanted to pluck one, but settled for turning a log into an instant canoe. Add to water and stir vigorously.

Sue and I went further along, threw our clothes off and swam, but not for long. It occurred to us that nudity on a prison island, in a society that punishes men for baring their chests in public, might need a re-think. We put our clothes on and scuffed sand back towards the prison.

Four Tongan men lay on the beach.

Maybe I've seen too many tropical prison movies like *Papillon:* human wrecks struggling through fever swamps, picking leeches out from under leg irons while guards use clubs to discourage the mosquitoes.

The 'paradise' prison island of Nomuka Iki. Sue and boys with
all the prisoners (two), all the guards (two), and the ferryman.
Prisoners and guards shared eating, working, fishing and playing.
They slept in the same huts. Can you tell them apart?

When the introductions to Joseph, Mark, Venisula and John were over, it was clear we'd just met the two guards and two prisoners of Nomuka Iki. But it wasn't clear who was who. We certainly couldn't tell by looking. All four were in late teens or early twenties, all four were a testament to good health, all four wore jeans and smart shirts. In fact they out-dressed us, having just come back from church on the main island. No one works on a Sunday, so the ferry longboat had to take them on Saturday and return them on Monday. That Draconian regime forced the prisoners to join the local community for the weekend meals, accommodation and socialising.

Today was Sunday. They had just arrived.

I pointed out the contradiction and Mark said that a friend had brought them back. That, apparently, did not amount to labour on the Sabbath. He nodded down the beach towards a longboat, where the unofficial ferryman was bent over the outboard. It all begged another question which we didn't get time to ask because Mark pointed to Joseph.

"This is my brother."

Joseph grinned hugely at Andrew and Sam.

"You are guards or prisoners?" I asked.

"We are prison officers."

"Ah." We nodded, darting a glance at Venisula and John. They didn't seem to resent our presence and smiled shyly at the boys. Joseph went to the day hut and brought back a kauri shell for each boy.

"Malo," the boys chorused, examining the subtle designs with delight. *"Malo aupito."* Thank you very much.

Mark seized Sam in a bear hug, holding him like that for a photo.

Joseph hoisted Andrew to his shoulder, with muscle-rippling ease. Taking a photo in Tonga is usually no intrusion. When you've finished, the subject is likely to thank you for taking it.

I found Mark beside me.

"I am not allowed to ask you for beer," he said firmly.

"Uh huh."

"However, if you wish to walk around the island and you wish to give us some beer for it, that is all right."

"If it's safe to row back from the boat, I'll bring beer," I promised.

With instant concern, Mark looked at the sky. I had my own doubts. The southerly was starting to lift spray off the water. Quarter of a mile out, *Alderman* was tossing its chain moodily, the weakest link holding everything of value that we possessed.

Down the beach, the unofficial ferry had been joined by a dinghy from the Australian boat, and the two skippers were bent over the ferry outboard. We went down to help. The longboat was little more than a sieve. Nails and glue may once have existed, but mostly the planks were held together by habit. The petrol supply was an open bucket with a hose, even though a new sealed tank lay unused in one corner. The outboard prop had been run at indifferent speed into a hundred coral outcrops. At a hundred and one: the prop shear pin had gone and the Sunday ferryman had no spares, no tools and no idea what to do next.

We found an ancient nail around the prison huts. *Boozewater's* skipper came up with pliers to shorten it, and soon had a makeshift shear pin in place. The next problem was harder because the ferryman's English was poor. We resorted to semaphore and bastard pidgin.

"Use one time. Only one time. Go to Nomuka, not stop. You in gear, not go neutral. In neutral, it will fall out. You savvy?"

He didn't.

But if he lost his pin in this wind, his next stop would be Fiji, if he was lucky. We brought Mark and Joseph into it, explaining the mechanics and watching as they explained volubly in Tongan. The ferryman's expression lit up.

"Not stop," he agreed.

He and Mark chatted some more. But it was in Tongan, so we left them to it. The Australian went back to *Boozewater* and we organised our own water transport as the ferry outboard roared into life. As we pulled away from the sand, the ferry grumbled down on us, bearing not only the skipper but the entire population of Nomuka Iki.

It reached us and went straight into neutral.

"We will tow you back to your yacht," called Mark.

"But ... " I pointed helplessly at their outboard. "What about the-?"

"It will be all right," Mark assured me, surrounded by nodding heads, including that of the ferryman. For all they knew, the informal shear pin was nestled in sea lettuce right now. The fact that the southerly would push us back to *Alderman* without needing even an oar was almost beside the point.

Obviously the word 'beer' had been heard on the sand.

I shrugged, raised eyebrows, spread hands and accepted the inevitable. That brought almost a round of applause. Not a slow learner this *palangi*.

So the Brown family accepted a tow it didn't need by men who weighed the certainty of a beer against the chance of being swept away and drowned, and chose the beer. They sang, they called out jokes, they laughed together. And suddenly we realised why distinguishing guards and prisoners had been difficult. It wasn't the lack of uniforms, or the similarity of ages. These men were behaving as if they were one family.

We came alongside. The outboard went into neutral again and fell silent. Guards, prisoners and the ferryman of Nomuka Iki clambered happily on board where we plied them with chocolate birthday cake, cigarettes and beer. Sam offered more sweets, watching carefully to see that nothing unusual happened. All these things were passed around as politely as if the parson had come to tea. The guards, sitting closer to us, passed each offering to a prisoner first before taking one himself.

"This is not a hard prison," I said. "Many New Zealand prisoners would like to be here."

"No." Joseph dealt with this superficial nonsense as it deserved. "It is difficult for the prisoners. It is hard for them. They are not with their families."

Both prisoners gave a quick nod of agreement.

I watched more closely as we talked. There was a pecking order after all. An understanding. On board, the two prisoners, John and Venisula, talked less. They expected that Mark and Joseph would carry the conversation with us. But it was not the pecking order of guard and prisoner. Rather older brother, younger brother. Teacher, pupil.

As we talked, meaning unfolded.

The justice department of Tonga, like every other, had very little money. It put guards and prisoners on the island with a herd of cows and said to the guards, "Go to it. Work together. Bring them back into the community."

But it wasn't just a matter of economics. All four maintained their huts together. They fished together. They worked the garden together, growing taro, kumara, yams, breadfruit, bananas, kasava. They played together. They went to church together and slept in the same huts.

"I am prisoner for six month," John said. "I stowaway on Samoan ship to New Zealand." He was sixteen years old. Venisula said. "I take alcohol," He was sixteen also, with a two-year sentence for the theft.

"These are small crimes," Mark said, as if asking me not to judge them harshly. "Big crimes are murder. We don't have that in Tonga. There are thirty-five prisoners in all of Tonga."

There was another round of cans, New Zealand beer particularly prized. If Steinlager only knew.

"How old are you?" Joseph blurted to Sue.

Mark rounded on him, rattling off a reprimand for bad manners, but Joseph spread his arms and re-directed his question. "If you don't mind, I ask. Thirty-three?"

"No, I'm forty-four."

"Ah. I am very close."

He was twenty, his brother twenty-three. Which put the average age for the prisoners and guards of Nomuka Iki at less than nineteen. Even now, Sam remembers word-for-word the next exchange I had with Mark.

"Mark, if all of you eat and work and sleep and go to church together, who are the guards and who are the prisoners?"

"Ah." A nod, understanding the question perfectly. "I don't know." He inspected a tiny cigarette end regretfully and flicked it overboard. "When the ministers come, we are prison officers and prisoners. When the ministers are not here, we are brothers."

"Then what happens when the prisoners leave to go back to their families?"

"When prisoners finish their term and leave here, they cry."

The outboard started, the prop engaged. The longboat returned the boy-men to Nomuka Iki, and then went safely all the way back to Nomuka. Maybe when that longboat disintegrates and the outboard corrodes to dust, the old nail will still be trying to hold it together.

The wind throbbed in the mast track and plucked at the stays.

Thirty knots. *Alderman* moved from side to side on the chain, fretting and rolling. It was looking as if we might lose the gamble that conditions would improve.

I gave Dudley tender loving care, cleaning plugs, drying out leads, checking ignition. There was no improvement in his behaviour. The boys rolled eyeballs but had the sense not to utter a word.

It was too rough for correspondence school lessons, which required a lot of flat space. We gave the boys a choice: write in your diaries, or write to someone at home. Andrew paced about, chewing a pen.

"Should I write to Ellen? I can't decide." (Names have been changed to protect the innocent.) "I might get rejected. I might get hurt. My fear is that I'll get hurt. Yet again." He was standing with his hand near his heart.

"Tough decision."

"I don't want to make a big thing of it. Shall I just talk about what we've been doing?"

"Writing to her from overseas is making a big thing of it. Does she know you've been thinking about her?"

"Sort of. And she smiled at me once in camp." He kept pacing. The wind reached gale force again by eleven p.m. The rolling and agitation became violent. Sleep was impossible; a drug-like coma the best we could manage.

Just after midnight, Andrew and Sam came running to our cabin calling out.

"Mum! Dad! The anchor's dragging."

If I touched down between bed and cockpit it was probably on boys.

But we were not dragging. The ferocious wind and frenzied movements of *Alderman* had excited their imaginations. At midnight, when they couldn't close their eyes, I showed them how to watch near and far points to judge movement. As always, my own lessons were not far ahead of theirs. And, as always, this thought: *What right do I have to put my children in danger, when I'm so inexperienced?*

12

To head out into a gale deliberately you have to have screws loose in the automatic pilot. Ours were rattling after days of skewing and rolling at anchor. We wanted calm water so badly we were ready to go through a wetter and wilder hell to get it. We were fully reefed even before hauling anchor. We knew the way out between the two Nomukas, and the Ha'apai Group was only a few hours away.

But first, we established *code red*.

It was an answer to sluggish responses by crew. Crisp commands no longer had the boys cycling their feet like Roadrunner. Which, they pointed out, was my fault. It seems I had never distinguished between an order to stop the mast falling and an order to stop picking their noses.

So at the boys' own suggestion it was decreed thus: if they heard, *'Code red,'* they would know the next bunch of orders affected the safety of vessel, life or limb and had to be obeyed with the speed of moggies dropped in a dog pound. Furthermore, *code red* status would require a standby 'vessel awareness' even after execution of said orders. Only *code blue* would allow a return to sloth mode. The downside, of course, was that any order not coded red could get filed in the tomorrow basket.

But for this gale and for sailing on the rest of the voyage, *code red* worked. The boys never failed to respond, though Sam occasionally lapsed into *code blue* before the signal. It consolidated their reliability, it gave us more faith in them and they knew it. We were in high spirits when the gale kicked us out of Nomuka, and we stayed that way through to the first of the Ha'apai Group islands.

On VHF we heard that a New Zealand yacht, a twelve metre cutter, had been on the rocks near Ha'afeva. She was off again, but had lost her dinghy in the process. There were immediate offers of loans. Later *Southern Lady* came on.

"Anyone out there got three-eighths copper tubing?" Several boats responded.

Then, I made the sort of mistake that looks at you thereafter out of every glass of whisky on the rocks: I tried to use the satellite system to navigate into a tight set of islands. That must sound reasonable on the face of it. After all, the GPS is the most accurate civil navigation system known. No one disputes it. Imagine, you're out there in a million square kilometres of wet and a little glowing box instantly locates you on the planet within fifteen metres. That's the length of *Alderman*. You could even call it accuracy overkill, more than enough to run a gauntlet of islands.

But GPS figures mean diddly-squat when the charts are as much as two nautical miles out.

When Captain A. Moystyn Field, R.N. plotted tiny Tofu Island and others on to the chart, he came within a shave of turning us into a kiwi version of the Swiss Family Robinson. Not his fault; he was using sextant and chronometer, the hi-tech of 1898. The mostly submerged reef of Tofu Island should have been half a mile from us - Tofu to port, Tongua to starboard, equidistant. But in the heavy white-capped conditions we first saw the coral dentures 200 metres off the port bow. They were sucking in the gale and any dinner guest it cared to bring along. The choice was: forget the superbly accurate GPS figures and move over, or follow the GPS and tell the island to move over.

We pulled away on a combination of sail, full depth centreboard, and full power engine. Centreboards are unusual in a yacht our size. I doubt now if I will ever cruise without one.

There's a saying in circulation now - *GPS assisted groundings.*

Quite a phrase for the scientific wizardry that was supposed to end navigation headaches. Which should ring crystal bells in salty memories; when radar was invented, the same thing happened. One of the world's worst maritime disasters, the collision of the *Andrea Doria* and the *Stockholm* was a 'radar-assisted disaster' because one of the skippers thought the new device provided near immunity to collisions in fog. No, heading into the islands with faith in GPS is like memorising the route through the lion cage and putting on a blindfold as you march in.

The gale shovelled us into a calm lagoon in the lee of Ha'afeva Island. Andrew and Sam were perfect on anchor and depth sounder and the debrief was short. The sudden cessation of movement was a bath of bliss and exhausted muscles sagged with relief.

Mystery Girl was there. Brendan and Jo called up, *"Well done."*

But the GPS blunder was too fresh and I managed only a weak acknowledgement. Ian's dinghy was already drawing a line between us and *Kindred Spirit.* We turned him away. We needed peace and quiet, to collect scattered, battered thoughts and catch up with ourselves.

And we had to reorganise our systems, including a stem-to-stern clean-up. Below decks looked like a town tip after a nor'wester. Also, we were due for an all-off clothes wash which involved throwing the whole horrible harvest in the shower and trampling on it. In sea water. That meant the clothes would come out stale and revert to sticky as the salt sucked moisture from the air. Another edict was to overcome the problems of forcing correspondence lessons into boys' brains. In anchorage, lessons would be held between nine and one, attendance compulsory, starting the next morning.

Somewhere in the clean-up Sam lost the top off the navigation highlighter pen, used on black and white charts for the little matter of distinguishing reefs from water and land. There's a children's story of an ant that sneezes, unleashing a chain of events that ends in the burning of a city.

"Am I still required to look for it?" Sam demanded hotly after half an hour.

"Yes."

After dark Andrew wore out the deck with his feet, worried a pen with his teeth, then put courage to paper:

Andrew at navigation desk, writing to prospective girlfriend.

Dear Ellen, I hope you don't mind me writing, but I am writing because I am thinking about you from time to time.

It really is hot here in Tonga. I have sailed to many islands, one island called Nomuka Iki (the prison island for Tonga). It had prisoners who loved their prison guards like brothers.

I have been snorkelling at some incredible reefs. I saw one fish that was about two metres long that you couldn't tell which end was which.

It ended with a return address at an island ahead. He didn't know Ellen's home address, so he sent it to the school secretary, with a plea for low-key delivery - the one horror worse than rejection was having to endure the class kookaburra chorus if they found out.

That evening we turned on frequency 4417 in time to hear an excited voice talking to another boat.

"Turn to 4445, it's interesting listening."

We took the hint. On 4445, Radio Kerikeri was describing two mean-looking pressure-lows building up over Vanuatu. If they chummied up, we could soon be sailing a cyclone. We called *Mystery Girl* for advice - they'd come the same route the year before. If a cyclone warning was issued, Brendan said, he would cut and run to Neiafu, the hurricane-hole of the Vava'us. Until then he was staying put.

Good enough for us. But in the meantime, the forecast was for 25 knots building to thirty-five. In other words, another gale.

"Why?" Sue shook her head at the radio in disbelief, her voice almost hurt. "Why?"

"What your name?"

I hadn't even shipped the oars and the eager Ha'afeva island youngster was already dragging us on to the sand. His eyes sparkled with fun and his face was radiant.

"Michael. What's yours?"

"Peter. What name you boy?"

I swung out while Andrew and Sam answered, both taken aback by the rushing momentum of the lad.

"What name yacht?"

"Alderman."

"You wife on yacht?"

"Yep."

"What name wife?"

Ha'afeva locals told us later that Peter was self-appointed as a cultural ambassador to the island's visitors. The diplomacy lacked something, but if effort counted Peter's job was secure.

It was through him and his sister, Star, that the boys first saw real poverty. They saw something of what it means and also of what it doesn't mean. With the Peacock family from *Kindred Spirit,* we walked across the island, led by Star, to visit her family, through fields of tapioca, taro, bananas, breadfruit, across a style and into the village.

The fence was to keep the pigs in the village and there were more of them than people. A monstrous black sow eyed Andrew. "Good morning," Andrew greeted it nervously, and jumped when the sow snorked loudly in reply.

Children came running, stopping abruptly at the distance where shyness outweighs curiosity. Their bodies were dirty but healthy, their eyes as clear and bright as Peter's, a few as young as five held machetes, the universal Tongan tool. Some youngsters had cut scars on their legs. They followed us, grinning, some hand in hand, a few stabbing the machetes perilously close to dusty toes. There were no streets and no fences within the perimeter. Just randomly placed houses of hardboard or corrugated iron.

Two small boys huddled behind a chicken coop, hiding from us. As we passed, they rose and rushed upon us having dared each other to chase the strange *palangi*. But they lost their nerve and fled, shrieking with laughter. Teenagers further back showed they had too much dignity to come so close so soon. In a distant window a bare chest was turned hastily away and covered.

Inside Star's house, the yachties sat shoeless and comfortless on the visitors' mat, facing Star and her family. Andrew and Sam were mute, confronted by irrefutable evidence of life without vehicles, without electrical appliances, without even the most basic furniture. Above all, without shops. But I could see that Sam's antennae were tuned in more than anything on the children playing around the doorway. Children who were different, but who obviously knew how to have fun the way he did.

Star's mother was introduced as that. Mother: *Fa'ai*. She nodded, hands busy plaiting *pandanis* strips. Star's *Tamai* was away in the plantation. The preliminaries were eased by the presence of children, the international language. Star beamed at Sam.

"Sam, Sam, come." He moved over shyly and was placed firmly in her lap. Hands tousled his hair. Sue reached out for a baby and was informed that her name was Olivia. Three months old and with eyes like starlit pools.

It was more a hut than a house, with one main room and three small. No internal doors. In the far room a very old man sat looking at us, but separate from the gathering.

"He is not a relation," Star told us later. "His mother and father die a long time ago. He never marry. He live with us now."

Star, it turned out, was a more likely cultural ambassador for Ha'afeva. Eighteen, shy but dignified, educated away from the island. When *palangi* were around, she carried unusual authority. She didn't know how many sisters she had and thought that two were now with other families. There were thirty years between the oldest and youngest of her siblings: Olivia was now sucking energetically on my index finger.

"Uh uh, no milk," I growled and the translation sent a ripple of laughter through the Tongans.

Star's mother rose, almost formally crossing into the space between the groups. "Sam. Sam," she said, giving him a *pandanis* bracelet.

"Malo," Sam replied, to an appreciative murmur. But a flicker of irritation crossed his face when the next hand stroked his hair and skin.

Lisa Peacock played 'Amazing Grace' on her flute. Star said she only knew Christian songs and sang one we didn't recognise. Sam and I sang 'The Gypsy

Rover'. Both sides struggled to find a tune in common, finally succeeding with 'I'm a Little Teapot'.

We asked to trade for food. And it was arranged more like mutual gift-giving. They gave us cooked stuffed octopus and small reef fish, plantains and breadfruit, throwing in bracelets and many shells for the boys. We produced nylon fishing line, biscuits, postcards. And a women's magazine: highly valued in the villages. We pulled out a Polaroid camera, which galvanised the family. They chattered over the detail as the shots developed, insisting on picture after picture, including one of the old man who made no sign that he knew what was happening.

On the return across the island, Sam conspired with like-minded brown-skinned imps to ambush me and plant a very dead fish under my T-shirt. The mass escape into the bush was led from the front by a blonde-haired renegade. I could have caught them, but I had company: Mary in one hand, Isaiah on the opposite shoulder and tiny Smaima skipping on the path ahead.

On the reef, Star and her family hunted for food with iron spikes, breaking up the coral for *vana,* sea urchins, *elili,* a shellfish, and especially *hulihuli,* a fat slug with a hard skin. The broken coral also disturbed scores of jet black, six-armed octopi, better known as the poisonous devil fish or *feke.*

Peter came to me.

"Gita?" he asked. "You? Yacht? Gita?" He strummed his fingers in the air. Guitar.

We took him and Star out to *Alderman* and discovered that she had never been on a yacht. She wandered around, almost afraid to touch things that had all been storm-battered anyway. Peter's reaction was something else again. When he first walked into the main cabin, he stood stock still. His mouth fell open.

"FUCK OFF OFF," he shouted.

Sam's hair stood on end. He watched to see if Peter would be incinerated in front of him. But with translation the words came out differently. *"Whaka ofa ofa.* It mean beautiful."

Peter used our guitar for an Elvis rendition that could have peeled paint off the bulkheads.

The visit roused furious argument amongst the yachts. Little wonder that Star had never been aboard, because many vessels made a policy of keeping islanders off. Confronting them with what we have rubs their noses in their own poverty, the argument went.

We said, "They've been hospitable, we can do the same."

13

The cyclone didn't happen. The two low-pressure systems flirted, abstained and spun out, dissipating their energies harmlessly. And yet the southerlies still came on through at 25 knots plus, more than a week after they began. The relentless moaning in the rigging wore us down, needling tempers. We built up our own pressure system.

Something had to give, and when it did I couldn't blame the breeze.

Andrew wasn't impressed when I wouldn't let him use the spear gun. So he developed his own, working much of the afternoon in the workshop with a length of hardwood, a peg, powerful rubber bands and two huge nails. It didn't work well.

"I have discovered the meaning of life," he muttered. "It is a bastard."

Even so, his diary says he and Ian used the gun to shoot two fish, *only to see a long, dark fin and streamlined body came racing in to attack our fish. We shouted Shark! Shark! And Dad leapt out of the water.* Which was news to me.

The battery-charging system stopped working. An intermittent fault which resisted analysis.

Andrew and Ian were once again excluding Sam from their adventures. "Sam can't keep secrets," was the hot complaint. True. Why tell Sam a secret when it was just as easy to use a megaphone? So we discussed boomerangs with Sam, extracted a promise of behaviour change, and declared *Alderman* a fight-free zone.

It didn't work. Tensions rose even higher. We kept Sam on the boat when the other two went ashore. Sam said, "Dad, I just want you to know I hate you."

The centreboard blocks seized. They had to be completely dismantled without losing the board.

Sue announced that we were nearly out of the staples: flour, milk, butter and eggs. She had underestimated the grazing habits of the human male at sea. She also developed 'Tonga Tummy', which was demanding on the facilities. Still, she was more restrained than Andrew who announced his plumbing emergency with "Clear the way, I'm going to blow."

We found that we needn't have suffered sleepless nights with graunching sounds coming up from the anchor. We hadn't been using the anchor at all. The chain was wrapped round a bombie. It had to be unravelled.

So did I.

At dinner - sauteed octopus and breadfruit chips - Sam demanded more salt. Sue said the chips had plenty of salt and he couldn't have any more. Please? No, and that was final.

"But I want some."

"No."

"But why?"

"No!" Me this time. "Can't you take no for an answer? Go on, hop it. Get out of my sight."

Sam left, greviously wounded. Andrew pulled his eyebrows back down, looked at the chip in his hand and thought about the danger in opening his mouth right then. In the aft cabin Sam made a humph sound. Andrew cleared his throat.

"Dad, you're having a bad day, aren't you?"

"No!"

"You're very crabby."

I thumped the centreboard casing. "Look, I have to make lots of decisions in this game. I can't stand it when there are endless arguments!"

Prolonged silence.

Unobtrusively, Sue pointed me to the for'd cabin for a chat. She didn't lay a finger on me, but somehow it felt as if she had taken me by the ear and hauled me away for a flea implant. Then she spoke quietly. Sue never shouted. Nor would she tolerate being shouted at - she'd been talking to Carol on *Kirsten Jane* who responded to shouting by folding her arms and dropping whatever she was holding: a rope, the anchor, or her husband dangling from the masthead.

"You're too tired," Sue told me. "You're too irritable and you're too hard to take. The boys are getting jumpy. Something's got to change."

Fair enough. I understood that. Obviously we all needed a break. We'd up anchor and doddle over to tiny Pudupua Island for a picnic, just one hour away. No shouting, nothing pushy, nothing strenuous, no work for anyone. And Pudupua was completely uninhabited.

We went back to the boys and declared our intentions. "Imagine that, boys, our own uninhabited island."

"Oh, yes! Let's go!"

The engine died ten seconds after we started up.

The hand primer diesel bowl was filled with brown gunk. Not healthy, and something of a mystery. Tony from *Southern Lady* came over, took one look and said I'd be better off using diesel because water didn't burn so well. No, I protested, it couldn't be that. The inspection bowl had shown no sign of a water/diesel mix. We opened the bowl, we tasted it. It was drinkable and fresh. In one great rush, condensation water from *Alderman's* seven tanks had flooded the whole fuel line. Fixing that involved pumping water from the bottom of the main tank, cleaning out the filters and bleeding the whole system.

Not my favourite pastime at sea.

I had all the tools around me when Andrew came through with a broom and a temper, choosing that time to do his chores and muttering, "Look out, here comes the grim sweeper." Sam, still in the kennel, snarled about the scarcity of fun around here.

I snapped at him. He responded. I responded. We had a tennis match. At deuce, he delivered his best and loudest shot. "I want to put a scorpion down Dad's pants!"

That did it. That was the one. The needle in my pressure gauge flicked right past critical and broke off in a cloud of steam. In a single bound I flew over tall spanners, carried Sam off to the aft-cabin, spanked him, thrust him howling into the berth and stormed out. An electrified Ian and Andrew followed me with swivelling eyes.

"Wow," Andrew breathed.

"I think I'll go back to my boat now," Ian added, perhaps wondering if there was going to be a general massacre.

"That," Sue said with slow and ominous emphasis, "was unnecessary."

There are two kinds of wretch. There is the ordinary wretch and there is the pathetic wretch. I started out as the first, putting my head in my hands, which were on the table at the time. I moved on to the second as a new kind of sound emerged from the aft-cabin.

"I hate you, I hate you, I hate you! I'm going to hate you for the rest of my life!" After a pause he added, "Dad's the witch of the Western world!" Later we would discover that the last bit was suggested by Andrew, acting as his advisor in the crisis.

Much later, when Sam had had sufficient time to think over the error of my ways, he went over my head. He went to Sue.

"There's something you should know. I need time away from you and Dad. I think two days, right away, no grown-ups, where we're left alone and not ordered about. You're just as bad as Dad sometimes and I just have to get away if we're to live together. Sometimes the things that happen just break my heart."

In other words, our seven-year-old was no longer spankable.

Another way had to be found.

It was. Sue gave me a cooling-off time so I, too, could think over the error of my ways. She gave Sam heart therapy, discussing his behaviour - and his Dad's. Then she came back and retired herself and me into the for'd cabin, this time drawing the curtain. With a clang. On the other side of the curtain I could hear the boys moving up the companionway so as to be as far away as possible. Whatever was about to transpire in the for'd cabin wasn't going to be pretty.

In the morning I spoke to the boys. First, I apologised to Sam, for losing my temper. Sam immediately apologised to me. Our tough little boy melted to the one we knew was capable of tears and hugs.

"I'm sorry I called you names," he offered with downcast eyes. "I'm going to change my behaviour."

I sat him on my knee. "Sam. I'm sorry too. But look, it's our last day here and Mum's going to be skipper for the day."

"She is?"

"Yes, I'm going to take a rest. Sound like a good idea?" Andrew sat bolt upright with a huge grin on his face. Sam's mouth worked into a wondrous circle.

"OH YAY!"

I limited my sulks to a short "Hmph" in the aft cabin.

Then, for the first time, I debauched in the style to which I always wanted to become accustomed anyway. I luxuriated in swimming and diving, books and beer, and the only tools I picked up were knives and forks. I waved decisions away and saw that I had been overrating their urgency and simply hadn't let go since the frenetic preparations in Lyttelton.

Brendan was so right; it had taken me close to six weeks.

Curiously, Sam found it hard to adjust to the change in his father. It puzzled him. He kept probing. He would creep up to give me mild frights. Or he'd suddenly tickle me while I was reading to him about Dick and Pongo's adventures in 'Famous Five'. But there's no doubt he approved. He asked the current skipper if she could stay on permanently.

Not that all would remain meekness and light, but the occasional skipper swap had come to stay.

Sue wants a word:

As Michael wallowed, beer in hand, in the for'd cabin, I took stock of my new standing. It was strange to be back at the family helm. I had to give myself a thorough rev-up to get back into the part.

I thought about the other yachting women around me. None of us fitted the gung-ho, dungarees and hairy armpits image. Few of us were strong physically. None had chosen an all-female boat, none tried to beat the boys at their own game. But, despite our age and experience differences, there was a common thread.

I couldn't name it, but it had to do with being extremely practical, strong-willed, inventive, unflappable but still unmistakeably feminine. We'd all had to rethink our views on equality of the sexes en route; without exception we were first mates to male skippers, most to husbands. However, we agreed it wasn't at all demeaning to find the men were the super-structure to the whole enterprise, and we the glue that held it together. The men took charge of the overall safety of the boat, and the women kept tabs on everything else. Life would have been impossible if we'd arranged things any differently. Certainly, there were some good male cooks in the fleet, and some proficient female navigators, but few did those jobs consistently.

The dentist is in.

The beard trimmer is in.

*A friend (English second language)
once remarked to Sue, "Ahhh... you very useful wife."*

Michael emerged just as I was considering ordering his cooking skills back into action. As duty skipper, I could surely make him produce the evening meal. But I didn't do it. He'd been at concert pitch for so long now, it was wonderful to see him relaxing finally, easing off on to Island time. How could I shatter that longed-for equanimity? As the boys fired a volley of questions at him, he waved them away.

"Go ask the skipper!" he said with a smile.

They blinked, disoriented by the new regime, then left him alone.

Later, I went into a huddle with women from other yachts, over provisioning, cooking, and laundry techniques. At home, I'd have run, screeching, from such a mind-numbing session. Normally, I can't bear swapping recipes and discussing detergents, as though I'm in one of those simpering housewife commercials on TV. Here, such things had to be addressed with some intelligence. They were fundamental to survival.

I discovered we all had mentors, other women who'd kept the flame of adventure burning through difficult and often dangerous times.

Back in Christchurch mine had been Glenys Duff, though she probably didn't know it. She'd understood the strain of preparing a family to take to the high seas; she'd done it herself the year before. She'd coaxed me through my periods of doubt, encouraged me with stories of joy and exhilaration, and admired my plan to play both mother hen and first mate. Sitting in Ha'afeva now I knew I might never have her skill in sailing *per se*, but I was catching up on her ability to keep things in perspective. It was Glenys who wrote to pass on another Kiwi woman's dictum to me: Little gained from a life of ease, the sailor hails from stormy seas.

I'd found other mentors within the fleet: Jo on the psychological plane, Geraldine on the practical. Both taught me how to have fun when all the evidence was against such a possibility. Our 'up-to-the-fence' chats were remarkably candid. We were all married to very strong, ambitious, and mischievous men, so the bond was immediate. More than at home, we all needed a measure of feminine intimacy to offset the lack of privacy in everything else.

I took a closer look at the on-board relationships around us. We were all, I

The versatile shower / washing machine with shapely twin agitators, for washing everything more substantial than knickers – in sea water. Clothes dried from a sea-water wash swiftly became sticky and unpleasant to wear.

noticed, asking a monumental amount of each other! After all, there'd be very few couples on land who spent every waking and sleeping second together as we had to; almost none who didn't have work, sport or hobbies to provide a counterfoil.

Perversely, I took some comfort from the sounds of occasional 'domestics' floating across the water – there was a frisson of reassurance in hearing that someone was being unbearable. I saw one couple conduct their dispute long distance – one shouting from the mother ship, the other roaring around in a dinghy with no obvious destination. They were all signs that the most stable of relationships has to have steam vents, and there's every justification in letting 'em rip occasionally.

An odd realisation came to me as I continued my skipperhood.

Despite our need for other people to bounce off, we wouldn't want anyone else living with us now. Like Jo and Brendan, we were learning that we wanted to find our own way, in every way.

Jo told a story of a man who'd stayed on *Mystery Girl* the year before. He was a charming, well-educated and witty man, but he'd not learned the essential social graces of life on board. Jo said he was permanently on transmit, and never on receive. His antennae simply didn't pick up that people living in confined spaces have very different needs from people anywhere else.

We now understood exactly why he'd never been asked back.

We liked being able to call our own shots without interference. We liked deciding when to be on transmit, when on receive, when to call Roger, over and out!

'By the end of my day in charge, I was absolutely pooped. But I could feel a nicer tension in our family fabric. It was obviously still frayed at the edges here and there, but the central weaving was no longer awry. I hoped we'd recognise the signs of trouble sooner next time. We now had a way to fix it up fast.

I'll hand back to Michael.

14

Then, for many wonderful days, everything came right. As if our universe had only been waiting for us to get our family act together. It felt like entering a magical cocoon – a place where our original romantic notions of cruising life were no longer naïve.

And we found an island like heaven on earth.

Half-way to Uoleva Island, when it was still below the horizon, the southerlies relented, shifting to east-southeast and softening to a warm 15 knots. The swell eased too, down to slight and lilting. So we went northeast on a movement so gentle it was like the canter of a horse projected in slow motion. We passed island after island, green stones set in shimmering blue as if in some ancestral dream. When the boys were below, asleep, Sue and I found new closeness as *Alderman* rose and fell through the cobalt sea.

Uoleva must be one of the world's most beautiful atolls. There's a long scallop of pale gold sand, topped with a sweep of palms that slow the trades to a soft, cooling breeze. Within the outer reef there's no coral to foul the anchors, just sand. There is no inner reef, so the lagoon bottom runs unbroken to the palms. On the eastern side, kauri shells and spider conches nestle in the coral, and inland, in season, the coconut groves are alive with monarch butterflies.

And there's almost no one there. Just one family in a couple of huts at the north end. The sand is untouched except for the prints of a few cows and the sow that takes its piglets for a swim in the cool evening.

Now, it was early afternoon.

Sam and I walked hand-in-hand on the shore. Sam dragged a stick, making snakes, then threw it into the water, disturbing a school of tiny fish. A wave of flashing, panicked silver broke out of the surface and hissed away along the shore. Sam chuckled and looked for another stick.

Out on *Alderman,* Sue's blonde head appeared then vanished below. A surprise, because she had promised herself rest, read and sleep.

I had dreamed about Sam and me: we were painting a roof with many colours. Wanting to change into old clothes, I put him in a safe place where he could keep painting without danger of falling. I went away, but was distracted from returning by a car with a television set playing a cheap western. I became part of the western. I found myself trying to rescue a damsel of the distressed kind, only to be set on by two of the bad guys. I started to lose. It seemed terribly important to tell them that

Sam would do a quality job and they would often see that in a seven-year-old boy.

Now I sat doodling in the sand, watching him. He'd found a new stick and was attacking a coconut.

He'd been a confident, hard-headed little blighter even before we started. Yesterday, he'd talked me into letting him up in the spreaders to bombie-spot for anchoring. Harnessed to the mast, bombie-spotting over pure sand, but up there without me. And no false modesty - by anchor-drop the entire floating complement of Uoleva knew about it. Whatever Andrew did, Sam had to do, as if four years could be spanned by the force of will.

"Dad, I can do this myself!"
Even with close supervision, Sam's boundless confidence was often terrifying.

Along the beach, Andrew and Ian were building a hut from palm leaves, aiming to sleep on shore.

If anything, there was even more change in Andrew. We could see it in his eyes, a new shine, a sharper focus, in contrast to the post-television couch-potato glaze I remembered. I had read to both Andrew and Sam from the sea classic, *The Last Grain Race,* about the apprentice who climbed the ratlines and nearly fell to his death. Both boys had then, unknown to me, talked themselves on to the eighteen metre gaff-rigged schooner *R. Tucker Thompson* and then up the ratlines to the crows-nest. Back home Andrew had been reluctant to get on a bicycle. Both boys were now flexing minds, muscles and tongues beyond anything we had hoped.

Andrew and Ian set out to swim to *Alderman*, a hundred metres from shore. They had probably forgotten some detail for the hut's defence systems. Or it was feeding time again.

Still on the beach, I removed my shorts and lay back in underpants so brief, so worn, so loosened by the cruising life that I might as well have been naked. It should have been safe. The only Tongans around were the family in the bush up the far end of the bay.

I heard a scuffing in the sand and opened my eyes. Three Tongan beauties were seating themselves beside me, all in the prime of their late teenage lives. I remembered the Tongan laws and sat up with a jerk, nearly dislodging the briefs altogether. The girls grinned at me.

"Excuse me please. My name is Hina."

"Hi." I caught my hands trying to cover up the essential facts and froze them.

"These are my friends Tema and To'ilose."

"Malo e lelei."

All three were fully dressed, as in dresses and shoes. They didn't look the least bit put out about my state of undress. I looked around bewildered as to how they had appeared on a nearly uninhabited island, but saw no clues.

Hina held up an exercise book. A school book.

"I ask please you help with English. Tomorrow I give talk in my class."

I badly, badly wanted to reach for my shorts, but they were too far away so I hugged my knees and walked my toes to block critical angles of view. My father had once told me admiringly of an Egyptian girl who lost every scrap of clothing in the surf in front of a platoon of soldiers. She recovered with such poise and aplomb that the platoon stood as one man and applauded as she left the beach. So I could surely sit here in my underpants and give a Tongan girl an English lesson while waiting for the morals police.

"Io. OK. I'll help."

"Ah, thank you, thank you."

"What's the talk about?"

"The name of my talk is *How to Make Friends with a Boy*."

I glanced at her. Confidence would never be her problem in making friends with a boy. But, to work. She told me what she wanted to say, I suggested changes, checked back with her, then wrote it down:

Thank you Brother Tad for allowing me to give this talk to the class. The topic is How to Make Friends with a Boy. First I say hello and I ask him his name. Then I ask if he would like to be friends with me. Of course he says yes. So I ask him when he would like to meet me. I take him to my house. If my parents like him they ask him to come inside.

Most parents back home would be astounded to have such priority in the romantic aspirations of their daughters. But modesty, chastity and honour are heavily built into the traditions. Typically a boy wooed a girl by arriving at her house with three or four friends and a root of kava, and asking the parents to let the girl pound the kava for them. For centuries this apparent drudgery has in fact been a night of excitement for the girl. She rubbed on sweet-smelling sandalwood oil until her skin shone, she wore her best dress, she slid her hands through the ancient motions of kava making, and her *kiekia,* grass overskirt, rustled alluringly as she moved. It was understood that a word or two of love might be heard sometime in the evening. A virtuous girl was chased and chaste. Something of a contrast to the behaviour of King Lafetamaka II in the 1770s. The eighty-year-old gent considered it his duty to deflower every native maiden. Duty, Captain Cook reported in his journals, called the king eight to ten times a day.

Hina was delighted. I hoped Brother Tad would not question her too closely about her sources. She bounced down to the water's edge, where Tema and To'ilose were talking to Sam. She put a hand on Sam's shoulder and looked at me.

"You take a photo of me and Sam?"

Sam sighed, resigned but still passably gracious.

Later, I sat on the dinghy transom dangling my feet once again, this time for Sue to cut my beard. She still didn't need to do the top hair; after Gen's ministrations it probably wouldn't grow back before it turned white. Then I unhitched Dudley and tied him to a coconut trunk. For one wild moment I considered flogging him but settled for taking him apart piece by piece. I went right through the fuel system cleaning out satisfactory gobs of gunk. Back on the dinghy, he started first time and I took off at full power to an underwhelming cheer from the boys. Their leverage for a new motor had just lost steam.

That evening, when our magic cocoon was spun in sunset pastels and deep indigos, and the flying foxes were stirring with dreams of quarrels in the dawn, the cruising tribe came out of the boats and onto the beach. We dug a pit in the sand, setting orange flames into dried coconut fronds and stems and fruits. Children made their own pits, tending them avidly. Then they found coconuts still with milk and beat them on the points of dinghy anchors to break them open. Andrew and Ian refined their hut. They'd worked out a secret code with their torches, to be ready to deal with blackbirders and bandits.

Sam came running to us, aghast. "Brendan is very sick, a rat ran over his chest!" But a check revealed the original wording: Brendan had a rash on his chest.

When the flames fell, we laid meats and fish and vegetables into the embers, then sat murmuring to each other and watching our vessels setting in delicate marble. The moon sank with purpose, drawn precisely to the anchor light on *Alderman's* mast.

Lisa's flute came out. And our school recorder. Two, then three guitars. Songs sprang up and ran over the sand and through the groves. Some, old and worn at home, had new life in that place and international company. 'Alouette', 'Once a Jolly Swagman', 'Greensleeves'. Even 'Frère Jacques' carried new meaning when sung in appalling French to Pierre, Cristina and Annabelle from *Hibiscus.*

One by one, dinghies returned to yachts, over a lagoon so still they were suspended in the centre of a vast sphere of stars. The gentlest stroke of an oar tumbled galaxies.

While Ian and Andrew were collecting final provisions, bandits came out of the bush, trampled their hut and escaped, leaving hoof marks as the only clue. The boys talked of vengeance and beef stew, but gave up for the night and slept on board.

Much later, Sue and I returned to the beach to talk, to walk, to run along the sand under the starlight. We nearly ran into a bandit, stolidly chewing cud at the water's edge. But she accepted our apology and we ran on.

One evening, as darkness fell, Sue dropped her watch over the side. In the morning Andrew and I dived for it, an exercise in faith because the anchor radius was large and the watch was tiny, with exactly the same shade of green as the sea lettuce. Against all odds I found it. After fifteen hours in salt water it was still on time, and still is.

We had a friend on a fifteen metre Roberts Spray who did the same thing with his false teeth. When they went down chattering, he was fifteen metres from the bottom and a thousand miles from a dental technician. He couldn't stand the thought that his gnashers were down there laughing at him. Another yacht, with scuba gear, found him standing at the rail, hugging his spare anchor with a look of gummy desperation.

The days and nights merged, mixing time. The end of the cocoon was close.

We heard that *Karma* had been caught by coral on Atata Island and paid the price. She was completely wrecked. There'd been no loss of life, but another dream had been shredded by dead marine animals.

A canoe came alongside. The family from the far end of the beach greeted us, the mother speaking for them. She had the radiance of the truly contented and the body of a Buddha. In Tonga, an ample body is considered a sign of good living. Big is beautiful and knows it.

"Please you tell other yacht, we make *umu* tonight. We make feast. You come. They come."

I went straight onto the back foot. Our scratch budget was not too happy with commercial eating.

"I'll tell the other yachts. How much does it cost?"

"Cost?"

"How much money?"

"No, no. No money. You bring something for feast," My back foot was obviously in my mouth so she was merciful. "My grandfather. When he die, he tell me ask all yacht to *umu*. You tell other yacht. You come."

The family slaughtered a pig for us, turning it on a spit for most of the day. They fired up a pit of hot stones, laying breadfruit, taro and pumpkin on them and covering them with *fao* leaves. They laid out a huge banquet mat on the sand and wove palm fronds into eating platters. And when it was all laid out, along with dishes we had brought, they sat back and watched with pleasure as we ate. In Tonga it's good manners to let the guest begin first, and if the food is all eaten by the guest the host is delighted and flattered. *Nofo fakalata.* Making the visitor at home with descendants of the warrior empire .

In 1806, about ten kilometres north of our feast, the crew of the English privateer *Port au Prince* was massacred by the warrior king Finau 'Ulukalala II. It was at a time when cannibalism, baby sacrifice and arbitrary death were a way of life. But a fourteen-year-old boy, William Mariner, was spared and became the adopted son of the king. And when William Mariner returned to England years later, his often horrific story contained a flipside. In spite of being the king's adopted son, he was at first always hungry and reduced to stealing food. When he complained to his adopted father, the king was astonished. After questioning Mariner he was even more astonished to discover that Europeans expect strangers to eat their own food in their own house unless invited otherwise. The Tongan way, he explained to Mariner, is to go into any house where a meal is under way, sit down uninvited and eat. The Tongan way is better, he said. The European way is selfish. So William Mariner learned unselfishness and stopped starving.

Some yachts left Uoleva. We farewelled *Kindred Spirit* and *Mystery Girl.* More yachts came. We saw the family canoe go alongside one, repeating the invitation to an *umu*. Later, on the VHF, two puzzled skippers tried to sort out what it meant.

"What do they want then?" one said. *"What's in it for them, I mean what's their game?"* They never did understand it and arranged to collect $5 a head. The family said later they would donate the money to charity.

In Uoleva, our system of working in the morning and playing in the afternoon worked well. Correspondence lessons finally got a good run, in spite of the resistance. And every now and then a lesson was a hit. Both boys took to electricity and stripped the electrics cupboard of spare lamps, switches, batteries and wires. Both assembled a basic circuit, threw the switch and made the lamp glow. Andrew drew the circuit with appropriate symbols, then said his next project would be to design a Tomcat flight simulator.

Andrew, gaining confidence.

Sam, gaining freedom
(from 'totally unfair' restrictions).

I improved my leisure times by learning to make bread. Delectable bread it was and Simple Simon would never have gone for the pies if he had known about this recipe: *Mix 1 tbsp golden syrup, 1 cup boiling water, 1 cup milk, 2 tsp dried yeast, add 2 cups white flour and 2 cups wholemeal. Warm at 100 degrees until risen, then bake at 180 degrees for 40 minutes.*

Dinner was even better: *Poach parrot fish in coconut juice, then bake with plantains, onions, tomatoes, sweet basil and tarragon for 40 minutes at what our oven says is 180 degrees.*

When Sam finally laid down his fingers he said, "No offence Dad, but I can't eat any more." Not exactly a glowing tribute, but I said nothing - when I exact praise for my cooking, Sue adopts an expression of infinite patience.

15

At Lifuka we hit coral.

It was a cruel backhander for the extreme care we thought we took with navigation and eyeballing the water.

Wham. What are you? Not careful enough.

We were low on provisions and had to call into Pangai, the capital of the Ha'apais, on the west side of Lifuka. The approaches to Pangai were the most hazardous yet. The chart of the complex two-mile approach to the harbour is enough to make any navigator sit down for serious planning. And of course the GPS was a waste of time at such close quarters with ancient charts. The one glance we gave it placed *Alderman* on land, in the Tongan king's Pangai residence.

The weather conditions were easy. East-northeast 15 knots and fine. We came in from the west, making it safely all the way to the harbour entrance, past every reef, every bombie, through the complex markers and buoys, trusting none. We even crossed the line between the entrance buoys into the safety of the harbour.

Then we relaxed. Too soon. Andrew came down off the spreaders. Sue took the helm, I went forward to prepare the anchor. Sue kept to the starboard side of the narrow harbour for the turn and I knelt to loosen the anchor-winch clutch. Then, for some reason, I glanced over the side.

My heart jumped, hammering on my chest. Coral. An unmarked tongue, licking into the harbour, close to the surface, right under us. That's when the scraping sound started.

A losing hand of cards flicked across my mind in the fraction of a second it took to rise and turn towards Sue. The wind was blowing on to the coral. If we stuck, a rising tide might free us, but not side-on like this. Lifuka was an outpost with no resources. The chances of another craft pulling us off in this cramped space were remote. And an unusually high tide stranding us in bad weather would mean almost certain disaster. On the other hand, if we stuck lightly, I could weight the boom to one side, or run a halyard from mast to shore, or exercise some other academic textbook theory.

I yelled and pointed, sprinting for the cockpit and thrusting Sam aside even as Sue swung the tiller. Sam fell heavily on the deck and cried out with pain. Full revs. Forward and hard to port because with almost no stern steerage we could be blown to starboard anyway. Everything happened with merciless slow-motion. The scraping became a graunching; we checked, kept scraping.

And then we were free. I had no idea how many seconds it lasted.

But we had scraped the living fronds off a lee reef, which is taking a close shave way too far. Half a dozen people watched silently from the shore. After a wash of pure relief, I looked back at the coral, astounded. No markers. How could the harbour authority in a capital allow an unmarked hazard right on their doorstep?

The harbour was narrow with no swing space, barely the width of three yachts on end, so we needed anchors fore and aft. I was so affected by the incident that I dropped the aft pick anchor without unfolding it. I had to go through the whole process again, only grateful that the watching audience was too well-mannered to laugh.

Then reaction set in. I needed some long slow breaths.

The boys knew only too well that we'd been close to the end of the dream, and Sam demanded only a token dignity-polish. Andrew put his arm around Sue who had the shakes. She blamed herself for being on the helm and not spotting the coral. But later we found the hazard mentioned in one of the informal navigation guides. I had that guide on board, I was the navigator and I had overlooked it. My responsibility. Mine.

What are you? Not careful enough.

It made us, me, all the more determined not to become yet another careless statistic, yet another greenhorn who gets stuck on the coral, bleating for a rescue that might or might not come.

We were still in Pangai harbour when we had the first of a remarkable series of coincidences. As if some island god, fed up with being ignored, had kicked his dog and decided to show the *palangi* he was still around. Each coincidence taken alone was only mildly remarkable. Taken together they stretched the long arm of chance right up into the coconuts.

In the skeds with Ian and Glenys, they sometimes mentioned people they had met when they cruised the islands. Look for a woman called Langilangi, they had told us over 1500 miles of static. She runs a guesthouse on Lifuka Island.

We had almost finished provisioning.

The choice in the shops was limited and fantastically expensive. We had been warned off the local fresh water, so we decided to risk low tanks through to the Vava'u group where we'd be in a few days. We moved back to the harbour to buy veges from the tray of a vendor's ute, again finding very little choice: peppers, mushy tomatoes, cucumbers and ping-pong lettuces. The main streets were further inland, so apart from a yellow van coming along the road there was no movement and no one around.

"We're looking for someone who lives in Lifuka," Sue said to the vendor, just as the yellow van pulled up opposite us. "Her name is Langilangi. She runs a guesthouse."

"Yes. There." The vendor pointed to the van, where the driver was opening the door. A woman got out and began to head for the post office.

"No." It obviously wasn't clear. "A woman called Langilangi who has a-"

"Yes. That is Langilangi." She called out and the woman changed direction to join us. "These people are looking for you," the vendor said.

A shy smile warmed Langilangi's features and when we mentioned Ian and Glenys the smile broadened.

We didn't stay overnight at Fonongava'inga Guesthouse, mostly because we wanted *Alderman* safely out of the harbour. In a blow, Pangai was just a trap with coral jaws. But Langilangi was a fine hostess anyway. She took us around Lifuka, showed us how to husk a coconut, and loaded us down with coconuts and cucumbers. And she came aboard before we left, where Sue gave her an antibiotic and pain killers for her daughter who had tropical boils.

No one ever picked their way through coral with more meticulous care than the skipper and crew of *Alderman* when we left Pangai to the north. Just as well because the northern route is even more of a minefield than the western.

With the smell of near-disaster fresh, the teamwork was crisp. We refined *code red* further for the boys, eliminating a source of past errors. From now on, if an order came from the helm, its substance had to be repeated back. Very navy. The boys took to it because they could imagine Tomcats, Hornets, Sopworth Camels, the whole zoo taking off from the deck of an aircraft carrier.

"Bombie spot in the spreaders, Andrew."

"Bombie spot in the spreaders."

"Sam, turn on the depth sounder."

"Turning on depth sounder, *Captain.*"

"There's no need to call me captain. Just repeat the order."

"But I like it!"

"OK. OK."

So the aircraft carrier *U.S.S. Alderman* sailed efficiently and without courts martial to Ofalanga Island, our last stop before the passage to the Vava'u group.

If Ofalanga Island could move it would rattle in its reef. It's less than a tenth the area of its coral ring. Also, it cuts off the lagoon to anything bigger than a dinghy or canoe. We anchored at the south end, where island and reef almost touch, quarter of a mile from the beach, our first time without the dubious protection of coral.

The island was deserted, with no sign of human life except the huts of itinerant copra workers. The beach was smooth, the coconut trees like crossed teeth, pointing 25 metres or more towards different parts of the sky.

To the west, steam rose from the flat-topped Tofua volcano. In ancient times, condemned prisoners were thrown into it.

Next to Tofua in 1879, most of Captain Bligh's crew mutinied against his harsh rule. Fletcher Christian dumped him and eighteen loyal crew unceremoniously into a small open boat. Bligh attempted to take on coconuts, breadfruit and water at Tofua, but the natives hurled stones, killing one of his men - somewhat ironic for Bligh, who was Captain Cook's sailing master when Cook deemed the islands friendly. He and his men left without provisions, beginning one of the great ocean feats of navigation and endurance, a 6,500-mile journey in an open boat.

Andrew and I snorkelled the outer reef from the dinghy, always keeping someone on shark watch. After one look, we went back for the spear gun. The water was diamond clear in the sun and I had never seen so many dinner guests in one waiting room at one time. Fishing was sparse; even the locals were complaining about the weather from the south. The only fish we'd hooked in the last fortnight had, in one clean movement, carried away our deep sea, bungy-sprung, heavy duty, overkill trolling gear. But I doubt if I would have handled that one alongside anyway.

The great white hunter cocked his weapon and circled, looking for a fat innocent to slap on a plate. From one spot I could see at least thirty, sixty to ninety centimetres long, gliding around the coral ledges. And one, a grouper, a good 120 centimetres long and even lazier than the others.

I cunningly powered right for it, to stop it developing suspicions that I was up to something subtle. It glided under a ledge, in no hurry. I turned back to see if Andrew had noticed my skilful approach. He had. He expressed admiration by rolling his eyeballs and circling his finger round his ear, then pointed at the gun with an expression of great longing. Clearly he wanted to see more of my skill.

After thirty minutes of hunting, the only thing suffering in the water was Andrew. The fish seemed to know if they were pan-sized, and if so, they also knew, to the millimetre, the range of the spear. Those that weren't pan-sized ignored me, except for two that nibbled the tip of the spear and inspected my eyes through the goggles.

As we surfaced, Sue was leaping to her feet in the dinghy, alarmed, pointing towards the open sea.

"Fins! Fins! Move!"

At the same moment, she plucked Sam from the water. Being jerked out by the snorkel tends to put an end to happy snorkelling. Andrew and I churned water, reaching opposite sides of the dinghy at the same time. I thought about my toes, realising how attached I was to them. Andrew must have had similar thoughts because we nearly crossed in mid air above the dinghy.

They were dolphins. Either that or sharks have learned to somersault in the air.

Ashore, alone, we felt part of the island. *Alderman* mulled quietly beyond the reef. The boys tumbled and chased in the lagoon and built fantasies in the sand. Sue and I lay in the shade, talking, sometimes just dozing.

I hunted for milk coconuts, husking them on a sharp stick, cracking them on a trunk, forcing the crack right round the equator until the milk started to drip through. Then, throwing my head back, I poured the cool liquid into my mouth until it spilled over chin and shoulders and down my chest. When you sail 2,000 miles to crack a coconut on a tropical island, the milk is the sweetest nectar on earth.

We began the passage to the Vava'u Group when the full moon was just over zenith, so bright that the details of Ofalanga, its coconut palms and beach and even the slow lick of sea on the reef were clear and stark. The details stayed sharp as they shrank with distance. The air was warm, the wind five knots, the open sea utterly flat, a condition foreign to us. Even Frankie's quiet throb seemed intrusive. We all had the same question and none of us dared air it.

Where's the gale?

Andrew's first official watch, celebrated with black bubbly in plastic. His experiences over the last few weeks made him take the job very seriously. Nothing would divert his attention from the safety of the vessel and his family.

We were ready for a taste of civilisation. Neiafu, the Vava'u capital, would be a country town by New Zealand standards but the biggest centre since Nuku'alofa. We wanted its comforts so badly we saw their shapes in the stars: steaks with steaming mushroom sauce, icecreams and cold, cubed, drinks brought to the table on a real tray, pizzas crisp on the bottom and so thick that the Mozzarella takes forever to melt down the side of the slice.

While our minds luxuriated in that, our mouths actually experienced unripe melons and crackers with old tomatoes, and we drank from the our last litres of stale water. The one treat left was popcorn. When it rattled the saucepan lid and sent its aroma up through the hatches, Sam said it was the smell of God. But then Sam was pretty far gone with fast food withdrawal symptoms. If we were ever to

At last, the first passage with no gale or storm. This is dawn. Again, a cloudless sky lit up by dust from the explosion of Mount Pinatubo.

drift in the burning sun for two weeks, he would lift his head and croak, "Coke, for the love of God, Coke."

A piece of popcorn knocked a huge filling out of one of my molars. We thought about the dental kit on board and Sue's wide knowledge in every field but dentistry and decided to wait for Neiafu.

There had been some unusually spectacular dawns in recent weeks, often cloudless, creations of the volcanic dust and ash of Pinatubo.

But all our dawns will be compared to the one that climbed out of the darkness on the fifteenth of June. There are spectacular dawns that reveal themselves like a snapshot and vanish. This dawn was the feature movie. As the moon fell into the west, the colours began in the east, long before the sunrise. First deep apricot in the sky, then many shades of pastel one after the other which reflected in the silken water until the whole world writhed in colour: pinks and yellows and lavenders and deep blues. The first sliver of sun came up like molten bullion on a shelf, and became a furnace that burned the colours away. Sea snakes began to swim by, bright yellow and black, weaving lazily south, leaving the water almost undisturbed.

By then we somehow knew that for the first time we would complete a passage without a gale. We had clicked through 2,000 sea miles on the log to find it. We didn't care that this was the other extreme, we weren't going to pick nits and sniff for 15 knots. All the more extraordinary when we heard on the radio that a fleet of fourteen, setting out for the Vava'us from Auckland, had been hit by another vicious series of southerlies and only two yachts were still going.

The log records that Andrew did his first full official watch between 0900 and 1100 hours, monitoring safety of crew, non-existent weather, vessel direction and speed, radio, other traffic, engine revs, temperature and pressure. And ordering up more crackers. "Make them snappy, get it Dad?"

To celebrate the triumph we toasted him with a warm, shared can of the remaining Coke, which had joined the 20 litre jerry can as emergency drinking. We clinked glasses, he talked adult-to-adult, informing us of his new maturity and asking questions like what age is the right age for a boy to have sex with a girl.

Later, he spoke to the flunkey.

"Sam, now that I'm a full member of the crew, *code red* will only apply to you. From now on you've got to be really careful to do what we say when we say it."

Sam, after another argument, waiting for a wind to come and blow him away. The harness was a technicality.

Bad move. Sam didn't know the meaning of humble so it was a waste of time feeding him the pie. And some time later, when the Vava'us were close, he came up from below with an umbrella. On top of the doghouse, he opened the brolly, set his jaw and glared around at the clear blue, breathless day.

"What are you doing, Sam?" Sue asked.

"I'm waiting for a wind to come and blow me away."

She sighed, and resisted the temptation to point out that he was still harnessed to the boat.

The Vava'us were the last of the Tongan islands to be revealed to Western eyes. A remarkable oversight because they're clearly visible from long distances. Steep, thickly forested hillsides rise hundreds of metres, often topped by plateaux. Not coral atolls, but limestone clusters thrust skywards by molten muscle. The 34 islands have at least forty safe anchorages in spectacular, primitive scenery, making the Vava'u group one of the great yachting destinations of the world.

We hitched a ride on a newly woken breeze through the eight-mile fjord to the main harbour, sensing already that the Vava'us would be a very different dish from those that had gone before. New flavours. New spices. Not just in the physical looks of the islands, but the atmosphere and the people.

When the Spanish Captain Mourelle brought his ship up the same fjord in 1781, he found one of the safest hurricane holes in the Pacific. The fjord turns at the entrance so that the harbour is completely encircled by land. In a hurricane, a ship would have only the wind to contend with - no waves could penetrate so far. He called it *Puerto de Refugio* and the name lingers. Maybe his men, like us, turned slowly through the circle, breathing in the aromas and sights of the forested hillsides. Then, as canoes full of warriors set out from under the trees the sailors would have rolled the cannon forward, primed them and stood at the ready.

A canoe full of warriors powered towards our bow, uttering a chanted grunt on each thrust. It was an outrigger, of creamy-white fibreglass, the warriors young Tongans practising for a festival. Six postcard prime specimens, hunks with highly toned, sweat-polished biceps.

"Wow," said Sue.

"Neat," said Sam.

The warriors hesitated, looking at us. We waved them on and they crossed the bow with rhythm restored. A longboat skimmed past with a load of Tongans returning to a village. Below decks, our VHF radio came alive.

"The devil made me do it," a seductive voice announced and left it at that.

"Do you think there'll be a letter from Ellen?" said Andrew.

From the distance, Neiafu has the look of a frontier town. Rough buildings sprawl as if slung over the saddle and down the steep harbour sides. Instead of horses, there's a string of cruising yachts hitched close to the shore. And up the far end of the town, almost apologetically placed, there's a tourist hotel.

The choice over what to do first was clear. We could explore the town, meet the people, absorb a new culture. Or we could absorb a few long-lost luxuries. Without hesitation or deviation we cut a straight wake for the tourist trap, the Paradise Hotel.

In Neiafu, they tell a story about the hotel. The grand opening in '72 was a big occasion for the community. After all, it was built on leased Tongan soil, it would employ locals and bring many tourists. It was, supposedly, 'their' hotel and they were proud of it. But the Australian owner removed Tongans from the invitation list, a tactical move in the same class as removing your own nose with the garden shears. And he compounded the blunder by turning away nobles and commoners alike who turned up at the gate in all their finery.

The one exception on the invitation list was the King of Tonga.

He was already there, absorbing the news of the insult to his nobles and commoners, when he heard one Australian guest explaining to another the significance of the *sulu* or *ta'ovala*.

"Those skirts are for stealing the glasses," the guest said. "They hide them inside."

The king promptly departed for his Neiafu residence, without taking any glasses.

Just like that the Australian hotel owner realised that something was amiss. By midnight he suspected that he might even have made some kind of mistake. He sent an emissary - we'll call him Jones - to deliver an apology. In the early hours of the morning Jones took the gum out of his mouth, thumped on the door, and asked if he could have a chinwag with the king. It happened that the king was awake, so the request was delivered, the reply returned.

"His Majesty asks me to convey to you that should you wish to visit him at a respectable hour, he will be glad to receive you."

So the story goes.

Even now Paradise Hotel is one of the few places where Tongans have to work at their friendliness. More than likely some *palangi* has lectured them about service quality and told them they have to smile if they want to keep their jobs.

The story didn't get in the way of our debauchery. Bleary from the long day, we swam the pool, ordered the drinks, worshipped the steaks and icecream and allowed the sense of quiet, ordered luxury to penetrate by osmosis. We even absorbed the bill without asking where one could play Russian Roulette.

The boys are a species perfectly adapted to expensive hotels.

We went back down through the palm trees to where *Alderman* lay peacefully on the path of the moon. That was the night, June the fifteenth, that moon, earth and sun shuffled into line to the order of the Drill Sergeant and right dressed, passing earth's shadow across the lunar seas. An eclipse.

We slept long and well.

113

17

The impression of frontier town was confirmed when we walked through Neiafu. The short stretch of paving was ancient. Mostly, orange day clung to the feet or raised heavy dust.

The colours seemed more vivid here. The people were more intense, more volatile, the passions deeper, the conversations sharper, the teasing and laughter more uproarious. Adults with jandals in the dust wore ties on smart shirts. School children wore freshly cleaned, ironed uniforms that would never survive at the hands of a Kiwi fourth-former.

A woman chased an errant child with an impressive length of *fue* vine, but applied it with symbolic taps and a humorous tongue. A school brass ensemble tortured 'Silent Night', six months before its allotted time. A convoy of utes bounced through the main street, the lead vehicle's bonnet covered with a wedding *tapa*. The trays were packed with wedding guests singing into the clear sky with voices born to fly in formation.

The taxi company headquarters was little more than two square metres. It had an aerial around eighteen metres high but the operator didn't know the location of the visitor's bureau, which turned out to be one block away. There was a garage that was even smaller, with two pumps, a dozen chickens and six pigs. As I passed, a male piglet tried mounting a sow, but when high enough to see the target, changed his mind.

There were no fences between the houses, just grass kept short by livestock and immaculate with brooms. Owners don't have to know which pig belongs to them because the animals identify the individual sound of the household coconut scraper and come running.

We took on fresh water and more fuel. And we loaded up at the market, ending the limitations of the last few weeks: spinach, watermelon and vines, coconuts and kumara, papaya, peppers, plantains and pineapples. I crossed another item off the wish list by climbing back on board with a huge bunch of bananas on my shoulder, tying it under the boom. Later, Andrew practised his swordsmanship skills, teaching the whole scurvy bunch a lesson in manners with one hand behind his back. Most considerately he aimed just to nick the skins and was astounded when they sprouted great black scars.

Kindred Spirit came in. Which made Andrew very happy until he saw that it made Sam very happy. They both asked when *Chieftain* was expected. We didn't know the answer, but we were prepared to sacrifice our children to the gods if it would speed things up.

To our huge pleasure, there was a vessel from Lyttelton where our own journey began. *Chado* had also been dealt to by the southerlies, losing an LPG tank overboard. They couldn't heat even a can of beans. They tried every trick known to man including using a hair drier and, they said with straight faces, dropping a lit cigarette lighter into a bowl of water.

Hey Mister Tally Man... Michael bringing in supplies from Neiafu,
capital of the Vava'u Islands.

We picked up our mail. There was no letter for Andrew from Ellen. He bit his lip thoughtfully and said very little, brightening only when we pointed out that there was no guarantee his letter had even reached New Zealand. Then we basked in news from home. My brother Ralph had just helped his daughter escape from an unsuitable - that was the word he used - flatmate who got stoned, fired his crossbow into kitchen doors and said, "You can't trust *anyone.*" Friends sent us newspaper clippings showing blizzard-like conditions in Christchurch streets. The articles talked of power cuts and of the winter shaping up as the worst for many decades. Surprise, surprise.

"Tell us about it," Sue and I grumbled to each other.

We wrote home. Sam's pen almost entirely ignored the Wairarapa storm and the gales, dwelling poisonously on Dudley, which he described as a 'bottom scunger'. We assumed his class would know what he meant. Our letters dwelt on the blissful change from what we'd had. But Sue came out of her letter pad with a problem.

"You know, when you write it all down, it seems a totally hedonistic lifestyle that nobody could possibly support."

"That's a bit rough," I objected. "We've earned it. It wasn't exactly cruisy getting here, was it?"

"No. But we're here now. And they're miserable back there in deep snow."

"It's not as black and white as that. We've got problems like anyone, even here. Anyway, why should we apologise for it?"

"No. No apologies, but how can we complain about what goes wrong? Who cares if the outboard is playing up? Who cares if the gybe preventer won't move and if the water temperature drops two piddling degrees?"

I didn't have an answer to that. She had a point. It's a common perception back home that if you own a yacht you must be filthy rich, which is so wrong back there – and yet so right here.

Here's another coincidence.

I headed for the only dentist in the Vava'us to get a filling for the cavern in my molar. The rooms were in the hospital up the hill above Neiafu. On the way, I gradually closed on a boy striding along the road, in spite of a bandage on his knee. Even before he spoke I could see he was self-assured for his age. About eleven years, the same as Andrew. He spoke first. His tone was friendly but remarkably authoritative.

"Where are you going?"

"To the hospital."

"Me too, I have sore feet," he said pointing to his knee. This lapse aside, his use of the language was excellent.

"What's your name?"

"Tiki."

"Your English is good."

"Yes. My teacher is Pat Matheson."

I stopped. Pat Matheson was the married name for Patricia Ledyard. "Pat Matheson? The writer?"

"Yes."

"But I am looking for her! You live in 'Utelei?"

"Yes."

"That's... That's... Will you give her a message?"

"Yes."

I wrote the message and we walked on, talking about the village of 'Utelei, about his teacher, and about his ambition: he would get a job that would make lots of money so he could help his parents who had helped him. He was entirely comfortable walking along with an adult, a foreign *palangi* at that. In these overpopulated islands, I thought such a chance encounter worthy of notice, but like

116

the Pangai vendor, Tiki hadn't even twitched an eyebrow.

The Tongan dentist had the gentlest touch and inflicted the least pain of any I've encountered. The filling fell out three months later.

Alderman *at anchor in the hurricane-hole port of Neiafu.*
The harbour is almost entirely enclosed by land.

"Dad, can we play with them?"

We were anchored off the village of Talihau, southwest of Neiafu. Andrew and Sam were swinging on the sidestays, looking longingly at the beach where a score of youngsters milled around on the sand. Several were looking at us across the water. I wondered why no one was swimming.

I would have to go with them. There was a good quarter of a mile of water between us and the sand. But I was keen to do it, partly to reward Andrew who had handled the tiller competently during the anchoring. And partly to cheer up Sam who had botched the anchor-drop - a minuscule mistake, forgetting to unlock the drum and dropping the sod later than intended. He lashed himself mercilessly saying that he might as well throw himself over the side right now.

So we gathered swimsuits and dipped oars. Once again I did the work while taking flak about Dudley.

There was still no one swimming as we landed and we could still see no reason for that. The Tongan youngsters helped the dinghy ashore, planted the anchor and gathered around, ranks of bright, brown faces. Andrew and Sam took off into the water, thinking that the others would follow. They didn't. So the two white boys were left to flounder self-consciously in front of a fascinated audience.

"They're not coming in," Andrew complained.

"You'll have to tell them what you want," I suggested.

So Sam approached a boy twice his height and four times his weight. He grabbed his upper arms, made a movement as if to throw the boy to the ground and pointed at the water.

"Vainga!" an older girl shouted as understanding flashed through the assembly. Every boy rushed for the water. In seconds it was a maelstrom with two *palangi* heads surfacing and submerging. As Sam was so much smaller than the boys he went for, I watched carefully. But they looked after him and took as much care with each other.

Occasionally an adult appeared back on the grass, looked on with eyebrows raised, and departed. The girls didn't swim. But they did gather round the dinghy with obvious longing. I told them to go ahead, climb in, but they shrank back.

I didn't understand.

"Yote," one said, pointing at *Alderman.*

"You? You want to go to the yacht?"

"Io!" The girls' shout was unanimous. I looked around doubtfully. Coming ashore at a strange village and rowing away with the young women seemed to lack courtesy.

"First, ask your mothers. *Fa'ai.*"

The girls looked impatient. They discussed it. One of the shyest was pushed to the front.

"I ask mother. He say yes."

I took this to mean that there was a general prearranged agreement for youngsters to be taken to yachts - something of a change of attitude since the blackbirders dropped in. So while the final of the world wrestling championship raged in the shallows, I rowed five frilly-dressed and demure girls towards the yacht.

As the sides of *Alderman* loomed, the two youngest became set-faced and spoke sharply to the older ones.

"They afraid," the eldest explained. And even when we hitched on to the bollard alongside and Sue spoke to them from the deck, the two would not leave the dinghy.

"What you wife name?" the eldest asked me before tackling the steps.

"Sue."

"Soo ... Sooooo ... " The three brave ones climbed, practising the name, rounded lips issuing the sound like a breeze in the palms. They also had never been in a yacht. I stayed in the dinghy with the two young ones, who were so afraid they could scarcely breathe. They were vastly relieved when the others climbed down and we returned to the beach.

The next day, a dugout outrigger pushed out from the beach and doddled towards us, well down in the water, propelled by a large man with a smile as wide as the island behind him. He waited to be asked on hoard, then introduced himself. He was Auka Folau, Methodist minister of Talihau and he had something to say about the village children who swam with Andrew and Sam.

"They are forbidden to swim on Sunday. Yesterday I am busy. If I am here it not happen." He wasn't ticking us off, just putting us in the picture. But I expected something more strenuous about girls being whisked off to a foreign yacht on a Sunday.

"Have a banana," I said, pointing to the remains of the bunch Andrew had slaughtered.

"Ah," he said, taking the first of five and beaming at Andrew. "I know what make this banana. Boy with *hele*. Machete. Maybe knife."

Andrew's lower jaw dropped. Auka chuckled. "I have boy."

Sue and I laughed, warming to him.

"You rich man?" he asked me.

"In New Zealand, no. Here, yes."

"Ah." He was satisfied with this. He had been to New Zealand as a guest minister and knew something of our ways. He talked of what he had seen, making observations on details but avoiding judgements of a society that must have seemed like an alien race but for the religious link.

I checked something with him. Another canoe had been out before him, with a young woman who asked for money to help her child in hospital, the first time – surprising now that I think about it - we had come across a beggar. Something had not rung true about it at the time. When I told Auka, he was startled.

"What canoe?" he demanded.

"Yellow."

That meant nothing to him, in itself an irritation to a man who knew more than most about everyone in the village.

"Is there a child in hospital?"

"No, no!" he exclaimed in disgust. "These lies very bad." And his wrathful expression promised enquiries on return and dire consequences for the culprit.

Before he left, he invited us to one of his services.

But that was followed by an invitation from Auka's religious opposition, and it would give us an inside look at one of the most fascinating of island forces. We were asked to attend a feast with the missionaries of the Mormon Church.

The opposition, our guide to the enemy camp, was Auka's daughter, Tangimana. I feared a social clanger.

"You are taking us to the Mormon Church?"

"Yes. I join Mormon Church."

"Your father. Was he angry?"

"Yes. He very sad at me."

Tangimana was fourteen and fearful of the responsibility of looking after *palangi*. Her name means 'crying in the storm' which simply describes what happened when she was born. She's one of thousands of youngsters who have joined the Church of Latter-day Saints in recent years. They're attracted by eligibility for free schools, lunches, accommodation and sports facilities. Many are 'school' Mormons, dropping out after graduation. But the king is unhappy with the new 'fast-faith' religion and one Mormon Church in Nuku'alofa, judged too close to the palace for comfort, was told to move.

Tangimana took us first to her uncle's house, where a single missionary-sized pot bubbled in the backyard. In it was a dish of sweet dumplings in the making: coconut milk, sugar, flour and baking powder. All day the pot had been a cornucopia, pouring forth dishes for the feast. And it was one of many pots, earth ovens and primus stoves doing the same throughout the village.

Beside the pot was none other than Auka.

"*You* help make a Mormon feast?" I said, pointing out the bleeding obvious in the hope of getting a reason I could fit in my head.

"Yes," he said pleasantly. No problem. No big deal.

He stirred the pot while discouraging a dog called Saddam, which had been born on day one of the Gulf War. I squatted beside Auka, discussing food and the new village industry of harvesting *bêche-de-mer*.

Tangimana took us through open yards and houses of cards made of leaves and particle board. Past the village shop where there were no customers and where a lead pencil cost most of a dollar. Past a young man with wild eyes and deranged hair who called out to us.

"This man is... foolish," Tangimana apologised. "His mother and father they go to New Zealand and they not write to him now."

A wheelbarrow trundled past in the rain, laden with food for the feast.

Tangimana took us to the school where the teacher's house is a woven hut little more than the size of a Western bathroom, and where the classroom walls are bare concrete block. Teachers lack materials as basic as paper and cardboard. And yet they do have the richest resource of all, the one that has been lost in the developed countries: the teachers want to teach and the pupils are eager to learn. Even so, at Talihau, the teachers carry sticks to encourage the children and sling shots to discourage the dogs.

"Sit down."

"We are sitting down!" the class chanted in ringing monotone.

"Anna is touching the table."

"Anna is touching the table!"

Whack.

"Teacher hit for wrong speak," Tangimana explained.

At the feast, it was immediately obvious that those who asked us to come would not be eating with us. Vast quantities of the very best the village had to offer were laid on cracked crockery and a plastic tablecloth down the full length of the hallway of the Mormon meeting house. As well as the staples - papaya, roast pumpkin, taro and breadfruit - every kind of available meat: roast pork, chicken, fish wrapped in vine leaves, and the love of the Pacific island stomach, canned corned beef. While the ants were marshalling their forces, forty Mormon elders from the Vava'u region arranged themselves either side in *sulus*, white shirts and ties. They indicated politely that we should sit with them. The boys wriggled down beside Sue.

Talihau's villagers, including those who invited us, stood bare-headed in the rain, peering down the hallway through the open door, watching the consumption of their labours.

The missionaries, or elders, were Tongans, with one exception: the chief elder. He was a young sandy-haired American, hardly more than a boy, by the name of Andrew Douglas. He was twenty-one years old, given the respect of a prince, and comfortable with it. My first impulse was to try to nail him up on a conversation, but my Andrew got him first. The eleven-year-old had been scowling, looking between food and dripping villagers at the door. He leaned forward to direct the frown at his namesake.

"Why are we leaving people out in the cold and wet when we've got a big feast?" Right to the point. I was proud of him.

But Andrew Douglas smiled easily. "I can't do much about it. It's their custom. It would be an insult *not* to accept."

We looked again at the villagers. There was no doubt they looked happy. More than that, they had an air of pride and anticipation. So we ate. And we encouraged more explanations from this boy king.

We were invited to the Mormon feast, at Talihau village, in the Vava'u Islands. Those who invited us to join the missionaries stood out in the rain, looking in. Initially, we had problems with that.

Like his colleagues, Andrew Douglas lived a strictly regimented life with a male companion. The buddy system. Each looked after the other's 'security' (his word) watching each other's adherence to rules such as rising at 6.30 a.m., no alcohol, no videos, and a string of thou-shalt-nots longer than a shaft of lightning. He volunteered that the old rule forbidding dark-coloured races from becoming priests was now history. God had apparently revealed the new word through one of the top elders: all men could now become priests in the Church of the Latter-Day Saints. The moment of revelation, Andrew told us, had been one of great emotion and relief in the church.

How much money did he get?

He didn't. In fact he paid the church US$350 a month for the privilege of teaching the gospel. He didn't choose Tonga, he was assigned it, deliberately avoiding any familiar language so that in the effort to learn he would become one with his flock. As for the villagers waiting on him, he said, "I was uncomfortable about it when I started, but I'm used to it now. They expect this, they want it, they make it happen this way."

A villager began a formal speech. One of the missionary elders translated.

"This is a happy day for Talihau," the villager said, with rain dripping off his ears on to his shoulder. "We are blessed by the presence of the missionaries."

When we rowed back to *Alderman,* Auka's three children came with us. Tangimana, brother Tausinga and eight-year-old sister, Taiamoni. There was something particularly striking about Taiamoni. When she and Sam were side by side, they had a strange effect, like a silent sigh, on anyone watching. Maybe it was just the contrast of brown and white in the two equal-sized bodies, Taiamoni dark even for a Tongan, Sam blonde and fair-skinned.

On the way out, Tangimana and Tausinga went into a huddle, jabbering conspiratorially in each other's ear. Taiamoni bit her lip.

"What's the secret?" I asked.

Tangimana and Tausinga looked sheepish, Tangimana biting her knuckle to stifle a chuckle. She came out with it slowly.

"We saying, next week Sam and Taiamoni they get married."

And she and her brother burst into laughter. Dark-eyed Taiamoni frowned, knowing it was about her but not understanding. Sam's jaw went forward and his nostrils went sideways as he put the record perfectly straight.

"We hate each other."

Auka's children visit Alderman, *anchored off Talihau village.*
From the left: Tangimana, Taiamoni and Tausinga.

We anchored off Talihau twice, surrendering to an atmosphere we had never known on other travels. Of course, Talihau villagers had their problems like people anywhere. But the ebb and flow of their tides reflected the practical Tongan philosophies of living: *mo'ui fiemalie*, a contented life, *m'ui nonga*, a peaceful life.

Even if you are sons and daughters of a warrior empire.

18

24 June

We hovered *Alderman* in deep water, close to an unremarkable stone cliff face on the west side of Nuapapu Island. From cliff top to waterline there was nothing to distinguish the face from any other. We pulled down all sail, turned on the engine and moved along the cliff face at dead slow, peering into the shadows at the waterline.

Here's a riddle.

Imagine a hiding place so secret that it contains these contradictions: it is surrounded on all sides by rock, it is covered on top by rock so that not even air can move in and out, yet it is lit by the sun, and yet again it has no earthly entrance.

Impossible?

But it exists. And Mariner's Cave is central to one of the greatest of all love stories. Not great just because the hiding place is the stuff of fantasy, nor just because it has the classic elements of tyrant, young chieftain and beautiful chief's daughter, but because the legend could well be true. William Mariner was the first *palangi* to hear the tale from the ancient Tongan histories, and through his highly romanticised account in 1817 came a legend with that indefinable ring of substance.

Here's a short version of Mariner's account:

In former times there lived a tyrant governor of Vava'u. When his cruelty was no longer to be borne, a certain chief plotted against him. But he discovered the plot and condemned the chief to be taken out to sea and drowned and all his family and relations to be massacred, that none of his race might remain.

Now one of his daughters, marked for slaying, was a beautiful girl, young and interesting. She had a secret admirer, a young chieftain who until this time had entertained no hope that he might win her. She had been betrothed to another of much higher rank and had he opened his heart to her, he might well have forfeited his life.

But now the young chieftain knew that he might at last entertain hope, because one day, while diving for a turtle, he had discovered the cavern of Hoonga. The cavern was his secret alone. He too had plotted against the tyrant and had thought it wise to keep the cavern as his own place of hiding. There was no time to be lost. He flew to her abode, told of her terrible danger and declared himself her deliverer if she would but trust to his honour, and, with eyes sparking the most tender affections, he waited with breathless expectation for an answer.

Soon her consenting hand was clasped in his. They speedily embarked in a canoe from a lonely beach in the shades of evening. Upon arriving at tall cliffs he instructed her carefully, leaped into the water and she, trusting him, followed close after.

They rose into the cavern, resting on a ledge high above the water and partaking of refreshment he had brought. Early in the morning, to avoid suspicion, he returned to Vava'u but did not fail to bring back to her mats to lie on, the finest gnatoo *for clothes, the best of food, sandalwood oil and coconuts.*

For two or three months he tended her every need when he could safely do so. He pleaded his love with the most impassioned eloquence, and how much he delighted when he heard the confession from her own lips that she had long regarded him with a favourable eye. How happy they became in their solitary retreat where no tyrannic power could reach them, only longing that they might be together more often.

The time came when the young chieftain devised a plan that would free them both. He signified to his inferior chieftains that he wished them to accompany him on a voyage to Fiji, with all their wives and female attendants. When a large canoe was prepared they assembled. And they asked him if he would not take a Tongan wife with him. He replied, no! but he should probably find one on the way. This they thought a joke, but in obedience to him, said no more.

As they passed near the cavern, he directed them to a certain point. Without explanation he sprang into the water on the far side of the canoe, swimming deep under it and up into the cavern to where his greatest treasure lay.

Those on board were exceedingly surprised at his behaviour.

And they were greatly alarmed when he did not return to the surface, imagining that a shark must have seized him. Their wonder was increased beyond all powers of expression on seeing him rise to the surface of the water and come into the canoe with a beautiful female, whom they took at first to be a goddess. Their astonishment was not lessened when they recognised her countenance as one who had assuredly been killed and they then took her to be an apparition. But how agreeably was their wonder softened when the tale was related.

They arrived safely at one of the Fijian Islands and resided there for two years, at the end of which time, hearing of the death of the tyrant of Vava'u, the young chieftain returned with his wife to Vava'u and lived long in peace and happiness.

That's a movie waiting to happen.

Though we had been told where to look, we saw nothing by staying safely on board. The water was too deep for anchoring, so Sue took the helm. I jumped in with a friend, Warren Matthews, and snorkeled along the base of the cliff. At one stage, I thought I had found it, a man-sized black hole not far below the waterline. But when I surfaced inside, it was to a tiny pocket of air a few metres across and fifteen centimetres high. Not a pleasant experience. I came out much more quickly than I went in.

We continued. Warren seemed completely unconcerned, but with deep water very close I couldn't keep my mind off sharks.

Then, once we saw the entrance, there was no doubt: about two metres below the surface, a ghastly jagged shape, like a mouth from a nightmare and wide enough for a dinner party of six. We had been told what to expect – even so it took a moment of nerve-steadying to dive into the blackness of that mouth and further into the throat. Warren went ahead and I followed on his heels.

It got easier. The throat was a short fat tunnel about four metres long and sloping upwards. Once inside the mouth the surface within was visible and obviously opened into a place with enough light to see.

We came up into an atmosphere I won't ever forget. The sunlight was at our feet, bent through the cavern mouth, filtered by sea water, an oval spring of dazzling golden blue light. It illuminated the cavern, which was about twelve metres across and fifteen metres high, an irregular dome hung with stalactites that looked at first glance like Gothic arches. As long as we kept our eyes off the brilliant light below us, more and more detail around us became clear.

Ahead and to the right, about three metres above where we trod water was the legendary shelf, sloping upwards to the right but certainly wide enough to hold a Tongan chief's daughter and her lover.

Warren prepared an underwater video camera he'd brought with him. I sat on a rock at the edge, listening to the crisp, echoing detail of every tiny sound.

And then I saw the phenomenon I had been told about and hardly believed. Every ten to fifteen seconds, a mist formed, faintly masking the ledge and walls and roof. Then it cleared, just as quickly. I watched to see if this was a passing event, but it continued all the time I was there. It was responding exactly to the surface of the water which rose and fell to the force of the swell outside the cavern, misting on the rise, clearing on the fall.

I thought about that. Mist, created and expunged, four or five times every minute of every hour of every day for tens of thousands of years. I'm not going to do a calculation, Sue would laugh. She knows me too well.

The mist answers an old question. Many have looked for an open air entrance to Mariner's Cave, as it's now called. But the mist forms when the rising water increases air pressure and condenses airborne moisture. That could only happen if the air had little or no escape. And if there were a tiny entrance, we would surely have heard a wind breathing out and in as the mist formed and faded.

Some who accept that there's no land entrance have cast doubt on the legend, saying that if there's no air supply, the chief's daughter could not have survived two to three months. But they forget that the cavern is huge and the constantly changing sea water is highly oxygenated.

I slipped back into the water. Warren handed me the video camera with its wide angle and idiot-proof button. On the thumbs up, he took a deep breath and dived down towards, then into, the dazzling sunlight, flippers flickering behind him. Even through the lens it was a sight out of a dream in which gravity has no place and could just as easily have been an Ascension in a religious painting. I was so taken with the moment I didn't switch off the camera, but kept rolling as I followed on into the light and through to the outside world.

We broke the surface, and waved to *Alderman,* circling fifty metres off with anxious faces in the cockpit. And once on board, I spent some time in rapturous descriptions.

A few days earlier, Sue had said that she might give it a go. Her confidence in the water had been increasing all the time. But now she looked at the wind-driven slop at the base of the cliffs and shook her head.

"I'll do it," Andrew said. Now I looked hard at the chop under the cliffs and the very deep water below us and remembered the boy who once burst into tears when tipped off a dinghy in sheltered water. That was just one month ago, but it now seemed many months. So I made a potentially dangerous mistake.

"Are you sure?"

He paused a moment. "I'm sure. Let's do it."

We spent some time talking over detail, then leapt in. Neither of us saw the apprehension in Sue and Sam left behind. Andrew didn't have a lifejacket, of course, because buoyancy is the last thing he needed in the coral-lined tunnel. Warren was there, too, as we approached the entrance.

I could see Andrew becoming uncertain and slowing down and then the matter was decided beyond any doubt. He suddenly yelled with fright and began to gasp.

"Jellyfish! I've been hit by jellyfish!"

"OK, come on, we'll swim back." I waved both hands towards *Alderman.* She began to turn in towards us.

But Andrew's gasping increased and his voice rose as he started to struggle and panic. I remembered my mother, a first-rate swimmer, saying how difficult it is to help a panicking swimmer. I'd heard stories of lifeguards having to knock swimmers out in order to save them. But I wasn't a lifeguard and Andrew wasn't yet in full panic. So I slapped him sharply on the cheek and the shock brought him to an instant halt. He trod water slowly, wide-eyed, staring at me. My huge relief made me overreact cruelly.

"You want to die? You go ahead and panic."

He nodded, eyes even wider, then swam back with me, under perfect self-control. On board he was fine. He didn't see the skipper, below at the table, eyes closed, trying to breathe calmly.

As we raised sail for an anchorage at Port Mourelle, he showed off the mild rash that appeared on his chest. I'll never know whether or not I need to thank a jellyfish.

Then he developed an appetite for plantain pikelets and set to, grating some of the fruit into a bowl. His banana massacre had led us in desperation to the less-edible plantains and a little experimentation produced some delicious pikelets: *Grate two green (not ripe) plantains, bind with an egg, add salt, pepper, basil and tarragon and fry half an inch thick on a hot pan.*

In other words, he recovered faster than a sick schoolboy on a Friday afternoon.

His father's recovery took longer.

What are you? Still not careful enough.

We prepared for other assaults on Mariner's Cave, but wind and water and sun never teamed up to make it possible. Even if Tonga had nothing else, all four of us would want to return for that magical cavern with the irresistible legend. Each of us for our own reasons.

19

It wasn't easy to meet the Vava'us' best-known expatriate, American-born writer, Pat Matheson. Tiki had delivered my message, but then Pat and I kept leaving messages for each other that didn't quite bring about a meeting.

Finally I relied on Dudley to get me to her house because the anchorage off 'Utelei village was exposed and a southeast blow was rising. For one third of the trip, Dudley complained of arrhythmia. For the next third he called for the last rites, and for the last I rowed the slop, snarling about what I would do to him if he didn't start for the trip back into the wind.

Once beached, I walked up the sand in a filthy mood, through agitated trees to a very European-looking house and knocked on the door. This would be the house that Pat Matheson and her late husband, Farquhar, had built decades ago. Solid concrete. In one of her books she tells how the house sheltered a hundred and forty-three villagers while the great hurricane of 1961 took two passes, destroying the village and all green things. Even this house had been badly damaged. Now it looked solid, including the thickly timbered porch that looked out through an extraordinary variety of plants to the fjord.

An elderly woman came to the door in dressing gown, slippers and a mood to match mine.

"Yes, who is it?"

I told her.

"Don't come near me," Pat Matheson crackled. "I've got the sniffles. Something going round." Her hair was white and straight, she looked frail but stood straight up and down and the gleam in her eye said she didn't take any kind of nonsense from anyone. She certainly didn't intend to stand jawing forever at the door, so I was ushered at a don't-touch-me distance through to the porch. There, she offered me her cold cure, a vodka fruit juice concoction with a wallop that dumped me on the cane seat.

She didn't go for drawn-out preliminaries.

"Glenys wrote that you're an unusual family. What makes you unusual?" she grated, peering at me round a glass of neat whisky.

I winced – thinking of the events of the last few weeks – but decided against calling a lawyer. "Maybe because we don't want to get to our deathbeds wishing we had tried this or that when we had the chance."

"Hmmph," she snorted, but there was a small grin. She looked at me sideways, speculatively. "You could be a candidate for the 150s club," she said. She was seventy-nine and held that with a lively mind and body you could rake in nearly twice that number of years.

I returned with the whole family a week later, this time anchoring off 'Utelei in spite of another stiff southeaster. And this time we met the woman whose character so influenced Pat Matheson's books.

Tu'ifua also was snow-haired, around the same age as Pat. Her skin had the grey tinge of age. She was slightly stooped but still had the bearing of dignity and timeless patience we had been told to expect. She brought the lunch tray out to the porch along with her smile which looks shy but isn't. She placed it between us so that a loaf of newly baked bread steamed deliciously in front of me.

"Shall I cut it?" I offered, lifting the knife.

"Yes. That is a good place for you," Tu'ifua said, her eyes flashing with mischief. And I glimpsed why the two had been friends for so long.

In 1949 the young Pat Matheson came to take over as headmistress of a mission-run girls' college in Vava'u. She took an instant dislike to the missionaries. Those men of God were alarmed by her talk of likeable Tongans; they talked love but breathed hostility, and they had a talent tor turning Tongans into laundresses, yard boys and house girls who should work for nothing because they loved the church. Pat saw Tu'ifua, then the head teacher, dismissed like a servant from the presence of a missionary, and referred to as quite intelligent and reliable... for a Tongan.

So Pat Matheson and the missionaries established a long-lasting relationship of incompatibility. Long-lasting because the missionaries were thankful to have anyone willing to take on the remote Vava'u outpost. They left her to it. Under her maiden name, Patricia Ledyard, her book *Friendly Isles* describes how the friendship with Tu'ifua strengthened as polite distance was replaced with trust.

Being intelligent and quite reliable... for a *palangi,* I cut the bread. We slid pleasantly through half a bottle of whisky. The boys were astoundingly well behaved, possibly awed by the presence of the two women.

In Pat's *'Utelei My Tongan Home* there's a passage describing what happened when the great hurricane passed:

> *'Malo mo'ui ... thank you for living,' Tu'ifua called to me when we met for the first time after the storm, and everywhere I went I heard people echoing her. 'Malo mo'ui ... ' and as I looked at their faces shining with friendship and with love I knew that the beauty of Vava'u would never he destroyed because it lies deep within its people.*

I asked what Pat thought of a local dignitary with a high public profile. She snorted and said, "I have a shallow mind. I like people to be good-looking."

"What do the people here think of you after all this time?"

"They still think I'm peculiar," she replied, and Tu'ifua smiled her Mona Lisa smile.

Pat described Tu'ifua as one of noble birth. But Tu'ifua murmured, "No, no. Very common." An interesting modesty in Tonga, where nobility is held in much more esteem than in European countries.

"Are you a Christian?" I asked Tu'ifua.

"Yee ... ees." The affirmative dripped with qualifications.

As we talked and as the level of whisky sank, the two women lifted the veil cautiously. I asked about Pat's school. At nearly eighty she was still writing, and still took class on her porch for the village children.

"At your age, how do you deal with naughty kids?"

"I want to smash and smash them. But that doesn't fit my upbringing so I separate them all over the porch and tell them what 1 think of them. It doesn't do any good, but I feel a hell of a lot better." Another cackle.

We asked to see the famous library and left them both sitting on the porch. In Neiafu I had followed directions to the capital's only bookshop, and found just two books for sale. Two volumes. Both were by Pat.

Her own library could be the biggest private collection in the South Pacific. There were literally thousands of books, completely filling a large room and spilling into others with a range revealing an all-embracing thirst for ideas and knowledge: everything from *Anne of Green Gables* to *The Septic Tanks Manual* and *The Ascent of Man.* An entire length of a wall was taken up with hundreds of *National Geographics.* Andrew borrowed *The Story of the Secret Service,* Sam look *Peter Pan in Kensington Gardens.*

Pat and Farquhar had built the library up over the decades. There were photos of Pat's daughters, Tami and Tupou. I didn't see any copies of her own books, but I remembered a passage:

> *In 1967, Farquhar died. The village people quarrelled, and out of my sorrow I loved them; for they quarrelled over whose part of the cemetery he would be buried in. Our wise town officer opened up a new section for our household and there, overlooking the harbour that he loved, he lies.*

Come sailing with us," we said to the two women. "We'll take you out on a day with a light breeze, not too strenuous." We didn't really believe that two women nearing their eightieth years would even consider it. But on the day we rowed ashore, they were waiting, bags in hand, bare feet in the water, keen to be off.

When we coasted up the fjord, they told us of a startling possibility. One of Pat's ancestors, a John Ledyard, refused to serve in the king's army and was offered a choice: go to prison or sail with Captain James Cook. For the three months that Cook was laid up in Nuku'alofa, Ledyard had a passionate affair with one of Tui'fua's forebears.

"So," Pat cracked gleefully to Tu'ifua, "We may be cousins."

Tu'ifua snorted with derision. A ridiculous idea.

Patricia Ledyard and companion Tu'ifua on board Alderman, *both made famous by Pat's book 'Friendly Isles'. Pat invited us to join the 150s club. That's the number of years we and they could live, as long as we kept "a lively mind and body".*

20

About the time of the Vava'u Regatta, Sam took a big step towards independence. Confidence was not the issue; he had a truckload of that before he started out, in fact his lack of fear terrified us. No, his ambition was getting 'big boy' skills that would free him from little-boy shackles - lifejackets, harnesses, jackstays, and knuckle-biting parents.

The first step just happened. One day he couldn't row, the next he could. Everything fell into place and I suppose that's not too much of a surprise. So we double-checked the knots tying oars to rowlocks and gave him solo rowing freedom near sunset when the wind was down. No problem. He even managed the ship-side oar himself when coming back alongside. Great. More freedom won.

That led to the second step, and to as much radiant triumph as can fit on the face of one seven-year-old. We had friends on board at the time, yarning in the cockpit while Sam mucked about in the dinghy.

"Does that bother you?" one friend asked, nodding out the back.

I followed his glance. Sam was tugging on the outboard start rope.

"No." I laughed and took another swig of beer. "The compression's way too much for him. Anyway, Dudley isn't starting for anyone right now."

Thirty seconds later, Dudley roared into life. Sam picked himself off the bottom of the dinghy, seized the tiller and dropped the clutch with a sickening crunch onto full screaming revs. As he took off, his high voice came triumphantly back to us.

"Yeeeeeeee . . . haaaaaaah!"

That miserable, pathetic, sodding excuse for an outboard motor performed for Sam like a new thoroughbred.

Frantic hand signals had no effect on Sam, and our shouts couldn't penetrate the duet of crowing boy and roaring motor. He did heart-hammering wheelies and came back in his own time.

Then it was all on. He accepted a few pointers to keep him from passing through other people's main cabins without saying please, but there was no stopping him. He begged and pleaded to handle Dudley at every opportunity and that swine of a motor did seem to respond better to Sam's biceps than mine.

The boys fought over who was going to pilot Dudley in the regatta dinghy race. Andrew won. Ian arrived to announce that his two-horse outboard had a dial that could turn on eleven horsepower for a race. In other words, he would waste Andrew and Sam. Andrew countered with the little-known fact that Dudley had an afterburner. To my knowledge, only jet fighters have afterburners.

Sam, finally allowed to run ancient Dudley (clipped to the back of the dinghy). Dudley's performance appalled the boys and they mounted a relentless campaign to replace him.

I gazed into my crystal ball and went to see the organiser, arguing that our four-horse should be put in the two-horse category. He had no problem with that: Dudley had developed a reputation.

The boys came last. In the two-horse section.

Their shame was beyond the power of words. After they rowed over the line, they climbed out with stooped backs and drooping shoulders, faces like spent balloons. Sam was inconsolable, and Sue and I realised just how competitive the boys had become.

They had plenty of adult company. In the so-called fun sailing race for the cruising yachts, the racing fanatics took over. The only difference from a cut-throat cup race back home was the veneer of relaxation adopted by the skippers: you lean back and smile pleasantly at the opposition, you don't look behind you (bad manners), and above all you don't shout orders. Threatening to rivet sluggish crew to the masthead by their bollocks is something you scribble on a piece of paper while you smile at the yacht passing you. There's a game to be played.

Andrew and Sam swore at our opposition and had to be brought up sharp. So they contented themselves with abuse like, "That's *our* wind you're stealing." And, "You're cheating, your prop is turning." Andrew forgot who was skipper and sprinted the deck, giving orders to tighten or loosen the sheets. Sam spent 45 minutes - we timed it – pointing a battery-powered fan forward onto the genoa to help us go faster. The laws of physics did not bother him.

Lord Barrington, one of the fastest, passed us on the way to the front. John and Barbara gave us a cheerful wave. They had ignored the advice of the doctors in New Zealand, returned to their yacht in Nuku'alofa and sailed north to rejoin the fleet. John had regained almost all control of the muscles in his face, only slipping back when he got tired. He and Barbara were now having the time of their lives, living each day as if it might be the last. Which it might.

In this regatta, there were plenty of locals on board the yachts. They did seem to enjoy themselves, but we wondered how such an extravagant event, involving massed riches beyond dreams, went down with the local community.

I asked Don and Jenny Mundell, and they answered by telling me about a school poster competition they'd been invited to judge. The children had been asked to make posters about the good, the bad, the ugly and the beautiful of tourism. Most children had seen the 'good' of tourism as *palangi* standing on their yachts throwing money down to Tongans with outstretched hands. Most had seen the 'bad' of tourism as *palangi* on yachts shooting and stabbing each other and injecting themselves with needles.

"You're exaggerating," I protested.

"We're not," they said firmly. "That's the way the children saw it." Maybe that perception explains something of why Tonga has been so stand-offish with modern influences.

Even so, there was a good rapport with many locals. They mounted an exhibition to show and teach *palangi* ancient skills like basket weaving, and the *palangi* women and girls were eager pupils. There were exhibition competitions amongst the village champions of coconut scraping, basket weaving and fire making. The firemakers rubbed a stick of hardwood *fukofuka* on soft *fao* and the winner, Halamaka from Pangai, lit a cigarette from the glowing dust in less than a minute.

Sione, the amiable host, pointed to a hugely grinning competitor and announced that he had been disqualified because he was not good-looking and not Tongan. Sione looked over the results of the basket weaving, bearing down on one in particular. It had been woven too tightly in the centre and was shaped like two baskets woven together. He held it aloft and sighed into the microphone.

"I wish that you do not experience this as a basket." He made motions with his hands to indicate that it might be better used as a bra, which in local pidgin was known as 'basket-belong-titty'.

The woman responsible for the outrage smiled cheerfully.

Inevitably, the regattas put severe strain on livers. The rounds of people passing from one vessel to the next required hospitality. Here's a potent bit of hospital fodder: *One half Malibu liqueur, one quarter fresh coconut milk, one quarter fresh pineapple juice.* But most of us couldn't keep it up. Some vessels had alcohol-free days, including us. We developed our own liver saver: *One part tonic, one part freshly squeezed limes, sugar to taste, crushed ice.*

It was on one of those socialising rounds that I heard it. The music. The tune. It wriggled into my brain and confided that I had been waiting for it all my life.

We were partying on *Mystery Girl,* singing at the tops of our voices. Sam was reading a book. Andrew wasn't because Jo had just looked at his reading material and confiscated it: *All The Girls,* an expose of the skills of the prostitutes in the kinkiest brothels in the world. To this day, we don't know where it came from, but books flow from yacht to yacht in greater volumes than alcohol.

Andrew had a satisfied grin on his face.

"Listen to this," Brendan said to me. "I've got something you might like." He pulled a dubbed audio cassette from his pile, labelled in ballpoint pen. He inserted it, shuffled tracks and set it in motion.

It was a flute piece, backed by guitar, so filled with haunting pathos and wild open spaces that I stood right up along with my hair. How many ways are there to say *exquisitely beautiful*?

"What is it? What's it called?" I panted when it finished.

"I don't know." He was pleased with himself for reading me so well. "You'd better borrow it."

It was in my hands before he stopped speaking. I didn't have a flute. But I could force a note or two out of my old school recorder, which had been resurrected in the last two months.

It took me days of playing and replaying the tape just to write down the complicated music. Then more days to see how I might adapt it to the recorder. No one seemed to recognise the piece, so it became, simply, *The Tune.* By the time I was ready for serious practice, Sue and the boys were ready to cast me adrift. So I took recorder and music and climbed high up on the Pangaimotu ridge, far from sensitive ears, I thought. But I miscalculated how far the sound would carry. After just an hour Brendan appeared out of the trees. He listened without wincing to the recorder equivalent of a child's first three months of violin.

"There's a big talent quest at Musket Cove," he said, straight-faced. So cruel.

"Go away!"

He laughed and slid back down through the bush.

At Nuapapu Island, it was Brendan who told us about the whales. The island is shaped like the bone hooks of old Polynesia and we were anchored inside the curve near the barb, where the limestone falls away steeply into the deep. Brendan and Jo brought out a photograph taken from their yacht last year, then anchored in exactly the same position as now. The print showed a humpback whale longer than *Mystery Girl* immediately alongside. It was one of a pod that had come in amongst the anchored boats, gently exploring them, so close and so sensitively that at times they moved in between yachts and tethered dinghies, touching ropes yet doing no damage. Many of the fleet yachties were affected by the sight and called out to the whales to put on the show with their tails. As if understanding, the whales moved 200 metres off, put on the show, then came back for more investigation. Brendan described it as a fantastic exercise in communication.

Any lingering hopes that we had escaped the winter vanished in the southerly that came with July. The rain was endless, the wind gusting to 30 knots and shifty with it. At night, *Alderman* sleep-walked, stumbling around the anchor with the dinghy attacking the hull. Our own sleep played hard to get.

We heard that *Santana II* had been taken by Minerva Reef. A passing 767 picked up the distress beacon and the crew was plucked off the coral in a rescue mounted from New Zealand. The vessel was wrecked.

The weather flogged our morale. And it was the same on other yachts.

"Doesn't Noelle look elegant?" one skipper said on the radio, in reference to a woman on another yacht. In the background, his wife called out, with vehemence, *"Noelle has an iron!"*

A yacht in the Ha'apais lost a piece of stern to a shark. Which reminded me of another yacht in the habit of hanging freshly caught fish off the rear end. A crew member hung her rear end over the back to relieve herself just as a shark came up for the fish. She bolted below, burrowed into a sleeping bag and didn't come out for three days. Which leaves serious questions about the state of her plumbing.

Sam's beloved was still in foreign ports, so when Ian came over to play with Andrew, the three created purgatory on water. One night when Ian was sleeping over, he and Andrew got to discussing girls in general and sex in particular. At

138

midnight. They lowered their voices for the last bit, which made Sam's ears rotate and lock on. He was discovered eavesdropping at the aft cabin door. Somewhere in the ensuing shouting match, Andrew declared that sex was perfectly natural.

"Yes," Sam agreed. "Perfectly natural, nothing wrong with it at all."

So, having agreed with each other, a scapegoat had to be found to explain how bad they were feeling. Me, for keeping them apart.

Sam dreamed that he had a mean boss who made him work in a mine when he was supposed to be camping with his heroes Batman, Robin, Snoopy, Huey, Duey and Louie, and James B. Junior. The boss grew so much he couldn't get through the tunnel and James B. Junior pushed him into the lake where the devil lived.

Andrew dreamed that he and Ian were fighter pilots on the Royal Australian super carrier 'Scourge'. Together they intercepted MIGs, waxed bandits, bailed out, got rescued by the enemy, were tortured, led to the gallows, karate-kicked their way to more MIGs, waxed everything (with the help of 60,000 rounds, two sidewinders, Hades and duster bombs, and seven Phoenix, Sparrow and A111M9 missiles), returned to base, and then noticed they were both wounded.

Sam relieved boredom by using the rain cover to collect water. His delight at the results was unrestrained. His bucket became sacred and the water was 'too lovely' to put in the forward tank with ordinary water.

I had a man-to-man with Andrew about little brothers. How it was to be the younger one with no one to play with. I told him about the song with the line, 'He ain't heavy, he's my brother.' I painted a picture in his mind of being so strong - a cunning ploy I thought - that he could say to his friends, "He's my brother, he gets to play too. Like it or lump it."

"Yes," Andrew nodded, thoughtfully. He liked the sound of that.

Privacy was a rare commodity. One morning Sue and I were enjoying a wake-up cup of tea in the for'd cabin. We finished the tea and looked at each other. We listened – yes, the boys were still asleep. I flared my nostrils, Sue flared hers. We pawed our hooves, and we were just on the point of getting frisky when Sam bounced down the boards and up on top of us, waving 'Famous Five' and demanding the continuation of a story.

"Aaa ... aaaggh," Sue groaned.

"What's the matter?" Sam asked. "Read to me."

Resigned, I read: *"Chapter 21. Dick has a great idea."*

"No, no," Sue whimpered.

I kept reading. *"'Listen,' said Dick in an urgent voice. 'It may be Pongo-'"*

Sue put a pillow over her face and tried to strangle herself.

Sam said, "You guys are really weird sometimes."

Sue and Sam in the Vava'u islands. Alderman *at anchor*

Lester Parkes flew in from New Zealand to join us for the passage to Fiji. He didn't turn up in Neiafu when and where he was supposed to, so we went on with other things in the meantime. I was walking along in a different part of town when I heard a bus around a corner behind me. I walked back up towards it, somehow certain even before I saw it that Lester was on it and intending to get off right here. Which he did.

Another piece of strangeness.

Lester had only the clothes he stood in and his camera bag. The Vava'u airline told him he was the first ever to have luggage misplaced on their planes, a claim he proudly shares with many others. He didn't get it back until long after his time with us, which was a strain on our rotting wardrobe.

During a break in the weather we shifted round to the west of Talau mountain. The anchorage there is particularly beautiful and we'd been told to listen out for the dawn chorus.

Legend has it that flat-topped Talau had its peak stolen by a visiting devil who planned to install it in Samoa. But he was intercepted by a Tongan devil of extraordinary ingenuity who raced to the suddenly flattened top, faced away from the thief and touched his toes. The thief, looking back over his shoulder at this terrifying sight imagined he could see the sun coming up. In his fright he dropped the peak in the bay. That is now tiny Lotuma Island, used for the naval base.

Before night fell, we heard a commotion from the dense bush: a great deal of barking and a pig squealing, followed by human shouts. That went on for some minutes. Then there was a shot followed by an odd whimpering. Ten minutes later a very disgruntled sow appeared on the beach and trotted south. At almost the same time, a man with a rifle appeared further up the beach carrying a limp dog. He went north with two more dogs slinking behind.

We heard the dawn chorus in a rare lull in the wind, when the water was gloss-black and the overcast cloud cocooned us between mountain and hills. According to the ornithologist Douglas Cook, many people reply to enquiries about island birdlife with, "What birds?" But he identified 43 species, and to us, nestled up to Talau mountain, it seemed that every one of them was there, singing to us.

21

"Go to the Spanish restaurant on Tapana Island," we were told. "You haven't seen the Vava'us till you've been to La Paella." We liked the sound of that. Sue and I did much of our courting in Spanish-speaking countries. And we all needed a change.

There's no phone - you make the bookings by VHF radio. When we made ours, the restaurant owner was in the middle of a rapid-fire conversation with someone in Neiafu. In Spanish.

"Don't forget the beans!"

"I won't forget them!"

"You always forget the beans!"

"I never forget the beans if you write it down!"

I chipped in. Beans or no beans we were keen to make the booking. Could we make a booking for tonight?

"Yes, Alderman, that is all right tonight."

"What kind of payment do you take? Do we pay in pa'anga?"

"No, you pay gold, diamonds or two virgins."

We were so keen to get there I made a nearly disastrous mistake. I chose the short cut east between Mala and Kapa islands. The local guidebook, published by a charter company, gave a depth of two metres at low tide. I decided to trust the advice because the company would have more than a passing interest in keeping its yachts afloat. It was half-tide now and with our draft that meant minimum clearance of one metre. That was the theory.

The problem was that past the point of no return, the channel became impossible to pick. Within five minutes we were sweating it out over half a mile of coral. Communication between spreaders, helm and depth sounder tuned up like a guitar string on the way to snapping point. I called directions from the spreaders trying to distinguish between the subtle shades of colour below *Alderman*, Lester steered, Sue called the depths down to absolute zero and then tailed off because there was no point. She came out with spread hands and wide eyes.

It all came down to my eyes in the spreaders.

I still don't know how we made it. When we came out into deep blue on the other side I shook all the way down the mast and sat for a while with closed eyes. Sue's complexion matched mine she made her feelings plain: being down below and watching the sounder bottom out was not an experience she wanted to repeat. Ever.

Got it.

Lester was polite. In fact he was the voice of restraint and reason, a hard virtue to forgive. *Never again,* I wrote in the log. But how could I be sure? There were too many potentially deadly first-time blunders to make and the sea was not known for its generosity with second chances.

I suppose I shouldn't have been surprised at what happened when we anchored at Tapana Island. The contours were simple, the coral problem almost non-existent, but my state of mind must have been catching. When I put Andrew on the helm, his usual confidence had gone.

"I'm a bit nervous," he admitted, and I just nodded. Under the circumstances, what could I have usefully said?

We worked together and dropped anchor in fifteen metres. We over-tested it, pulling back on the chain with Frankie on high revs. It was a good holding. Then we did our own thing for a while, saying nothing to each other.

Still not careful enough.

A school of tuna painted a kaleidoscope below us for an hour.

Tapana Island is about 800 metres across each way, completely covered by bush. In the binoculars we could only see trees. There was nothing man-made on the whole island except La Paella restaurant, we'd been told, and the thought appealed to us.

"*Whipjack!*" Sam shouted, pointing to a small cruising yacht nearer shore.

I should explain something about names. Generally, cruising people don't know each other's surnames. Not because they're ignorant but because person and boat become glued together in the mind. The name of the vessel becomes the surname. Ken and Hilary from *Celebration,* Brian and Louise from *Astron,* 'AB' and Adrienne from *Dawn Treader* and so on.

With a few hours to spare, we rowed over to see Linda and Marco on *Whipjack.* They were New Zealand doctors who needed a rest, so Tonga was home till further notice. Marco was a G.P., Linda a gynaecologist who'd been on call to the police and seen rather too much of man's inhumanity to woman. The two were delightful, stimulating company. When you're on a rising tide of '89 Cabernet Shiraz, the answers to the world's problems and age-old philosophical conundrums are quite obvious.

"Thought," said Linda, "is greater than electrochemical activity and leads to it."

"Thought is the source, brain activity the outcome," I agreed.

"Thought *is* electrochemical activity," Marco argued.

"I thought," Sam said to him, "that you were going to take us for a hoon in your dinghy."

If you tipped a roller-coaster ride on its side, that's what Marco gave the boys on water. It included a loop underneath the catamaran *Pyxis.* The boys returned full of how wonderful a Mariner 8 was in comparison to other outboards... like, for example, Dudley.

Right.

Next, Marco found a place in the boys' hearts with imitations of sewing up his own lips, a man eating a slug, and an angry duck. The last one hit such a chord in the boys that they rushed throughout *Whipjack* practising at the tops of their voices.

So we restrained them. Which didn't go down well. When we departed, Sam said with ominous emphasis, *"Whipjack* is a nice boat."

"It's the people in it really," Andrew observed. "Yes, *they'll* make good parents."

The first of La Paella's charms is that it's hard to get there. You walk on a track through the bush, or take a dinghy over coral in falling light. We walked the track, found the place and wondered if we'd made a mistake. The only building was a grass hut.

It wasn't a mistake.

"Buenos tardes, I am Eduardo. Can you sing?"

"Buenos tardes. Yes we can sing."

"Good, good, come in." Shaggy-haired Eduardo looked fresh from the flower-power sixties.

The rumours had not exaggerated. This was like no other restaurant. It wasn't just the hut, though that alone was unusual. The cooking was over a fire, with a chimney so badly cracked we could see everything cooking from the outside. Not that we needed a menu anyway, there was no choice. The loo was out through a flock of chickens to a long drop in the sand.

Inside there was a bar, with a game of liar's dice under way. The RT hissed soothingly on the wall, occasionally bursting into life on a marine channel. Bookshelves were filled with Spanish translations: *Zane Grey, Rio Perdido,* Wilbur Smith's *Viene el Lobo.* The tables were rough-hewn, with kerosene lamps and candled bottles engorged with old wax. A couple of divans drooped in the corner. In the music area, tapes and instruments lay about: guitars, cymbals, clarinet, mouth organs, triangles, castanets, drums. There was half a guitar, a keyboard without batteries, and clubs and a three metre drainpipe in the percussion section.

"Can I have a Coke, please?" Sam said at the bar.

"How old are you?" demanded Adam the attendant.

"I'm seven."

"Hmmm. I suppose that's old enough."

Sam paid up and vanished outside to play with Flamenco, a yapping hound that turned somersaults, vibrating with joy at having a willing playmate.

It wasn't the meal that made La Paella special, though that was excellent: croquettes, marinated fish, calamari, potato rissoles, tortillas, paella with baby clams, and watermelon. Nor was it the guests: an interesting international mix, including the astonishingly loud character from a multimillion-dollar vessel who felt it necessary to boom an introduction to all diners.

"Yes, sir, I'm from South by God Carolina, right in the heart o' Dixie."

"Glad we've got that straight," another customer said, and Sue added *sotto voce* that someone should put his Southern lights out.

A few years back, a New Zealand yachtsman was off the coast of Florida when a multimillion-dollar extravaganza - with all the turrets, bells and electronic tackle - loomed out of the fog and pulled up next to him. The owner, in dazzling whites and braided cap, called down to him. "Hey, buddy, do you know the way to Miami? And don't give me none of that compass crap. Just point."

No, the special nature of La Paella restaurant was in the staff, if you can call them that, and the atmosphere they wove around the music, if you can call it that.

For Maria, Eduardo, Pepe, Adam and Emilio, La Paella was a way of life. Eduardo and Pepe are brothers who sailed out from Spain, each in his own tiny yacht, each solo, to get away from an authoritarian regime. Eduardo, the chief musician, at home with his guitar. Wild man Pepe, even shaggier than Eduardo, looking like a manic Che Guevara, but in reality kindly, shy and thoughtful. Maria, the organising force behind the scenes, had a tongue like a rasp for business and a heart like a teddy bear for friends. Adam was an anti-American-establishment American. And then there was Emilio, a wealthy Spaniard who heard of the special atmosphere at La Paella and caught the next plane.

One of the youngsters found a six-inch nail lying under her seat.

She showed Pepe, who inspected it and was amazed.

"This nail from Jesus Christ cross!"

A guest fell right in. "Looks a bit fresh."

"It is galvanised," Pepe said gravely. "It lasts a long time."

And then there was the music. The staff of La Paella loved to make music and they didn't give a tuppenny toss who liked it and who didn't. More than that, they handed out instruments into the crowd and urged everyone to take part, take over, do solos, whatever.

"What? You can't play? Of course you can play! Everyone can play!"

We had found another Dead Poets Society.

A few guests brought up on professional restaurant entertainment and recorded music didn't get it and went away early. The others stayed on for the party. Sometimes the music was superb, sometimes it fractured teeth, but nothing is quite so contagious as genuine enjoyment. Pepe, on percussion, was the human equivalent of Animal in *The Muppets*. At the climax of one song, he used two driftwood cudgels to beat the borer out of a packed dining table, causing the guests to scatter.

Several children rushed outside to make up a performance, rehearsed for two minutes, and came back with a reproduction of a television quiz-show.

A ferocious row erupted between bits of music. Emilio, Eduardo, and another Eduardo from Buenos Aires waved their arms and threw machine-gun Spanish at each other. But it wasn't the prelude to the O.K. Corral. They were discussing the relative merits of two different Spanish dialects.

"I'll sing!" Sam announced, to prolonged applause from Eduardo, Pepe, Adam and thirty guests. He made his way to the microphone. "Dad will help me."

"I will?"

"We'll sing 'The Cat Came Back'."

The fact that Sam had not yet sung a note in tune and didn't know the lines didn't bother him at all. He hoisted the mike and hit the high notes about the cat that survived eight determined assassins. I did my best, but knew even fewer lines than he did, so when he stopped to think up more words, I started to edge a leg off the stage.

"There's one more verse, Dad!" he bellowed into the microphone, to a shout of laughter from the guests. When we finished, or rather he finished, there was a roar of approval and thunderous applause.

"*Bravo, bravo, malo, que niño*! Splendid. What a boy!" they shouted and Sam floated, glowing, back to his seat.

"You want to play?" Maria asked me.

"Got a school recorder?" I said.

One was found. It was solid with tropical gunk right down the centre.

"I will fix," Maria said and bashed the instrument mercilessly on the floor. A cockroach ran out and scuttled for a comer. I flushed the rest of the gunk out in the kitchen sinks, then returned to find Eduardo playing on his own and looking at me significantly. Of course I couldn't yet even begin to play *The Tune*, but to my delight I found myself doing something I had always wanted, but thought beyond me: ad libbing music with someone else. Quite brilliant music it was and the four rums I'd had did not blind me to the fact. One confused sailor put his hand on my shoulder afterwards and said he had the same problem.

When we left I didn't have the readies in gold, diamonds or virgins, but avoided the dishes with travellers cheques. I produced my passport for identification, but Adam waved it away.

"We all came here to get away from that bureaucratic bullshit, man."

In the early hours when the chickens were still and the birds silent, the crew of *Alderman* stumbled back along the bush track, Andrew hand-in-hand with Sue, and Sam with me. When we reached sight of the dinghy, we had a family pee in the trees. When does a family ever pee together? After that we stood looking out over the star-rich water.

"Why do we always have to leave people we like?" Andrew asked.

We didn't have an answer.

"Why do we have to leave people like Linda and Marco?" he said. "Why do we have to leave Tonga?"

"I feel like crying," Sam said.

Sue says this shot is a swindle. True, I did ask her to lie in the hammock for the camera. But that was partly because she didn't take enough time to relax. We were both guilty of that. It took us many weeks to learn how to switch off fully.

22

Back in New Zealand the *Pacific Pagnag* took on the Wairarapa coast and lost tragically. She'd been one of the better-known vessels in the deep south, endearing herself to Port Chalmers by starting races with a cannon that turned cabbage into coleslaw. She went on the rocks and three people died. Another was found unconscious on the beach.

For us, the heavy weather lifted slowly and it looked good for the passage to Fiji. *Kodiac* and *Harlequin* left for Suva. *Mystery Girl* cleared for the Niuatoputapu Islands, known familiarly as New Potatoes.

Our morale took a night and a day to lift into line.

It might have been sooner if it weren't for what Sam did when Ian and Andrew took him to see an old Cessna in a Tongan backyard. They got permission to look it over, but when Sam jumped up and down on top of it, the owner took exception and showed them the gate. Sam was surprised. And he was even more surprised when a furious Andrew and Ian denounced him and ganged up on him. They did it so ruthlessly that I chewed Andrew over for breaking his promise to lighten up on his brother. I told him to return Ian to *Kindred Spirit.*

Andrew's face fell. Sam patted me urgently on the leg. "Dad, I want a word with you."

"What is it? I'm talking to Andrew."

"I need to talk to you in private. In the for'd cabin."

Uh oh, the for'd cabin. Tromping sounds.

"Dad, I want you to lay off Andrew."

"What! I'm doing this for you. Not that you deserve it."

"I know. But he's been told off enough and I don't want him to be without his friend."

Aha, a whiff of large rodent. Too bad, Ian could stay away and give all the magma a chance to cool.

On top of that, discipline had been frittered away by spending too long in undemanding anchorages.

So I decided on a new strategy. I would have heart-to-hearts with the boys in the best white liberal tradition. Yes, I would really, really, listen to them, treating them like mature adults. Oh, oh, if hindsight could only be forwarded in advance.

It was a complete failure. The boys spotted my vulnerability and eagled in. I got an ear-flattening litany of complaints like: *it's so unfair* and *adults always get their own way* and *I'm old enough to run my own life.* And the long chorus was topped off with this concession: *But Dad you can make the decisions about danger if you want... when we're under way.*

Really? How kind.

So much for the new strategy.

When the boys were asleep that night, Sue and I went rowing under the starlight. As usual when there was a problem, we began in silence, dipping oars slowly and smoothly in the night sky. Then I wondered aloud how we'd got ourselves two such high-octane boys. Sue reminded me. She also reminded me of one of the saddest sights we'd seen in the Andes of South America: the 'good' children who made no noise, who moved slowly, whose eyes were dull and reluctant to focus, who might never answer back to their parents. Fair enough, but the memory didn't solve the immediate problem.

"I thought they were mature enough for that kind of conversation," I complained.

"They're not little adults. They're boys."

"Well if I can't get better discipline that way, it's going to have to be more punishments."

"More? No, you can't get any tougher on them. We're raising two very strong characters. You'll just have to put up with it. Is it that important?"

"But you can't run a boat like this!"

"Why not? When it really matters, they jump-to, don't they?"

"Yes but... "

In the end, the decider wasn't any kind of reasoned argument. Next morning I got a little too much backchat when my head was in the electrics cupboard and my fuse melted. No juice left in the patient tone circuits.

In seconds the boys were standing bolt upright, wide-eyed in front of me.

"Right, boys, hear this. As of now, what your mum says and what I say is what goes. You'll do it straight away, you'll do it right, you won't answer back. You won't fight in front of adults. You'll use a respectful tone to both of us and to all adults. And you'll take a respectful back seat when we're talking to other adults. Have I made myself perfectly clear?"

Their heads went up and down as if on the same camshaft and the jaws were still open.

It was as if I had thrown a switch.

Within half an hour, Andrew set about making Sam an airship. He used hose, wood and aluminium tubing and he said it would work because he had done the research. And the two were in perfect harmony when they divided up the ownership of *Alderman,* attaching written titles to everything in sight.

They combined to put fake treasure maps in bottles. The maps were traced outlines of Uvea and Futuna Islands and contained a cross with the words 'Sunken

149

treasure ship here'. Sam placed his inside a completely enclosed lagoon. Neither boy showed pity for future treasure hunters excited by their maps.

Still later they showed affection for us, with spontaneous hugs. Though I suspect Sam's mood was partly due to discovering a faster way to change VHF frequencies. All boats in a radius of half a mile must have heard him tell Andrew that he had shown me something I didn't know.

"Andrew, have I been a pain?" Sam enquired after the bedtime story.

"No, you haven't."

"Yes, I have. I've been a pain. A ball in a china shop. I'm really sorry."

"Sam, please go to sleep."

In other words, my authoritarian command worked – against all my previous understandings of how to treat and bring up children. I had been inconsistent. That was it. My crimes had been inconsistency, uncertainty and unpredictability, swinging between punishments and mateyness. We were at sea, often in danger. They needed totally clear, consistent boundaries. I remembered an old saying about kittens. Put them out in an open field and they'll be terrified, but with solid walls around them they'll have fun and play.

Okay. Another lesson learned.

So, was it all perfect then?

Of course not.

Nessa came the next day. Geraldine called us when they were six hours away, to find out exactly where we were. Within sixty seconds of *Chieftain* dropping anchor, a dinghy roared out from under her stern and flew towards us with Nessa's long hair flying from the bow. The mutual relief on *Chieftain* and *Alderman* was almost palpable.

So what happened at the Lisa's Beach feast was all the more poignant.

We might not have gone except for another of those chance encounters. Sue - mostly these simultaneity events happened to Sue - was sitting at a café reading a letter from Glenys, which said that if we ever made it to a feast on Lisa's Beach we should look up a woman called Rosalind, the wife of one Isaiah.

Sue finished the letter, put it down, and sipped her coffee.

"Hello," a voice said. A very black, tall, cadaverous Tongan stood in front of her. "Where are you from? My name is Isaiah."

The same Isaiah, married to Rosalind.

He invited her and us, to a feast. It was commercialised, created for the tourist dollar. The food was set on coconut leaves under a woven roof beside the sea. Dancers swayed in the light of tin-can lamps, bodies gleaming with coconut oil.

The boat children grew bored quickly and moved out the back, throwing rocks at a crumbling cliff face, or down to the water helping crabs to fly by putting them in snorkels and blowing hard.

Somewhere amongst them were Nessa and Sam.

Tongan dancing is much gentler and more graceful than the frenzied hip swinging often associated with the islands. The rhythms are slower, the movements more subtle, relying on flowing arms and hands and fingers to weave the tales in the *tau'olunga,* the *lakalaka,* and the *ma'ulu'ulu,* the sitting dance. The one exception is the *kailao,* a blood-surging, foot-stamping, drum-pounding remembrance of the times when their warrior ancestors overran much of the South Pacific.

The food was superb: lobster, roast suckling pig, octopus, clams, pawpaw baked in coconut milk, marinated fish and more. The children ate quickly and went, unimpressed by the lavish spread, keen only to play with each other beyond the range of parents' tongues.

After the meal I was down by the water talking to someone when Sarah from *Kindred Spirit* arrived at speed.

"Sam's hurt!"

I found him sitting in the remains of roast suckling pig, blood pouring down over his face from a head wound. Sue was trying to find the source and both were encircled by *palangi* and Tongan women. Nessa, paler than Sam, was trying to hold his hand. Isaiah brought ice in a teatowel to stem the blood. He wanted to pour kerosene on the wound as well, but no one gave him a chance.

Once cleaned up, it turned out to be no more than a scalp wound, probably not even needing a stitch. That news had two effects: Sam began to enjoy the sympathy and played his suffering like a virtuoso. And Nessa broke down and howled. Like the others, she had been throwing rocks into the dark and one of hers had bounced off Sam's skull. She flew to her mother, sobbing and inconsolable while Sam was helped to the dinghy. He bore his terrible wound with noble dignity.

"Would you like a cuddle, Mum?" he offered. "After my hurt, you're probably shaky."

Next morning, Nessa turned up alongside. With grave anxiety she handed Sam a get-well card she'd made herself. It said: *I'm sorry I hit you on the head with a rock. I didn't mean to. I hope your head gets better.*

Sam adopted the expression of one who suffers beyond all understanding yet is too manly to complain.

We prepared for passage to Fiji. Diesel, food, water, endless checks of fittings, rigging and engine.

We had to borrow oars. It had been a fine idea to tie the oars to the rowlocks. We might have got away with trailing the dinghy so close that it hit the hull. We might also have got away with forgetting to lie the oars completely inside the dinghy when moving. But the combination cost us an oar and a rowlock and there were no oars for sale in the Vava'us. A small-scale lesson on a sailing truism: disasters often come from a combination of small details. The survivors in the fleet were those who attended to detail.

Then there were the farewells, friends we'd made on shore and amongst the fleet. Some yachts we wouldn't see again.

We anchored one last time off Talihau village and went ashore to say our farewells to Mavava'u, to Tausinga, Tangimana and Taiamoni, to Helala and Mafi, Anna and William, and Paula at the school. But we didn't find Auka and no one else could. We waited on the beach, while children buried Andrew in sand and Sam used William's machete to turn driftwood into chips. But still there was no sign of Auka.

We went back to *Alderman*. I checked once more on condensation water in the tanks because we'd had more problems with surging revs.

Then, as we prepared to raise anchor, a canoe set out from shore. Once again it was well down in the water, but this time the very recognisable figure of Auka was waving to us and paddling fast. We reset the step-ladder and he came up panting, carrying a package. We took him below, where he thrust the package into our hands. It was a patterned *tapa* cloth, a big one that kept on unfolding until it was as wide as I am tall.

This was no ordinary gift. It had been made for us by his family, from scratch. They had to strip bark from a mulberry tree, beat it into fibrous lengths over an ironwood anvil and bind the lengths with arrowroot adhesive. Then it was decorated in a manner similar to brass rubbing: but instead of brass they used pattern boards, *kupesi,* of stitched ribs of coconut leaves, and various red, brown and black shades of juice from the bark of the *koka.* Tongan handicrafts are amongst the best in the Pacific, because the products are used, not just produced for tourists.

Auka had tears in his eyes.

"You and your family bring us things. You come and talk to me and the village. Thank you. God bless you."

The boys gaped. Sue and I looked at each other and we both shook heads in disbelief. We had done little but enjoy ourselves. I found myself giving one of the very few formal speeches of my life.

"No, no, Auka. We should thank you. Our gifts were very small. They were nothing. We thank you, not just for this wonderful gift, but your hospitality and for letting us know something of your culture."

His eyes screwed up, trying to understand.

I tried again with pidgin semaphore. "I mean we thank you for... for letting us talk with you and your family and the village. It was good for us. It made us happy.

152

And this *tapa,* one day we have a house. It will go on a big wall. We will look at it and remember Talihau."

His wrinkles vanished, he beamed his understanding through the tears, and then he ate five slices of banana cake.

At last the wind softened to ten knots from the southeast. The time had come. We tied up at Neiafu's wharf for the clearance formalities and for last-minute provisioning from the market. At a lull in the proceedings, a dozen schoolgirls in bright maroon uniforms came to look at us. And that's when Sam had the wind taken out of his confident spinnaker.

The girls were about twelve years old and shy. But not too shy.

After Andrew went below, there was a burst of chattering, then a bit of nudging. A girl spoke up, pointing to her right-hand neighbour.

"She like your son."

"Oh. Sam?"

"No, no ... " She held a hand high. "Older."

Sam, sitting on the doghouse at the time, was dumfounded. "Andrew?" Sue asked.

This time the girl in question spoke up for herself. "Yes, I like Andrew."

"What's your name?" Sue said, delighted. Sam looked from one to the other, unable to believe his ears.

"Lesley. I like Andrew. I like to talk to him."

I went below. "Andrew, there are a lot of girls up there. One of them likes you and-"

"Oh my God!"

"-and she wants to speak to you."

"No way."

"Her name is Lesley."

"I'm not going up there! I'm not. You think this is funny, don't you? I'm not going up there."

But after certain despicable tactics on my part, like words about the importance of being an ambassador for one's country, he breathed in deeply, grabbed an unused postcard from the navigation desk and emerged.

"Right, which one of you is Lesley?"

"She is Lesley," the first girl said, pointing. Lesley had now adopted a becoming shyness.

"Hello," Andrew said, "I've got a present for you." He handed it over and promptly vanished below. Sam had recovered his wits and launched himself on to the boom, swinging like an orangutan on the topping lift in a desperate bid to recover the limelight.

The girls were having none of that.

"We all like Andrew. We like talk to him."

When this further news was conveyed below, Andrew realised at last that heaven was on earth expressly for him. A huge smile spread over his face and a subtle nonchalance entered his gait as he emerged. In seconds he was lounging in the cockpit, basking in admiration.

In the clearance shed, the customs officer took half an hour with the forms, printing the words letter by meticulous letter against a ruler to be absolutely certain of a straight line. Then he handed over the paperwork and passports.

"Thank you for coming to Tonga and being here. God bless you." We were not supposed to stop on the way out. But for a few hours we anchored at Port Mourelle, partly because Lester was so taken with the bay. Just before we left, a woman came out in a canoe, selling shells. As we talked to her the sun shone on her kindly face and on our backs. Behind us, beyond Hunga, the open water and the sky was tranquil.

The passage west beckoned.

"Mou o a," the woman said as we drew away. "Goodbye. Thank you for your smiling faces to us."

PART THREE

23

23 July

It looked and felt as if we had finally outstripped the winter. As Tonga's northern islands sank behind and the sun sank ahead, we could not have asked for more benign conditions. The gentlest of seas, cobalt blue, blackening for the night. And ten knots from the sou' sou' east, precisely the same wind that pushed Captain Bligh away from Tofua in his overcrowded longboat. His log, written while seas broke over the stern and while his men bailed continuously said: *My intention is to steer to the W.N.W. that I may see the group of islands called Fidgee, if they lie in that direction.*

That's thought to be the beginnings of the word Fiji. The true word was Viti, but Bligh heard the Tongans' attempts at pronunciation as Feejee or Fechee and added his own.

Ahead lay the great eastern barrier to Fiji, the maze of coral reefs that tore ships apart for two centuries. Most of our fleet had gone north, choosing the Nanuku Passage through the reefs. We chose the slightly faster Lakeba Passage through the forbidden Lau Group, where no foreign vessels are allowed to anchor.

I took the midnight watch. Everyone else was asleep, or trying to be. Lester found it difficult that night, perhaps because it was his first ocean passage.

The vessel was silent but for hissing water and creaking sheets. The moon was half an orange, rising on a column of mist. I lay back and saw a shooting star and a satellite in quick succession, a rerun of the hare and the tortoise on a vast field of stars. For a long time the masthead waltzed in the Milky Way. It seemed suddenly as if I was touching sky and wind and water all at the same time and all without moving. I could understand, in that setting, the belief in Gaia: the earth as a living being in which the elements, the water, rocks, trees, animals and humans are all living interconnected cells. And I recalled a scrap of history, words spoken by the Red Indian Chief Seattle in 1854: *All things are connected like the blood which unites one family. All things are connected.*

The following afternoon, 120 miles out of Tonga, a bank of cloud rose and a deepening swell opened up. The wind came a couple of hours after the swell. From the south, wouldn't you just know it. Sue shook her head as if trying to dislodge a persistent headache.

By six in the evening we had a deep reef in the main and just a patch of furler out front. Then a completely separate swell swept in from the east and the combination sct us to plunging and corkscrewing unpredictably. The log has a single understated phrase in barely readable scrawl: *sea getting lumpy*.

We forgot to bring in the trolling line. Close on dark its three signal pegs snapped off and six thicknesses of stretch cord were pulled up taut. Back behind, throwing itself around on top of the rollers, was the biggest fish we had ever seen. Yellow and green.

A mahimahi.

For months I had wanted to catch a mahimahi. I had anticipated one in a giant pan many times. But now I couldn't handle it. It was too big, I was too sick. The gear was too expensive to cut loose. The first decision was to keep dragging it till it drowned. But I couldn't stand it and forced myself to start hauling the beast in. With 30 metres to go, it gave a great heave and was free. There was a pause, a last flick of golden flank, and then it was gone on a howl of protest from the boys.

"You idiot!" Sam screamed out over the stern.

I dropped into the cockpit, too ill to check whether the idiot was me or the fish.

Tonga to Fiji. Yet another blow.

He and Andrew helped batten down for the blow, fastening the engine cover and navigation desk top, locating vent covers, latching the electrics cupboard, tidying away or securing loose objects. Even though I was at war with my stomach, I noticed there wasn't the slightest bit of tension between them.

"Another passage, another gale," Andrew said ruefully.

158

"Yeah," Sam agreed disgustedly.

At eight, Sue and I went forward to change sail for a full gale, pulling the main down altogether and raising the stays'l. Sue kept some humour going but it was an effort to cover the dread of yet another relentless hell. Every now and then, while lashing the main, she spat out some choice expletives - unusual for Sue. I knew what was bothering her most. For her the discomfort still counted way less than worries about the boys, even though the boys were mostly boat-safe now.

An awkward lump hit us from the south, thrusting the deck sideways. It threw Sue towards the edge and hard against the lifelines. She came back on to her knees, with a paint-blistering oath I didn't know was in her vocabulary. Lester watched us anxiously from the helm as we returned. His face was the traditional green you hear of but don't often see.

He always made the effort when it was needed. Once again we had been lucky with the friends who joined us. We knew of vessels where crew were useless for entire passages, one locking himself in his cabin, refusing to answer calls and reappearing cheerfully in port as if nothing had happened.

To my intense annoyance I was the only one to surrender my stomach. For the skipper to be alone in turning the chicken dinner into a firehose has to be one of the great injustices of life. I could feel the inevitable and didn't want to set anyone else off, so I went forward and lay along the deck with head over the rail - a waste of time because my actions only alarmed everyone into watching me anyway.

Once again Sam and Sue were immune. But then they were hardly blissed out by the conditions. Unwashed dishes clanked in the galley, wedged to stop them smashing from one side to another. Damp, smelly clothes and mattresses made life miserable below. No one ate more than crackers and crisps, and all the fruit began to spoil, starting a trail of wasted pineapples, melons, coconuts and tomatoes bobbing in our wake. Our faces were haggard with exhaustion, hair matted thick with sweat and salt spray.

Nicholas Monsarrat wrote a famous book called *The Cruel Sea*. I would have called it 'the indifferent sea'. Sue thought otherwise. She went to the bowsprit, shook a fist, and screamed to the waves.

"You bitch!"

Then she lurched back along the jackstay with a satisfied glint in her eye. It became her gale-welcoming ceremony.

I tried to read Sam a story. My stomach put a stop to that, but I felt a surge of affection for Sam when he was instantly understanding and went about asking what he could do for people. The lurching motion threw Andrew out of the doghouse and he only just saved himself from a nasty spill down the companionway.

"Never again," Sue threw in my direction. "No more passages after this trip."

I said nothing. I remembered the couple who summed up their ocean passages with one sentence: "When we tie up, we have a bloody good scrap then we make up and it's shit hot." But it was hardly the time to mention that to Sue.

Fifty hours out of Tonga, we began to peer ahead, trying to pierce the weather with our eyes for the lethal shoals ahead. This was the way many of the first Europeans came to Fiji, dreading the coral but drawn hy the riches in sandalwood. One shipload bought from the natives for a few broken-down cutlasses could make their fortune in Canton. To the Fijians, the first sight of the Europeans was the tops'l rising from the horizon. They called the Europeans *kai vavalagi*, the men from under the sky.

Kai is also a common Polynesian word for food.

The radio sked made it plain that we weren't the only ones suffering, By going north, the rest of the fleet had only delayed the gale by a few hours. And they would pay for the reprieve in Nanuku Passage by having the southerly on or forward of the beam for much longer than we would in the Lakeba.

Night would fall as we entered the Lakeba. Even with ancient charts, it was certainly wide enough for us to rely on our GPS.

That was the theory.

24

Just before dark dropped on us we caught our first sight of Fiji, a chilling set of fangs rising thirty jagged metres above a reef. A fitting introduction to the land first known to Europeans as the Cannibal Islands.

As we entered Lakeba Passage, still in gale-force winds, pitch blackness hid everything. The swell eased slightly, reduced by the reefs. And it should have been safe enough, but an hour before midnight, the GPS flickered and died.

That is, it went into a coma and refused to display a latitude and longitude. If the whole set had died completely I would have worked out what was wrong sooner, but the screen was still lit. I beat up a few buttons, the read-out woke for a few seconds, then died again and wouldn't budge. For long moments I gathered my wits for sailing through the Lakeba on dead reckoning - that navigational guessing game in which you work off the last known position and project ahead based on heading, speed, wind and sea conditions, with error growing every minute.

Once more, fear.

But then I noticed how dim the galley light was and nearly choked with relief. The auxiliary batteries were flat. The problem was fixable. The last two days had been too cloudy for the solar cells to feed the batteries and we'd used a lot of power on radio and lights.

We were saved by the old practice of reserving the engine battery only for the engine. A touch of the button and Frankie came to life. By the time Lester appeared from his berth, asking what was wrong, the problem was over. The recharging system laid twelve lively volts across the auxiliary batteries and the GPS flicked on, performing instantly.

By dawn we were through the Lakeba, past Cicia Island and into the Koro Sea. The Koro is about 10,000 square nautical miles of deep water, surrounded by the Lau islands and reefs to the east, the two main islands of Vanua Levu and Viti Levu to the north and west, and Moala and Totoya Islands to the south.

Sam brought out the foghorn and serenaded while Lester raised the Fijian courtesy flag and the 'Q' flag. Then we turned northwest towards SavuSavu, driven by sea and wind, encircled by Fiji.

Tonga might have claimed the title of The Cannibal Islands, but Fiji was so much more deserving. Europeans left Fiji well alone until the 1800s, partly because of the terrible reefs, partly because the ferocity and cruelty of the Fijians nearly outstripped European belief. If you were a chief, quality of life was measured in how many slaves you buried alive under the posts of a new house, how many young girls you used as rollers on which to launch the new canoe, and - a new wrinkle in spectator sports - how many living prisoners watched while you cooked and ate their flesh bit by bit.

As late as 1867, they were still taking missionaries with a grain of salt, and herbs. The missionary position – no pun intended - was uncomfortable for nearly three decades. And yet it's widely recognised that in Fiji, the much-admired courage of the first missionary families was a major factor in converting the warrior chiefs to Christianity.

A few of the first European beachcombers took sides in local disputes and many took part in the savagery. Some offered instruction on how to use firearms and were welcomed with open arms, the most notorious being a Swede with the apt name of Charlie Savage. He knocked over the finely-balanced scales of power, and for the first time, one Fijian took widespread control: Cakobau, from the disproportionately tiny island of Mbau. He proclaimed himself King of Fiji in the 1840s and kept his position by ceding Fiji to Great Britain as a colony in 1874.

Entering Fijian waters. Lester Parkes raises the courtesy and quarantine flags. Sam provides the ceremony.

Again, we were out of phase with land and light. As SavuSavu Bay clarified through the sheets of rain, night fell. Even in perfect weather we would not have tried the entrance at night, so we doubled back to shelter behind Koro Island.

Even there the reefs were too numerous to risk anchoring, so we hove-to, a system of setting the storm sails with a fixed rudder in which the boat is pushed slowly sideways by the wind.

The radio kept blurting the movements of the regatta fleet. Those pushing down the Ninuka passage were getting a thumping in 35 knots. Some very sick skippers barely kept the skeds. *Lord Barrington* gave their sked, John Senior's voice firm and clear, but the next one just gasped out, "We're where Lord Barrington is." Another was so desperate for shelter he called a vessel already in port to ask for the GPS co-ordinates of the entrance and ran it blind, no small-scale chart, zero visibility. And he made it. Madness or faith? I would have to ask him what religion he practised.

We kept watch all night, drifting five miles in four hours, then motoring to the lee of Koro and heaving-to again. We didn't dare go closer than two miles off Koro, but that was close enough to quell the worst of the sea. We stayed in relative comfort, eating again, our empty stomachs greeting a simple omelette like gourmets sitting down to a banquet.

Across the reef-ridden black, faint lights showed on Koro, perhaps only tilly lanterns, but our first hint of Fijian civilisation.

The first British governor, Sir Arthur Gordon, created modern Fiji almost single-handedly. Enlightened British colonialism is almost a contradiction in terms, but he achieved it. While others like him were laying colonies waste with arrogance and stupidity, Gordon set out to do something almost unheard of in British history - he civilised while preserving the culture, ruling indirectly through the existing chiefs. He ordered that native land could not be sold, only leased, that Fijians could not be made to work on European plantations, and he ordered the end of 'blackbirding' Solomon Islanders and New Hebrideans to the plantations.

That created a labour shortage. And Gordon's well-intentioned solution then laid the groundwork for bitter strife a century later. He brought in 63,000 Indians indentured to cut sugar cane for five years, then allowed them to lease their own plots of land from the Fijians. Today, half the population is Indian.

In 1987, after an election that shifted the power base, indigenous Fijian Lieutenant Colonel Sitiveni Rabuka marched into parliament with armed soldiers and shifted the power base back again. That was only in part because indigenous Fijians feared that the Indian Fijians would take over their country. It was also because the high chiefs saw the beginning of the end of their Fiji: a racially divided society with power and lease money firmly in their hands.

In the morning, we were thankful we had waited. Even in the daylight, negotiating the entrance safely depended on spotting a thin pole stuck in the coral quarter of a mile past the lighthouse. Even then, with poor water visibility, we were cautious to the point of paranoia.

Anyway, we no longer had faith in lights, buoys, or marker poles. And we weren't the only ones. *Astron* complained to Suva that the light on the west tip of Kadavu wasn't behaving. The authorities came back with the classic reply: *"It's a perfectly good light. It is only the phase that is wrong, which makes it go in the day and stop at night."* In Samoa, *Triton III* went straight on to coral beside five red lights. Nothing wrong with the lights as such, the authorities explained; they were in fact brand-new, very good lights. But no one had got round to painting two of them green.

And watch out, we were warned, for hazard markers at Lautoka that are totally submerged at high tide. Totally submerged? No, I scoffed, surely not. No port authority gets it that wrong. Surely that story had to be a myth.

Once inside SavuSavu Bay entrance we were directed to a small inner bay to anchor and await instructions for clearing into Fiji. A few houses sprinkled colours, reds and browns, amongst the coconut trees. A couple walked along the beach, hand in hand, our first sight of people in Fiji.

We were busy on the deck when a woman's voice called from the beach, 150 metres away.

"Sue! Sue!"

We looked in some amazement. We knew no one in Fiji. Well, no, that wasn't quite true – Sue had once acted on stage with a woman called Jo Collins who moved to Fiji. But she lived in Suva, the capital, 100 miles to the southwest.

The couple had stopped on the sand. The woman was waving frantically.

"Sue! It's Jo! Jo Collins!"

"I don't believe it," Sue said, awed.

At that distance, conversation was reduced to threads of sound. But we did establish a phone number. And the fact that Jo just happened to be on holiday, taking a walk on that particular beach at that particular moment and recognised the name of our boat.

The radio summoned us into SavuSavu port.

SavuSavu means 'Hidden Paradise'. It's the main port for Vanua Levu and it's Sitiveni Rabuka's home town. It's also a hurricane hole, a narrow inlet between a coral island and the mainland. SavuSavu itself is little more than a single street along the shore, a small town in a huge and beautiful setting: the rugged mountains of south-western Vanua Levu, and down SavuSavu Bay towards Kumbulau Point.

In a country with a love of complex ceremony, we shouldn't have been surprised by the clearance formalities: twelve forms to be filled in, some in triplicate. Skippers massaged cramped wrists under the eyes of bored officials and over the light of a single 2000 watt bulb (I checked) set on a chair, answering questions like, *Are you aware of any plague amongst the rats and mice on board your vessel?*

A buzz of surprise went through the fleet when Fijian Affairs announced that no skipper would get a clearance to visit the Yasawa Island group, one of the most desired cruising destinations. Why not? The crew of an American yacht had just desecrated a sacred beach. Instead of apologising they argued with the villagers who told them to stop, then pressed home their diplomatic initiative by insulting the chief. So the villagers went away and came back with machetes. The Americans retreated, clearly recognising the validity of the argument.

But the regatta organisers, Don and Jenny Mundell, pleaded for special clearances for the fleet, pointing out which country we came from, and offering to take responsibility for our behaviour.

Success. There was a whole new round of paperwork.

Alderman was something of a mobile post office, bringing late mail across from Tonga for other vessels. But there was also mail waiting for us. We expected it, partly because Brendan told Andrew there was a letter for him. Andrew went a deep shade of scarlet and tottered towards the SavuSavu Copra Shed yacht club to pick it up. He returned in disgust, holding a letter from the Correspondence School.

Suva authorities picked up a Mayday from a yacht on a reef near Beqa Island. But the long-range radio held out only long enough for a longitude reading, then faded. Later we heard that the yacht had been found and successfully pulled off the reef and towed to safe harbour.

Suva issued a strong-winds warning. As if what we'd just had was a breeze. The fleet sorted itself on to fixed moorings. There were too few to go around, so many had to double up, rafting side by side. But, we were assured, the moorings were safe, weighted down by old engine blocks. This was, after all, an established hurricane hole.

The engine block holding *Geotta* and *Lesumai* must have been a Fiat Bambina because they eloped, waltzing off through the night with the mooring for luggage. They went half a mile before a watchful security guard caught up with them in a dinghy and woke their crews. They were well downwind in the fleet, so they managed that *pas de deux* without damaging themselves or other boats.

We had a mooring to ourselves. So did others with children on board, because most yachts preferred peace and quiet. Even so, we tested our mooring, throwing the engine into full reverse. More excessive care. We couldn't afford to drag - we had half the fleet downwind of us, then coral. The mooring held.

So we could count on it, couldn't we?

25

6 August

SavuSavu was alive with movement and vivid tropical hues. Buses bounced through the pitted open-air terminus. People of more than the two main races drifted along the street, bringing country colours to town. In that lush, mountain and sea backdrop, SavuSavu might have lived up to its paradisical meaning if it hadn't been for the rubbish and discarded cans. But compared with the towns of Tonga, it was wealthy. The one street paraded an astonishing variety of shops and goods, from the most modem cosmopolitan banks to the hive-like market and the store that advertised second-hand underpants.

The most striking thing was the chasm between two races, indigenous Fijian and Indian Fijian (I'll call them Fijian and Indian for short). It wasn't the physical differences - brown Fijian skin, near-black Indian skin, Fijian frizzy locks and straight Indian hair - it was in their demeanour.

The Indians were reserved and sullen, smiles appearing only with the prospect of business and rarely reaching the eyes. They seemed money-minded, but of course it's a role forced on them by a regime that denied them land and encouraged them to invest money in business. They had found political power through democracy, and then lost it by coup. There was even ill-informed talk of shipping Indians out wholesale, away from the land they'd been born in.

The Fijians, on the other hand, were open-hearted and warm, smiling quickly and easily.

"Bula, bula." Hello, they called out to each other and to us.

Almost all Fijians were villagers, living along the rivers or coasts, working communal land. We saw none in business. The price of the strong communal ties is that individuals trying to rise above the group are stifled by the demands of relatives.

Fijians didn't greet Indians. The two races seemed not to see each other in passing, the gulf far more pronounced in SavuSavu than anywhere else we went in Fiji.

The restaurant we chose, however, was Chinese. "Can I book a table for tonight?"

The owner's eyes expanded with astonishment. "You want reserve table?"

"Yes. Don't I need to?"

"Yes! Yes! Reserve table!" In his haste to find a pen he trashed the contents of an entire drawer. He wavered like a dart player looking for the target and settled on the calendar, drawing a huge circle round the 6.

"You are from yacht?" This was SavuSavu's first organised influx of cruising yachts.

"Yes."

"Name please."

I spelled it out, but he wrote it DROWN. I looked suspiciously at his innocent wide eyes and decided to leave it alone.

Jo Collins had to return to Suva quickly but we took her husband Paul to the restaurant. He told us of post-coup tensions in Suva, of the flight of foreign expertise, of 'honorary' cardiologists who now left off the word 'honorary', of an 18 metre yacht seized for dope smuggling. The skipper was held, pending extradition. In spite of a 24 hour security watch, the yacht was stripped by thieves down to bare hull and mast.

A policeman came into the restaurant. He was tall and powerfully built, an imposing presence and with the only forbidding Fijian demeanour we had seen. He ordered food and left with it. We didn't see money change hands, but an old man came out from the back and set the abacus beads flying with long gnarled twig fingers. Sam investigated the plumbing and complained that the hole-in-the-wall urinal was too high. He enlisted Andrew's help and they returned saying that Andrew had to lift him five times.

As we left the restaurant, the clouds unloaded. The rain roared on the awning and the wind came in a flurry of punches. An expensively dressed Fijian woman was there with us, holding a child.

"Are you waiting for a taxi?" we asked.

"No. I am waiting for my husband. He is a policeman. He is there." She pointed round the corner, where a ute was parked. There were two dark shapes in it, one cigarette glowing. The woman explained. "He is dealing with someone. I am keeping out of sight."

As we stood wondering what to do, a tarpaulin-covered truck rattled by at high speed. The driver spotted us, stood on the brake and did a spectacular U-turn, stopping opposite. We yelled above the rain where we wanted to go, climbed in the back, and the driver dropped the clutch, jerking us violently into the wild night.

"*Bula*," a couple of shy voices murmured in the dark.

"*Bula*," we replied. As our eyes adjusted, we saw two young Fijian women sitting with us. First the teeth, then the spherical frizz of hair, then the smiles.

"You are from the yachts?"

We introduced ourselves.

"Baby!" one of them beamed at Sam, then grabbed him and planted him on her knee. His scowl was fleeting and lost in the dark. He even neglected to tell her how big he really was.

"Who are you?" I asked. They looked at each other and their smiles changed subtly.

"We are daughters. We live at the police station."

"Who is he?" I pointed forward to the driver who seemed bent on reaching his grave early, with us for company.

"He is drunk," was the answer.

At the water's edge, I volunteered to row out to *Alderman* to collect everyone's rain gear. As I took the first stroke with the oars, already soaked, the boys told me there was an outboard shop in SavuSavu. I shouted through the rain that Dudley would get one more chance, this time with a mechanic.

Back on board, the wind was even wilder. The gusts, turned belligerent by the mountains, gave us left and right hooks, making *Alderman* reel around the mooring. But we had checked the mooring's holding power with full reverse thrust. It had to be safe, didn't it?

That night, *Triton III* and *Pacific High* turned up off SavuSavu Bay in the gale, without GPS. They tried to come in by searchlight, but the waves were too high. The Cousteau research ship *Alcyone*, anchored within a mile of the entrance, used its sophisticated radar to shepherd them in. Even inside the entrance they were close to disaster, saved only by a local European resident who looked out his window in the night and saw that they were close to a bombie. He leapt to the radio telephone in his front room.

"Stop! You're heading for a wall! Three more metres and you're gone!" They stopped in time. Some days, the glass falls and no wine is spilt.

Like what happened the night after Lester flew home.

At four in the morning, there was a fierce pounding on our hull. *"Alderman! Wake up, you're moving!"*

As a wake-up call, that's effective.

I reached the cockpit as Andrew reached the engine controls, looking up at me, waiting for the order.

"Switch on!"

"Switching on."

Outside, we all gaped at the unbelievable. Somehow we had drifted through half the fleet, some dozen yachts at that stage, and we had not touched one. We were to find out later that we had left on the spreader lights, so those who first saw us move assumed we were awake.

The coral was 50 metres away. I engaged Frankie, Sue snatched up the searchlight and trained it forward. Andrew went on depth sounder and when it wouldn't go, sorted out a loose-wire problem himself. Then we pushed the mooring back through the fleet to the right spot. But this time we dropped the anchor as well. Lesson number seven thousand and fifty three: a supplied official mooring with a short cable may be safe at low tide but unsafe at high.

"Andrew."

He looked at me.

"Well done. I'm proud of you," I said.

He tried to look nonchalant. Sam slept through everything.

26

When the wind stopped, two days later, mosquitoes rose. We had a choice: close the boat and suffocate, or get air and let the squadrons have their way with us. We tried lighting the mosquito coils, but they only repelled humans. We tried the local remedy, leaves of the pawpaw tree, and we might as well have sacrificed to the local gods.

Before dawn they were even getting my flesh through the netting, so I went for a row. The stars were still bright. The first hint of dawn drew the outlines of the mountains so faintly that sometimes they seemed far away, sometimes so near they could fall over on me. I thought I heard a sound like hands clapping, a fish jumped, but apart from that, everything was still. It was one of those times when you dip the oars carefully to avoid the intrusion of a splash.

"*Bula*," a voice called softly.

I looked around. It had come from the SavuSavu yacht club.

"*Bula*. Come, drink kava with us."

There was a circle of Fijian men in the dark under the awning, eight of them, some in a uniform I didn't recognise. They seemed courteous rather than friendly.

Intrigued, I sat with them round a bowl filled with a muddy grey liquid, kava, joining them in the ritual brought by the Tongan invaders centuries earlier and which the Fijians have made their own. Combine the social significance of alcohol, tea, and prayer and you have the Fijian national drink, their universal social catalyst. Legend says the *yaqona* plant sprang from the grave of a Tongan princess who died of a broken heart. In past ages, young girls prepared the kava by chewing the *yaqona* root, spitting the result into a bowl and mixing with water. Now, the root is pounded before mixing.

This was social kava drinking, the simplest of the rituals. Clap once, accept the dipping bowl with two hands, drink without stopping, say *maca!* empty! and clap twice or three times, slowly. Normally, there is little more significance to social kava drinking than inviting in the neighbours for a cup of tea.

But when a *palangi* takes part, there's a subtle change because the Fijians know that to a *palangi*, kava looks, smells and tastes like cold dishwater, the only difference being the numbing effect of the narcotic on lips and tongue. *Maca!* is pronounced 'Mother!' *Palangi* don't usually stay for a second round.

However, after five rounds the mosquitoes didn't bother me, the dawn looked peaceful and the men friendly. They decided I was worth helping with the finer

SavuSavu, Fiji, at dawn.

points of the language, correcting, for example, my pronunciation of *malo*, another version of 'thank you'. Apparently I had been expressing grateful thanks by saying, 'underpants'.

They were plain-clothes police and security guards: Inoke, Seru, Etiki, Isaac, Ruveni and three more who were not introduced.

"All of you? Guards and police?"

"Yes. Some of us are secret police."

Friendly of him to tell me. "There are many of you for one small town."

"We are here because of the yachts."

"Us? The yacht people do no harm."

"No. Because there might be trouble. After the coup."

I resisted the impulse to ask how they expected to protect us by drinking kava on the blind side of the yacht club. In any case, the conversation moved on to the attitude of Fijians to foreigners. Then the hard-bitten cops became animated.

"Fijians very friendly. You go to village, they show only friendly face."

"There's another face?"

"Not understand."

"They have other feelings about *palangi*? Some bad feelings?"

"No! No!" In spite of the soothing effects of the kava, three of them nearly came out of their seats in alarm. "What Fijian show on face is what is in heart. Only one face. Not two face."

I returned to the possibility of trouble.

"No," they assured me. "There is no tension between Fijians and Indians. Most people are innocent. They do not care what the politicians do in Suva."

Isaac – a self-declared secret policeman - came out to *Alderman,* to join us for breakfast. He was softly spoken, but with the kind of physique that causes women to go weak at the knees. Isaac may not care, but I have changed his name.

The boys complained to him about Dudley, saying that we would have to buy another one. Isaac listened, well disposed to them and to us.

"You want to sell this outboard?"

"Yes," I admitted.

"Yay!" shouted the boys.

"You want me to tell someone to buy it?"

"*Tell* someone?"

"Yes. I tell someone to buy it. How much you want?"

That was a world we didn't want to explore.

A navy patrol boat came in, an obsolete Israeli gunboat in Fijian paint. It tied up at the yacht club and the elderly district paramount chief was helped down the gangway.

He welcomed the yacht fleet to SavuSavu in the Fijian way, a kava ceremony known as *sevu sevu.* Fleet representatives presented the required gift of *yaqona* roots. Five warriors prepared the kava with intense concentration and gravity. And for a paramount chief there was no compromise on the full tradition. The pounded *yaqona* was handled by warriors with leaf bracelets on ankles and upper arms. They strained it through water, using the shredded bark of the hibiscus and a bowl of *vesi* hardwood.

"*So lose oti saka na yaqona, vaka turanga,*" the mixer said. The kava is ready, my chief.

And so it went, the cup bearers presenting the dipping bowl to one guest after another, each movement of hand and arm and foot, each clap, each murmured word potent with past centuries. The warriors looked ready for a time warp. Flick the clock back just a century and a half and they would have been cannibals. Their paramount chief would have shown contempt for a vanquished enemy by drinking kava from his skull.

Jean-Michel Cousteau came over from *Alcyone.* In fluent, articulate English he urged the cruising yachties to take care of the sea they travelled in. He was asked how much involvement his famous father, Jacques, still had in the Cousteau Society.

"It is gigantic," he said. "It is monumental, it is massive. He is eighty-two years old and still diving. He drives me insane."

Later we found a piece of Jean-Michel's writings on Fiji. It said:

> ... *it is important for Europeans to see how a person can have a high quality*

of life when one lives in an environment where the forests and reefs have not been destroyed, where the traditional values give a person a sense of belonging. We want these visitors to realise that... happiness comes from the heart and from relationships with other people, not from things. We believe the Fijian culture can demonstrate this as well as any other culture on this planet.

Jenny from *Dancing Wave* was walking down a beach at Waya Island when she

The Cousteau research vessel Alcyone. *Under wind power alone, the steel turbosails can push the 100 tonne ship at seven knots.*

Below: Sue with Jean-Michel Cousteau on Alcyone. *Brendan Neilsen from* Mystery Girl *in the background.*

met a chief's son walking the other way. He was not only a 'hunk' and an athlete, he had degrees from Oxford and Harvard. He could have conquered much of the world, but had chosen to come back to live in his village.

"Don't you want to go back to the real world?" she asked him.

"It holds nothing for me," he answered. "The only thing I miss about that world is having my beer cold."

The yachties were treated to a dance, made notable by the frogs the children put into the women's toilets. The children were politely asked to desist, partly because the animals tended to set up home under the seat rim, partly because they weren't frogs but poisonous spitting toads that could blind the children for life. For just two minutes, every child in the entire fleet was simultaneously silent and obedient.

Lacking an expensive resort, the sea kids adopted the yacht club with fierce enthusiasm, demanding fizzy drinks and pizzas and willing, if allowed, to spend an entire day watching videos set up for them. The only place they didn't reign supreme was the upstairs bar. If the party became boistrous, management put up a sign banning children.

To Andrew and Sam's disgust, Sue and I enforced that ban. Sam's diary entry next day reads: *I went in and then Mum sent me firing down stairs. Parents are greedy and drink too much and push children down stairs.*

By taking us into the Lambasa sugar mill, the regatta organisers put together Fiji's two greatest earners. The tour was the nearest thing I've seen to a living hell, a walk through endless heat and noise in the gut of a mechanical monster. And deep in the bowels there's a sign written on a steel floor plate in molten welding metal, underlining human torment: *Love thy neighbour but don't get married at 75 to a girl.* Some of the yachties may have been affected by that glimpse of Hades because they arranged their own church service dedicated to the philosophy that thirsting is a greater sin than drinking.

Then there was the race. Not a contest on a coastal passage, not a tussle between the big cruising yachts at all, but the race that really brought the competitive beast to the surface. The local children's sailing club offered their tiny sailing Optimists for a fleet championship. The craft are so small that grown men can barely squeeze under the boom when they go about. Even so, the local club didn't realise what they were unleashing. The skippers eagerly put their names down for syndicate racing. I was put on the same syndicate as Steen from *Chieftain*.

Steen came to visit.

"I would like to withdraw from our syndicate," he said, looking at his feet. What he meant was that I had no racing pedigree, he could not bear to lose, and he was too polite to ask me to bow out for someone with proven talent. If I was a mature adult and a gentleman I would have to offer a dignified withdrawal.

"I'm all right," I said hotly. "I won a race once. At school."

"I am very competitive," he apologised.

"I know!" I glowered. I knew that he had once ordered Geraldine to run down a competitor who got in the way on the wrong tack.

"I am sorry," he insisted. "I have a killer instinct."

"You should be able to relate to that," Sue said to me, grinning, and I directed my own killer glare at her. She laughed. Then the two skippers stood on the aft deck, sorting out whether they could cope with having each other on the same team in boats smaller than the length of our bodies. Suddenly inspired, I promised that if we raced in the same team I would whip the pants off him for his cheek. He promptly brightened. Maybe I did have 'the attitude'.

So we adults raced together in children's dinghies. I came in well behind him. But we won, giving no quarter, asking for none, yelling false claims for right of way to intimidate those who didn't know the rules.

There was a grudge match afterwards, between Steen and John Senior, two acknowledged racing experts. The interest, as much as anything, was in how John would perform after his surgery in New Zealand, then denying his doctor's advice not to sail again.

John won the match and Steen was the first to congratulate him.

Three-year-old Maddy, the human projectile from *Meridian*, overshot on the club veranda and plunged into the harbour.

John leaped in and pulled her out.

There was a raffle for an outboard motor. "We're going to win," the boys assured me, and we lined up at the draw in the upstairs bar.

John won the outboard.

Then he gave it away. He talked to the gathering quietly, with a catch in his voice, about the cruising fraternity.

"We've had such camaraderie here, I never realised ... It's like a family. I would like to donate it to the SavuSavu Yacht Club so they can develop the kids' sailing skills."

27

"Have you seen *The Gods Must Be Crazy*?" Andrew asked us.

"Yes. Loved it."

"Well, in that tribe they never scold their children. They don't ever speak to them harshly. Their games are inventive and creative and there is no violence between the children. Therefore the children are very well behaved."

"No kidding." For a moment, I wondered how Andrew would look wearing a well-placed length of packing tape.

But his point wasn't entirely lost on me. It had been difficult to maintain clear, consistent boundaries. I know, it should have been easy once I understood the necessity of unambiguous command. It wasn't. Nothing, nothing, tests child-raising ideals like being at sea with them. Whatever - I woke next morning at least resolved not to snarl at the boys for anything minor.

Half an hour later I found Sam tightrope-walking on the furling line, with a good chance of wrecking the gear that rolls up the genoa in a gale. That was not minor. That was entirely the other end of the scale. I ordered him below, batting his ears with my tongue.

Later I found him batting the centreboard casing with his forehead.

"There's no need for that," I growled. "You didn't know, but you know now, right?"

"You're always telling me off."

"You're mad at yourself, aren't you?"

Silence. Then, "Yes."

"Well, that's good. That means you've learned something."

"But mostly I'm mad at you."

I retreated to the aft cabin and practised *The Tune*. There's a sound on the front of it like the skirl of gulls on the wind. I was getting better at it. The wild thought came to me that maybe I could perform it in the Musket Cove Talent Quest. But I dismissed the idea immediately. The Quest was a sizeable bit of showbiz with an international audience of hundreds and playing a school recorder was one step up from playing a broomstick.

The Tune was doing me the world of good - great therapy for the tensions of cruising. It's hard to describe, but it was like playing something inside me at the same time as playing the instrument. But it did nothing for anyone else on board and there were complaints that my tune was accelerating the rust on the hull.

So I was delighted when the local school principal invited all the sea kids to attend class for one morning. I could get peace and play my tune, and they would see another kind of discipline.

Sue went with the sea kids. She can tell you:

The invitation to the school yard seemed perfectly timed for the children, and for Michael and me.

Life had hit about an E-minus at that point. I was fed up with demanding youngsters, days on end of torrential rain, mildewed clothes, and a nagging pain in my right shoulder. Our money was lost in transit from New Zealand. I'd had disturbing news about my business interests at home. I craved some totally inappropriate girlie fripperies and couldn't find any of them: perfume, nail polish, a satin nightie.

And, to cap it off, Michael and I'd had another spat. It was in the same idiot class as leaving the top off the toothpaste tube, and wouldn't have rated a complete sentence between us at home. But in this setting, it escalated to full argument. Neither of us fights well. For two articulate and mostly logical people, experienced actors as well, we're abysmal at verbal fisticuffs.

So, pleased to decamp for a while, I volunteered to escort the eight *palangi* children to the Indian school.

We were taken there in a battered old truck, me in the cab, the children out on the tray in the rain. After several attempts to cajole the vehicle up the school's steep and muddy entrance, the driver finally deposited us at the feet of the fawning principal.

He, suddenly alarmed at his own bright idea, squeezed us all into his tiny office and nervously assigned our children to classes according to age. Andrew and Ian looked huge and glaringly Anglo-Saxon beside their tiny, dark counterparts as they ambled off towards a shabby classroom. Its unhinged windows flapped crossly in the breeze.

The two older girls were borne off in a flurry of black pigtails.

I took Madeleine and Adam, both three, plus seven-year-olds Sam and Elliot, to a class of extraordinarily reticent children who thankfully had a smiling Fijian teacher. The class called her 'Madam'.

In the dark and dirty room, its blackboard serving as a wall to the next class, the children rose to say their prayers. The teacher gave me a "What can I do?" shrug as they chanted in Hindi for minutes on end, eyes tightly shut, hands pressed together.

The lessons were conducted in English, high-pitched and inaccurate. I'm sure the children barely knew what they were about. The teacher demanded absolute obedience, so the class was puzzled when she let my charges draw all over her blackboard, and walk about at will. She had no idea what else to do with them.

I noticed several left-handers in the class, and commented, really just to show I was taking an interest. The teacher took it as a criticism.

"I know. So sorry. I've tried and tried to right-hand them. But no use now. They're seven."

One little girl with a mask-like face did no work at all and kept leaving the room. The teacher explained sadly there are no schools available for children with special needs. That was when I decided we'd only just make it to break time. I took Madeleine to the toilet, which was a hole in the ground, the only one to serve hundreds of little girls.

In Andrew and Ian's class, I heard later, the lesson was taking an odd shape. First the Indian teacher insisted the boys talk about their homeland. Then he gave them no space to do it.

"Before we start, I give you time to mix with them kids," he told them. "Mix! You mix with kids. You mix!" He left the room abruptly.

The class became friendly enough, speaking English quite well, but re-froze when the teacher returned. The children were clearly terrified of him and our boys were stunned at what followed. He hoisted a metre long stick, then applied it with force to his pupils' upper arms, shoulders or chests for wrong answers. But then he suddenly stopped.

"Andrew. Do your teachers beat you?"

"It's very, very rare," Andrew replied in a shocked voice. "If you're going to be hit, you get sent to the principal's office first. Even then, if you do get hit, it's not hard. And you're never hit for wrong answers. Anyone who keeps getting answers wrong gets sent to a special part of the room with a special teacher."

The Indian teacher was astounded at the news.

When he insisted the *palangi* boys talk about New Zealand they were acutely uncomfortable. They spoke haltingly about New Zealand history, with stories of early settlers being killed by Maori. Andrew veered off on to the subject of lamb docking; Ian gave some details of our home climate. The going was uphill.

"Any questions?" the teacher asked.

No response.

"Are the sharks here dangerous?" asked Andrew, trying to fill the silence.

No response.

The teacher jabbed his finger at a boy. "You! Your father is a diver. Tell him!"

No response. The boy looked terrified.

Andrew battled on. "Do you have any questions for us?"

No response.

The teacher turned on his class.

"You are dull, dull, dull. Ask them some questions! Do something! Say something! Where are you going to end up, dull like this? Hmmm? Hmmm?"

No response.

178

At break time, our boys all but charged me down. "Let's go!" they said.

I nodded. You bet.

I gathered up the two girls, who had in fact enjoyed themselves, holding court with many admiring little Indian maidens. I faced the principal, muttered lamely that I had to get the little ones back to their mothers. He was deeply offended, and couldn't believe it when he realised we were all going to walk off back to the boats, on our own, in the rain.

We bounded back down the soggy driveway, past the hot springs, and back to the yacht club. I was grateful to the principal; he'd given us a valuable insight. I told anyone in the clubhouse who'd listen that the British Empire has a lot to answer for. My own empire looked much more appealing now, and the boys decided they were on the pig's back with this cruising lifestyle after all.

That inability to cope with the presence of *palangi* was even more marked at SavuSavu hospital.

But it was Michael who saw that:

Collectively the yachties decided to try to give something back to SavuSavu. They volunteered to help out with unskilled labour at the hospital because it was badly under-staffed. The hospital authorities accepted with delight.

But the staff didn't know how to handle forty 'rich' *palangi* turning up as slushies. They moved us right through to a dining room where they had spent precious resources on a fancy morning tea. We went through that out of politeness, but when the time dragged out, we had to make firm suggestions about work.

I got a mop and bucket and regretted that Sue wasn't there to witness. I did my best with it, moving amongst the astonished patients' beds.

"You like working in hospital?" one asked. Clearly I needed bed rest more than she did.

I assured her I did. But then I noticed that the charge nurse had her sights trained on me, and she wasn't happy. She kept looking away from me and back, sorely aggrieved by something. I went on working until she could stand it no more. She marched over.

"Excuse me!"

"Yes?"

"I am sorry!"

"Why?"

"In this hospital we do it this way."

Troubled by having to correct a volunteer *palangi*, she nevertheless took the mop from me.

"Not this way. This way. You spin mop in hands inside bucket to shake dirt out. Please you go out from patients. Do only corridor. I am sorry."

I apologized. I obeyed. I did the corridor, mending my ways along the walls where there were lists of defaulters, patients who have not paid bills of $1.50, even 50 cents. With my new skills I was eventually promoted back into the wards where I mopped without spreading dirt amongst the patients, the only yachtie in the fleet who had to be coached in unskilled labour.

28

Secret policeman Isaac came back.

He was in an excellent mood. The evening before, a *palangi* woman, a land-based tourist, had offered herself to him. True, he'd not understood the offer at first, probably because she was slurring her *palangi* words at the time. But she found ways to make the message clear. Booking a room and pointing firmly to the bed may have done it. Hesitating only long enough to ask why she wanted a black man, he had honoured her offer. Now he was happy; he had found a good woman who liked him as much as he liked her.

For us he had an invitation. "You come to see my village and my family."

But it wasn't his village, or even his family. When you join the police force in Fiji, you are deliberately posted away from your home village, away from the powerful ties that might stop you doing your job. He meant his adopted village, Nukubalavu, and by family, he meant a distant uncle and aunt.

On the way, he told us about the assignment he had when he wasn't protecting cruising yachties. Not so secret, it too sprang from the activities of a foreign yacht.

"Captain of big yacht, he go to village farmers. He tell them plant seeds for flowers in market. He give them marijuana seeds. We catch him."

"What happened to him."

"He go to prison for life. The farmers they go to prison for many years."

"That's rough..."

"Drugs. Very bad," Isaac said with a shrug.

He and other plain-clothes police travelled through the villages, asking the *turanga ni koro*, village headman, for permission to assemble the population for preventative drug education. Permission was always granted, no exceptions. The entire population was always present, no exceptions.

To get to Nukubalavu, we drove past a block of eighty hectares that had once changed hands for one shilling and ten muskets, and past the airport that had departed Fijian ownership for the price of one empty whisky bottle.

The village sits on the southern coast, where the coconut palms are more than 20 metres tall and the beach sweeps past islands so tiny they seem to have copied themselves from cartoons. Each has been undercut by water and each has a single tree. At low tide it looks from the shore as if each tree is sitting on one end of an apple core.

The Nukubalavu villagers were said to have totemic, spiritual links with sharks. In Fiji, even the tourists don't dismiss such things lightly. Some tourists pay fortunes to see village women call turtles from the sea in Koro and Kadavu.

The house of Isaac's uncle Emosi and aunt Noella was sparse by our standards. There were two chairs, set awkwardly against an end wall in a bare room. Otherwise there was just a mat on the floor and photographs on the wall. Amongst the family shots, a well-framed Sitiveni Rabuka, the coup leader. Every indigenous Fijian's home we saw had his image on the wall.

We matted ourselves, facing Emosi. His skin was almost African black, his eyes twinkling. I placed a gift of *yaqona* root on the floor between us. It would have been the height of rudeness to simply hand the bundle of roots over; he had to have the choice of picking it up or refusing it. And I gave a rehearsed guest's greeting: *Nogu sevu sevu gor.*

He nodded, pleased, picked up the *yaqona*, closed his eyes. The boys watched him with interest. They always took part in the kava ceremonies now, occasionally drinking small quantities. In a moment he spoke, rocking slightly as the words streamed out. The speech was unusually long, and afterwards, he and Isaac translated. Andrew and Sam, who had been fidgeting, cross-legged and uncomfortable on the hard floor, were transfixed.

"I ask kava god look after you on your journey home. Also I ask shark god protect you. Now, if your boat tip over the first fish to come will be a shark. Do not be afraid, speak to him as you speak to your brother. Say, 'Hello, how are you.' You hold him. He will carry you to shore."

The boys' mouths stayed open. I looked for some hint that Emosi was merely repeating ritual folklore, but there was none. Christianity had not replaced the old gods in this house.

A mere thank you would have been a miserly response, so I made a speech.

Formalities over, Sam got the lion's share of the attention as usual, especially from the women. He accepted it graciously and we nodded approvingly to him. We'd been through a heavy discussion about how to behave while being touched and what to do if he was touched too much for his liking. While the meal was still being prepared, Isaac took me to the mango tree to join the village kava circle. The men there were gravely courteous. Sometimes they spoke with me, sometimes amongst themselves, sharing cigarettes, poring over a Catholic newspaper. The atmosphere was without strain.

The tide was out. Isaac took us out beyond the beach where a naturally formed but perfectly spherical stone rested on three small rocks. It looked volcanic in origin.

"Its name is Vatukuro. It means 'the Storm Stone'. You must not strike it. If anyone strikes it, there is nine days of storm."

Sam backed off a centimetre or two, looking at the rock respectfully. But Isaac was smiling. He said, "All the men strike it when women come from another village, so that they cannot leave."

While Isaac told us about the Storm Stone, Andrew sat forlornly on the sand, drawing a heart and initials with a stick.

The meal was placed on plates, on the floor: *kasava*, silver beet soup, roast pumpkin and beans, corned beef and fried onions. And the delicious *palusami*: fish baked in a wrapping of leaves. The family had turned on its best. We could only guess how much time and effort had gone into preparations.

We asked about the village's links with sharks. "We respect the shark," they said.

We could understand that.

They warned us not to throw a stone at a shark because it would remember and come back for us.

We could relate to that too, but the next bit was harder. "When chief's father, he die, all sharks... forty, sixty ... they come to beach. Great white shark come up beach to chief s house, where body lie inside. He put head up steps close to body. Then he go back to sea."

I thought about that.

"How far from the water to the chiefs house?"

Isaac pointed out the door to a tumbledown shell. "That chief's house. We tear down house because no one must live there now."

Fifty metres there. Fifty back. My face may have betrayed something because a friend of Isaac's who had joined us leapt to his feet and earnestly elaborated, anxious that we believe.

"I see it. This big... this big... " He paced it out, using the entrance of Emosi's house to illustrate. Six to seven metres long. "Shark go like this... that... this... that... sideways on ground. His body... up steps. His head here inside... this much."

"Did you see it?" I asked Isaac.

"No. I was not there."

Ten years as a journalist had taught me a little about orchestrated hogwash. You can often see who's holding the baton. But there was not the slightest sign of it in the half a dozen indigenous Fijians in the room. Four men, two women. Either they were all Oscar material or they believed what they were saying. If they believed it, then where were we? It's said that at times of great emotion, minds will group together to create a shared experience that seems external and tangible. If so, then reality could never be a specimen in a scientist's jar.

But it wasn't the great white shark we remembered as we left to return to SavuSavu, it was the hospitality. We should not have been surprised. Experienced cruisers, those who were in it for more than the beaches and resorts, had told us to expect it. "Go to the distant villages, off the beaten track. You'll be shaken by the experience, bowled over, humbled."

Among the great-grandchildren of cannibals the quality of hospitality is not strained.

Three days later we set up for passage to Qamea Island in the northeast.

And to the delirious happiness of the boys, we bought a new outboard motor, a four-horse team with all four pulling their weight. On our running-in tour, half the fleet came out on deck to applaud, because our war with Dudley had been a fleet joke. The defeated machine now hung pathetically on the rail, waiting burial. Two days later, Sam didn't watch where he was going and ran the new outboard over a mooring line, stopping it dead. There was no damage done, but Sam went into a frenzy of self-flagellation.

Many yachts were leaving now, scattering throughout the islands. Most would not see each other again for many weeks.

Isaac paid a last visit, this time in despair. He went straight for Sue's international shoulder, telling her that his *palangi* woman had taken up house with two men, and wanted nothing more to do with him.

"I do not understand. She tell me many good things. In the morning we have breakfast in the bed. She say she like me. But she not like me now. I do not understand."

With me, he took a different line. As he spoke, the softly spoken, gentle Fijian allowed a steel snake to flex in his pupils.

"She go with two old men now. One man he is the man. The other man he is the woman. He have breasts. These things very bad."

It was Isaac who introduced us to Ruveni before we left. And Ruveni was the catalyst for one of the hardest decisions Sue ever made.

It was curious the way it happened. Isaac was on board when Sue and I sat looking through scuba-diving pamphlets. Diving was something she and I had discussed before, a tempting idea that I thought would never become reality because Sue was seriously afraid of going under the surface, terrified at the thought of going deep with scuba gear. And yet she badly regretted not attempting Mariner's Cave.

That was the moment Ruveni came alongside and climbed aboard. He was a diving instructor.

He was also a soldier, on leave from serving in the United Nations forces in the Middle East. His matter-of-fact description of what it's like to get 600 metres per second hornets round the ears reminded me of the reputation of Fijian soldiers in World War II. They so devastated Japanese troops in the jungle that they were never listed as missing in action. Just 'not yet returned'.

But Ruveni had found and delighted in another world back home, the world below the surface of the sea.

184

"In Fiji we have the best scuba diving in the world. You should learn to dive here."

Sue shifted position, turning a shade paler. "I know," she said. Then she was silent. Decision time.

Isaac and Ruveni saw that this was no time to open their mouths, so there were awkward silences. Sue's eyes had the faraway look of crisis. "I'm thinking," she muttered once. And she did so for five very long minutes.

Then, "I'll do it."

In fact, we didn't do the course with Ruveni. The weather was fair for the passage to Qamea, so we booked ahead for a course at Musket Cove.

In our last conversation with Ruveni, he was almost tearfully warm with his wishes for our journey.

Sue asked, "If you and your friends are like this, how can we believe we are in the Cannibal Islands?"

"Yes, it must seem strange," he said. "But we have always been a friendly people. Even then."

Some historical documents agree. Many of the earliest missionaries witnessed the worst excesses of savagery first hand. They often recorded their horror. Yet again and again they recorded that the same Fijians were a kindly people.

When we finally cast off, the staff and guests in the Copra Shed yacht club rang the bell, leaned out the upper windows to wave, or came out on to the decking. Town children waved on the banks as we slipped down towards the mouth of the harbour.

"*Moce, moce,*" they called. Goodbye.

Emosi called out to us from a boat, wishing us safe journey. "God bless you!" Sam shouted back. He put his head on my chest. "I feel like crying."

"So do I," Sue and I said simultaneously.

Sam stayed distressed, so I murmured in his ear that it was good that we felt like this, because it meant we'd had a good time. But Sam only mumbled into my chest.

"One day we'll come back," I tried.

His head jerked up. "Yes!"

"We'll see them again. Lino and Emosi and Tavida and Isaac and Ruveni and Osiro and -"

"And Walter?"

"And Walter."

For the night we anchored out by the entrance to the bay, ready for an early start. When the stars came out, Isaac came aboard with three friends, for a kava party. The guitar emerged and they taught us one of the famous songs of the South Pacific, singing their harmonies out over the tranquil water.

185

Isalsa vulagi lasa dina. Nomu lako au na rarawa kina. Cava beka ko a mai cakava. Nomu lako au na sega ni lasa. You have enjoyed our true friendship. When you leave I will be very sad. Why did you come to visit us? When you go I will be sad and lonely.

Vanua rogo na nomuni vanuawa. Kena ca ni levu tu na ua. Cava beka kowa mai cakava. Nomu lako au no sega ni lasa. Your place also is known for its friendliness. I wanted to come but the seas were too rough. Why did you come to visit us? Because when you go, I will be sad and lonely.

Isa lei na noqu rarawa, ni ko sana vodo ena mataka. Itau nanuma na nodatou lasa. Mai SavuSavu nanuma tikoga. How great my sadness will be when you go tomorrow. Think, then, of the happiness you had with us. Think, always, of my SavuSavu.

29

"Welcome to Paradise!"

They were the first words we heard at Qamea. For two days we had followed the route through Somo Somo Strait, picking up a blow and rain squalls to the north of Taveuni. Qamea had been veiled by the weather, and Naiviivi Inlet tricky to negotiate, so we'd not had eyes for the scenery. Remote though the island was, another yacht had found its way there, the *Kirsten Anne*. As we swung to drop anchor, a European woman came out on the stern, spread her smile and arms wide and welcomed us to Paradise. We wondered if they had heard the same stories and come for the same reason.

The chain rattled out, the anchor winch locked off. *Alderman* tested the holding and settled. We looked around as the sun pierced the clouds.

The inlet had the kind of breathless beauty that seems only possible in fantasy: vivid greens, wild untouched bush soaring hundreds of metres from water's edge to the peaks. On the south side one slope was gentler, pausing its plunge just enough

Approaching Vatusogosogo village, to a subdued reception.

In the top of the bag: a bundle of yaqona root, the traditional visitors' offering.

to hold a village. Vatusogosogo. That was where the sun struck: on traditional reed and coconut leaf *bures*. A few people moved around on the steep grassed area, some stood looking out at us. It would be hard to imagine a more spectacular village setting.

But we had not come for the scenery.

We had to wade ashore through the mangroves and knee-high mud, clutching the presentation bundle of *yaqona*. Curious children hovered at a safe distance. They were more reserved than usual, less ready to smile. Their faces were much darker than most Fijians'. As we washed the mud off our legs, a young man arrived.

"*Bula.*" Courteous, but not yet friendly.

"*Bula.* Can you take us to the *turanga ni koro*?"

"Yes. I take you. My name Alusio."

A brief shower came through as he led us up the slope, through the *bures*. Every adult who glanced at us or waved tentatively had the dark skin of Melanesia, not the usual Melanesian-Polynesian mix. A rooster drooped in the rain blinking at its loss of dignity. Another two were held in the arms of young boys. Smaller children stood with propellers made of strips of coconut leaf, but they didn't run with them to make them turn. Two young men cut the village grass with machetes, though it was less than two centimetres high.

To the Fijian establishment, Vatusogosogo was not officially a village. No *turanga ni koro*, head man, no *ratu*, chief, just a collection of huts with a few people. We had asked for the *sevu sevu* ritual as a matter of courtesy and expected them to be pleased. But when the unofficial *turanga ni koro* carried it out, courtesy was all he gave back.

His name was Moses. There was little warmth and an odd flatness to the atmosphere. We heard birds, an occasional bark, but no sound of children playing. Somewhere nearby an adult coughed, chestily and painfully.

We told them we'd heard that the history of Vatusogosogo was unique, that we were interested to find out what had happened. There was little response. Their minds were not on us at all.

But, very slowly, possibly because of the boys, they thawed. Alusio Kelepi warmed the fastest, introducing his mother, showing us his house and the village three-shelf shop. His shop. It had a few staples, corned beef, soap, school stationery, razors and cigarettes. On several visits to the village, we never saw anyone go in.

Outside, the boys exchanged nothing more than the occasional smile with older children, who weren't playing even amongst themselves. I might have asked Alusio why, but then I did see three very young ones in a running game in the distance and decided I must have been mistaken.

It took three visits before Alusio passed on the invitation we wanted.

"You come tomorrow. We tell you history of Vatusogosogo." As we left, I heard the coughing again.

On the other yacht, *Kirsten Anne*, we met Tom and Suzanne and their son John from Southern California. They were born-again cruisers, among the very few who find not just interest but magic in other cultures. Tom had been in the navy, engineering and electronics. As he described it, back then he'd been further to the right than Atilla the Hun. Then he'd opened his eyes to what the world was like.

"I'm a changed man." he said. He waved out the porthole lowards the impoverished Vatusogosogo. "I'm here to learn."

John was busy repairing a village outboard motor. Asked about it, he shrugged. "Giving back something of what I've been given."

Suzanne and John went scuba diving later that day. When they returned, Suzanne was so overcome by the experience we could see her radiance from forty metres away. She and Sue talked intensely about it, Sue visibly impressed when Suzanne said, "Sometimes it's like... like my soul has been there."

She also impressed Andrew with her wisdom and intelligence by describing his VHF radio personality as 'elegant'.

The next day, Moses, Alusio and Tomasi, another village elder, met outside Moses' bure. There was a quick conversation in Fijian that ended in Moses shaking his head. The conversation wasn't explained to us. Instead, they took us across to a *bure* about forty metres away, seating us on a coconut-leaf floor so thick and soft it was like a mattress.

Through Alusio, they gave us the story of the village:

In about the year 1870, on the island of Malaita in the Solomons, a young man came down to the beach attracted by the excitement of other villagers. His name then has not survived the years, but he would eventually be known as Jim.

Jim was between eighteen and twenty-five years old. He was probably wearing a bone or wooden bodkin thrust through his nose, or possibly a spike of turtle shell. Each of his ears would have had anywhere from one to six holes, capable of carrying clay pipes and decorative wooden plugs up to eighteen centimetres in diameter.

There was a sailing ship anchored in the bay, stern on. And a ship's boat was being rowed ashore.

Jim was carrying a club, tomahawk or a bow and arrows. He and the others knew other tribes had been hard hit by the ravages of the white man, who abducted men, women and children alike into the bowels of the great canoe so that they were never seen again. They knew also about the terrible revenges visited on those who resisted, revenges that wiped out whole villages. And there were the diseases that did the same. In one village, the revenge had been in a

189

gift, a small pile of clothes left for the villagers, taken from men dead of a white man's disease called the pox.

Yes, Jim was suspicious. But like his fellow warriors he was entranced by something that no one had prepared them for. In the midst of the sailors was a man dressed in robes so dazzling white that it hurt the eyes to look.

Crouching at a safe distance, Jim watched as the sailors ran the boat ashore and helped the great white man out on to the sand. One sailor carried a finely carved piece of wood with a flat top which he set before the white-robed chief. Now the chief held up a thing covered with animal skin, opened it and set it on top of the wood. The thing with the skin contained pieces of the finest cloth that flipped in the wind. Then, most marvellous of all, it spoke through the white chief's mouth.

Now another sailor, this one with light brown skin, began to speak the chief's words in Jim's tongue. He spoke of a "god belong white man" who was greater than all the other gods. He spoke of a "word belong god" and a "garden belong god" with plenty kumara, plenty taro, plenty breadfruit.

There were no firesticks to be seen. So Jim and the other warriors stood slowly and came closer, until there were many of them listening to the words from the god on the wood.

Then the man in the white robes beamed, stopped speaking and nodded to the sailors round him. Promptly, every sailor produced short firesticks hidden in their clothing and pointed them at the warriors. Soon, Jim and many others from his village were lying bound in the bottom of small boats on the way to the ship. Perhaps, on the way, he heard the laughing white man's word, "blackbirds".

"What kind of ship?" I asked Alusio. "How many prisoners? How long did the journey take?" But after discussion with Moses and Tomasi, he shook his head.

"We not know."

"Which country was the ship from?"

"It was British."

In Suva, Jim had changed hands for the price of a pistol and some tobacco.

Then he was shipped again, to the Fijian Island of Taveuni where he built stone fences for a farm. And finally he was taken to the cane fields, where the British plantation owner stripped him of his Solomon name. After all, it was important that a slave not waste energy by pining for the past. So he became Jim. Jim Ravugani.

The owner also believed in firm discipline. At sun up, the slaves would be assembled before him by the cane. He would pull a pair of glasses from his pocket and place them on a rock, facing the field.

"These are my eyes," he would say to his slaves. "They will watch you until the sun goes down." Or he might anchor an open umbrella on the ground, saying, "This is my head. It will tell me if you have not been working."

Those squealed-on by the glasses or the umbrella were put together in a sack in the sun. Or if they were too much trouble, they were shot.

Jim survived. He was about 105 years old when he died in 1941.

"He my grandfather," Alusio said.

Figures flicked in my head. "You must mean great-grandfather."

"Not understand."

"You mean grandfather's father?"

Alusio frowned and spoke rapidly with the other two. Both shook their heads firmly.

"No. Not great-grandfather. Jim my grandfather."

Which meant that Jim Ravugani must have been strong to a ripe old age.

The whole village, perhaps sixty people, was descended from Solomon Islanders like Jim. Two and more generations later they have not inter-married with the Fijians. Eighty years after blackbirding was banned they are still trapped by it. They don't own the land they live on; they work the plantations to pay the Fijian owners for the right to live there.

"You want to return to the Solomons?"

Alusio conveyed this rapidly to Moses and Tomasi and came back emphatically.

"Yes. We all want go back to Solomon Islands. They have land there for us."

"Land? Who has land?"

"Government in Solomon Islands have land. It is for us when we return."

"I don't understand. Everyone in Vatusogosogo wants to go back to the Solomon Islands? The whole village?"

"Yes. We are not Fijians. We are Solomon Islands."

"Then why don't you go?"

"We have no money. We not... It is hard to pay lease. Pay lease... no money."

So for Vatusogosogo village on Qamea Island, nothing has really changed. The veneer is prettier, the owners now have dark faces, but the glasses are still sitting on the rock, glinting in the Fijian sun.

The three of them talked together. Alusio nodded and turned to me. "Please you write village history so we ask visitors help with lease."

They meant a one page hand-out, explaining their situation and asking for donations. It would be given to the rare visitors in the bay. I was willing. But how strongly to express it? How much were they willing to offend the Fijian authorities?

So with an assembly of villagers around me under the breadfruit tree, I read out each phrase and waited while it was sieved through Alusio then thirty tongues and thirty opinions and back through Alusio. That led to a highly diplomatic single page, expressing gratitude to the authorities for their administration of the village, but which still served the purpose of declaring their desire and intent.

Tom printed it for them on *Kirsten Anne's* computer.

"Come back tomorrow," they said again. "We have party."

"Take a look at this."

Tom handed me a book. *The Cruise of the Snark*, by Jack London. It's an account of a yacht journey through the South Pacific, early twentieth century, when

After cautious first contact, a friendly welcome into Vatusogosogo village.

Alusio Kelepi (village spokesman) and his mother. His grandfather was kidnapped from the Solomons and sold as a slave. Now he and the rest of the village want to go home to the Solomons.

blackbirding was outlawed, but when Solomon Island labour was still needed. That was when the ships went back to the Solomons, this time offering wages, the sum of six pounds a year for three years.

They also offered God.

This time, the ministers who preached on the shore were real. Of course it wasn't easy. For some reason, the Solomon Islanders didn't trust white men any more. They hung back in the bush with weapons at the ready. But this time the labour-recruiting ministers used translators who had been blackbirded but converted to Christianity. And they discovered that Solomon Islanders responded well to the story of the garden of Eden.

Here's one of the classic pidgin English, sand-in-the-toes sermons of the Pacific, as reported by Jack London. You need to know that *kai-kai* is food, *tambo* means taboo, *gammon* means liar or to lie, *bokkis* is box, *fennis* is fence, *savee* is understand. *Mary* is the universal name for woman. And *What name?* is an all-purpose interrogative meaning anything from 'Why?' to 'What do you mean by this outrageous conduct?'

Altogether you boy belong Solomons you no savee white man. Me fella me savee him. Me fella me savee talk along white man.

Before long time altogether no place he stop. God big fella marster belong white man, himfella He make'm altogether. God big fella marster belong white man, He make'm big fella garden. He good fella too much. Along garden plenty yam he stop, plenty cocoanut, plenty taro, plenty kumara, altogether good fella kai-kai too much.

Bimeby God big fella marster belong white man He make 'm one fella man to put'm along garden belong Him. He call'm this fella man Adam. He name belong him. He put him this fella man Adam along garden and He speak, "This fella garden he belong you. "

And He look'm this fella Adam he walk about too much. Him fella Adam all the same sick; he no savee kai-kai; he walk about all the time. And God He no savee. God big fella marster belong white man He scratch 'm head belong Him. God say, "What name?" Me no savee what name this fella Adam he want.

Bimeby God He scratch 'm head belong Him too much and speak, "Me fella me savee, him fella Adam him want'm Mary. " So He make Adam he go asleep, He take one fella bone belong him and He make'm onefella Mary along bone. He call him this fella Mary, Eve. He give'm this fella Eve along Adam and he speak along himfella Adam, "Close up altogether along this fella garden belong you two fella. One fella tree he tambo along you altogether. This fella tree belong apple. " So Adam and Eve two fella stop along garden and they two fella have 'm good time too much.

Bimeby, one day, Eve she come along Adam and she speak, "More good you me two fella we eat'm this fella apple."

Adam he speak, "No."

And Eve she speak, "What name you no like'm me?"

And Adam he speak, "Me like'm you too much but me fright along God."

And Eve she speak, "Gammon! What name? God He no savee look along us two fella all'm time. God big fella marster He gammon along you."

But Adam he speak, "No."

But Eve she talk, talk, talk, allee time - allee same Mary she talk along boy along Queensland and make'm trouble along boy. And bimeby Adam he tired too much, and he speak, "All right."

So these two fella they go eat'm. When they finish eat'm my word, they fright like hell and they go hide along scrub.

And God he come walk about along garden, and He sing out, "Adam!" Adam he no speak. He too much fright, my word! And God He sing out, "Adam!"

And Adam he speak, "You call'm me?"

God he speak, "Me call'm you too much. "

Adam he speak, "Me sleep strong fella too much."

And God he speak, "You been eat'm this fella apple."

Adam he speak, "No, me no been eat'm."

God He speak, "What name you gammon along me? You been eat'm."

And Adam he speak, "Yes, me been eat'm. "

And God big fella marster he cross along Adam Eve two fella too much and he speak, "You two fella finish along me altogether. You go catch'm bokkis belong you and get to hell along scrub. "

So Adam Eve these two fella go along scrub. And God He make'm one big fennis all around garden and He put'm one fella marster belong God along fennis. And He give this fella marster belong God one big fella musket and He speak. "S'pose you look'm these two fella Adam, Eve, you shoot'm plenty too much. "

"I don't want to go, it'll be boring. I'd rather stay on board." Andrew was fed up with the lack of contact with the Vatusogosogo children.

Sue and I took sidelong glances and agreed with each other without speaking.

"You're coming," we said. "We're not going to have you miss out on something good and then complain about missing out."

Sam didn't feel as strongly about it. He'd been wiring up bits from the electrics cupboard and chose that moment to throw a switch and watch a bulb light up. His voice took on the tones of doom. "Aha, the death switch!"

Andrew pursued it. "I didn't have a choice on this whole trip, did I?"

"No. We've been through that."

"But it's not fair, I-"

"You were stuck on chips, fizzy drink and telly. What would you do if you were a parent?"

"Look, I admit that this has been really great sometimes and it's good to be here and all that ... but you knew I was interested in aeroplanes and you were obsessed with this boat and went right ahead and I got nothing."

I ground my teeth. "What you got was the ability to use your tongue. OK, that's it. This could go on forever. You're coming to the village because we say so."

On the radio we heard that a 16 metre American yacht was on the reef at the Nasonisoni Passage. An hour or two later we heard that it had been pulled off by *Chieftain* and was on its way back to SavuSavu for repairs.

The warmth that had been missing when we first arrived at Vatusogosogo was finally present when we landed. There were only six adults, which was puzzling, but the opposite was true of the youngsters. While Sue, Alusio and I drank kava and sang, the boys were taken over by two dozen local lads. Someone had told them it was all right to enjoy themselves with the *palangi* boys and they took to the task with a will.

The Vatusogosogo villagers now relaxed with us.
It's an international rugby test.

Soon the All Blacks versus Fiji rugby championship was rampaging on the sward. Many honorary All Blacks teamed up with the white boys. The bigger boys were dynamic and aggressive with their movements, but made sure the smaller ones landed softly. At one stage, Andrew raced past our doorway clutching the ball and shouting that he had two bandits on his ass.

I winced, hoping Alusio wouldn't ask for a translation. "Where is Moses?" I asked.

"He cannot be here," was the answer.

I looked at the riotous boys outside and again at the softly spoken adults inside. Something still didn't fit and I still couldn't put a name to why. My instincts said to ask questions, but I couldn't focus on what the question should be.

Talitha made coconut-milk scones for us, without using butter.

They were surprisingly light. We asked the word for 'tasty'. *Kanavinaka*. Thomas sang a gentle song and his three-year-old grandson danced to it as if it were a war dance. Alusio sang Fijian protest songs by a Suva group called Roots Strata and a song about Hurricane Rajah which laid the village land bare in '86. He sang them quietly. I kept feeling that I should sing softly myself and stopped altogether.

I asked for the toilet. Alusio delegated a teenage girl to take me, which she did with embarrassment but huge enjoyment. She giggled all the way, explaining her mission and my plumbing needs to every woman we came across. The adult women smiled, but didn't laugh. They too had a subdued look and once again I put it down to a cultural difference.

The girl pointed me into a tiny, perfectly clean, woven hut with a pebble floor.

I came out afterwards to find her suddenly quite distressed, dithering uncertainly. She vanished into a hut and reappeared carrying a toilet roll, trying to show it to me and hide it at the same time. She was vastly relieved when I flagged it away.

On the way back down, I heard the cough again. It came from a hut close to where we had met Moses.

We made our farewells. Two very happy white boys made a round of noisy farewells, addressing several of them by name.

"Sam," they called back. "Andoo, *Moce, Moce*"

It was high tide when we left, so we rowed out through the mangroves as they waved from the shore.

In the morning, as we prepared to weigh anchor, we heard the news: Moses' brother had died in the night.

30

No one does a non-stop passage from northeast Fiji to Musket Cove in the far west. It's through the smoothest, most sheltered water you could ask for, but the shelter is courtesy of vast shoals of coral. The trick is to anchor by the reefs each night, hoping you don't get caught in a blow and installed permanently.

We made two mistakes on the way. Just off Buthelevu, Taveuni Island, thinking we were far enough off the Somo Somo Strait to discount the current, we found ourselves sweeping forward and sideways over tight coral at four knots. The lesson was to head into the current, negating most of its speed, keeping lookout over the stern.

The second mistake was at the far southwest corner of Vanua Levu.

We'd made good progress that day, hard on the wind but at a comfortable seven knots, and we had an hour's safe light to spare before anchoring. We wanted an early start in the morning, so we previewed the morning's exit through the outer reef into Bligh Water. Just as well, because we chose the wrong exit. In fact when we found ourselves bouncing up and down in a two metre swell over coral three metres deep we decided it wasn't any kind of exit. There were two beacons in the area. I had looked for one, having overlooked a mark one millimetre long on the chart. One millimetre!

Not careful enough.

When we did turn out into Bligh Water the next morning it was to a perfect reach in only a slight swell. We hissed southwest across the 30 mile stretch between Vanua Levu and Viti Levu.

Almost exactly two centuries ago, Captain Bligh crossed our path to the northwest in his open boat.

He was on the crest of a stunning run of luck. Sure, the mutiny was an ace of spades, but every card that followed led to a flush. At the great eastern reef he blithely rowed his men through the night at one of the few points without coral. In the Koro Sea he passed cannibal-infested islands too far away to be seen from shore and uninhabited islands close enough to look up at the coconuts. When he did strike coral off Mokogai, the current took him right over it, pounding and jarring the keel without damaging the boat. Sailing on, Bligh and his men unknowingly chose the Vatu-i-ra channel through the vast shoals, moving out into another enclosed sea that would be named after him. Bligh Water.

Then came what he and his crew had been dreading. One of his men cried out in terror that canoes were heading towards them. Instantly the men lost their lethargy. Oars came out to help the lugsails. Even so, the double-hulled Fijian sailing canoes laden with warriors closed the gap as if the white men were at a standstill.

But ominous black clouds towered up into the sky behind the speeding canoes. Bligh would never be certain whether the warriors abandoned the chase because of the imminent waves, or because they would have to come down on them in storm winds on a dead run, the hardest point of sailing. Bligh and his men vanished into the storm to continue the fantastic voyage to Timor.

All he wrote in his log at the time was: *Heavy weather - much lightning and rain - caught six gallons water - chased by two canoes.* That's a laid back log.

Long afterwards he would return, promoted by the British Admiralty, to lay the groundwork for charting Fiji and opening it up to the outside world.

Sam on the genoa boom, freedom denied, yet again, by the harness.

23 August

We turned on to the extraordinary Ba Roads.

Scores of centuries ago, when the coral organisms were dying by uncountable trillions, water currents kept them either side of a channel between half a mile and a mile wide running the full length of the northern coast of Viti Levu. The result is a remarkable, natural, marine highway winding for seventy nautical miles. To travel the Ba Roads is the sailing equivalent of walking a shag-pile carpeted corridor with walls wired to kill if you touch them.

There was no question of using the windvane. It was tiller and eyeball all the way.

Andrew and Sam spontaneously turned another corner, significant because it involved a fundamental principle: anticipation. Andrew learned how to control *Alderman* on a dead run, which requires pro-active steering rather than reactive. Sam was suddenly able to anticipate actions like loosening the furler sheet when the furling line came in and bringing in the boom before dropping the main. Often on that marvellous day he was waiting, ready, prompted by a nod rather than an order.

Then they learned how to relate real movement to movement on a chart and to put numbers to it. Abandoning the formal correspondence had not been as much of a loss as we thought. For instance, we got Andrew to look at the speed and chart position then work out how long we had before crunch time. Discovering that the difference between 0.6 and 0.06, for example, was the difference between a comfortable sleep and abandoning ship gave him a whole new perspective on maths.

Sam did simpler versions of the same exercises. And he was twice as pleased with himself.

"I invented numbers, didn't I?"

"Sam, don't be ridiculous," Andrew scorned. "Numbers were invented before you were born, before Dad was. Even before Grandpa, I think."

We trolled as we coasted the highway, hooking a big one opposite Vatia Lailai Island. We caught it on the rod, and it put up quite a fight. The boys' excitement was so hard on the ears that Sue protested the noise. I reeled it in close enough to spot a silver body as big as mine, then it wrenched itself off and was gone.

Sam's world blew up in his face. Once again he leapt to the rear and screamed out over the aft rail.

"You idiot!"

"That's not the fish you're talking to, is it?" I said, resetting the line.

"No!" he steamed.

An hour later, Andrew started to wind in the lure for the night. He had it in all but six metres and it was yanked out of his hand. Andrew's pressure gauge also climbed into the red.

"I can't stand it!" Sue yelled.

In a few minutes we had a trevalli alongside. As I brought it up on the gaff, the savage inside Sam reached new and barbarous heights. He danced up and down, screaming with triumph, shaking his fist at the fish. When the only life left in the fish was the dying movements of the mouth, Sam's mouth was still working hard. He even got down to jeering at the victim and poking his tongue out a few centimetres away.

I snapped, "Cut that out!"

Sam was astonished. "Why?"

Good question. We had just applied the sticks and stones, now I was balking at the name-calling. What the hell was the answer? But as soon as I thought about it, the answer was simple. "How about some respect for the fish?"

"Oh."

Sam understood instantly. He even looked guilty and thoughtful. Andrew didn't need to say anything, but that has never stopped him saying it.

"Sam," he said loftily. "It died so we could live." He stole that line from a cartoon called Ninja Turtles.

The trevalli was delicious. *Kanavinaka.*

31

When the boys sighted the long-awaited Musket Cove they hugged, they shook hands, they clapped each other on the back. They fell over each other and us with politeness and offers to help with every kind of task. In the dinghy Andrew even offered to let Sam start the outboard motor, a major concession. Or maybe it was because they'd just heard that sea snakes enjoy taking up residence inside warm outboard covers. Their eagerness was spiced by the knowledge that Musket Cove was literally the last resort. Actually, the only full-on resort.

In three weeks we would turn the bowsprit for home.

But in the meantime we would get the most out of this renowned cruising Mecca. More than 100 yachts from all over the world picked at the southerly on moorings or anchor.

The boys hit the beach running and we didn't see much of them after that. Fijian staff were well used to keeping an eye on *palangi* kids, particularly those from the sea. Smaller youngsters who went missing were sometimes found down at the village, sleeping in a hut with a line-up of diminutive brown bodies. They had a pool, safe sea swimming, hydroplaning, surf-boards and endless beach to terraform.

Sue and I took on the academic side of the scuba lessons, with a PADI-qualified Fijian called Lino. He had a big frame, a bigger grin and a professional manner. His English cut a few corners. He was adamant, for example, that tanks had hydrostastic tests and that our suits must fit smugly. He lectured us hour after hour under the coconut trees, each two-hour session followed by a test. With each multichoice test we passed, he beamed and pumped our hands.

"You did good! You did great!" he would say. Every time. It was his trademark.

While our heads were down, a coconut dropped out of the palms with a thump that would have exploded a pumpkin. We inspected the fronds above us. Lino shook his head knowingly.

"It's safer under the water," he said.

Sam appeared, a dot in the distance coming towards us at full speed. We weren't his intended destination, we just happened to be next to his path.

"We're getting an outrigger canoe!" he yelled as he passed. "But..." I started. But he was already a dwindling dot in the other direction.

The boys bloomed. *Chieftain* and *Kindred Spirit* came in and those friendships were renewed. More were made. Meisha from *Gungha* bribed Sam with a Cook Islands octagonal dollar to let her dress him in skirt, make-up, high heels and bracelet. He shrugged off teasing, saying only, "It was worth it."

His confidence grew when we had thought it impossible for any youngster to hold more. Sometimes he was downright arrogant and we tried - seriously - we tried the meekness training we'd talked about. That is, we discussed concepts like taking a back seat, like seeing others as equally important, and the meaning of 'humble'. On the last one he didn't have the faintest idea what we were talking about.

"Hey Sam, we passed our written tests for the scuba diving."

"Cool. Hey is that outboard a forty-horse Mercury?"

"Bart!" I snapped. Bart is a TV show kid in permanent trouble.

"Very funny, Dad."

"Your mother and I did good, we did great, praise us."

Then he looked directly at us and his face softened and he smiled. The vulnerable small boy was still there under the tough-guy exterior. But although he ended his requests with please, he still issued them like orders. Even adults found themselves obeying before realising what they were doing. So we tried a bit of basic Pavlov, rewarding him for ending his requests with the upward inflection that suggests humility, instead of the downward inflection which assumes that the world exists to gratify his every whim. We weren't going to object if the world salivated at his feet one day. But just not yet.

Sam at Musket Cove, a serious contender in the hairy chest contest. The boys loved the resort.

There was no sign that winter's worst binge in fifty years was letting up. This from a long-range sked with Radio Kerikeri:

"We've got snow in Dargaville, over."

"Lost that, didn't have that right, over." Dargaville? Not likely. There's been no snow in recorded history that far north.

"We've got snow in Dargaville."

"Dannevirke? You mean Dannevirke."

"No. Dargaville."

Tregillis came in, reporting an ocean encounter with an 8.5 metre Swedish yacht with two years of weed, and sails mended with old jeans. The couple on board had been trying to get to New Zealand direct from the Cook Islands. After four weeks and three near-successes, they had been driven north by the southerlies. When they met *Tregillis* they were down to a can of sardines.

And Sue and I were ready to become sardines in rubber, in open water - a very big deal for Sue. She'll tell you this part:

Michael and I had to make four open-water dives to complete the scuba course and the prospect scared me senseless. Both of us had found the two days of theory challenging, but fun. We'd enjoyed being back 'in class' together. But now we diverged on to different emotional paths.

I became a quivering wreck, almost immobilised by my fear of the unknown and by a poisonous string of 'what-ifs'. Not for the first time in our married life I was nettled by Michael's insufferably positive attitude. He was euphoric, champing to get going. Why wasn't he overwhelmed by the gravity of this, a mummy and a daddy preparing to plummet to the ocean floor in hostile waters, leaving their two innocent little children alone and stranded? Why wasn't he churning? Why couldn't he at least fake it? Completely irrational of course, but the thoughts were there.

Fortunately, my Scots ancestry and sense of occasion rescued me from complete disintegration and the scorn of my sons for perpetuity. We'd paid a fortune to do this course, and I knew there'd be no refunds for not completing it. And finally, this persistent thought in my head: *You've got the proverbial once-in-a-lifetime opportunity anyone would surrender their eye teeth for. This is the best diving in the world. Ninny! Go for it!*

Chastised, I went for it.

As we were assembling our gear for the first dive, Geraldine and Steen idled by in their dinghy. We told them where we were headed.

"If I don't return from this," I called to Geraldine, "I'd like you to know that you can have my jewels."

"I'd rather have your husband!" she yelled back, bantering as always.

"Ungrateful wretch!"

With Lino and his boatman, we climbed into the dive boat to meet a very-much-in-love American couple, and a lone Kiwi realising his lifelong dream to dive Fiji.

We were all facing our first time.

The boatman threaded us through the yachts at anchor, the fizz boats, the kids on rafts, and the paragliders. We zipped past all the signs of a normal sunny day at a tropical resort, and out into open water. There was much to think of. I checked again that I'd taken all my rings off, even my wedding ring. Lino had cautioned that barracuda think shiny jewellery is dying fish. "They just can't help themselves," he'd said dryly.

At Rainbow Reef he briefed us on the procedures for the coming tests. He seemed to take forever, rabbiting rapidly as we fumbled with the hefty gear and got used to the strange balance of it all. I pondered again what the hell I thought I was doing here. But, I couldn't afford to let the question take root. There's a lot to be said for rote learning at such a time. The repetitive drilling Lino had given us during the theory lessons gradually paid off. The familiar instructions and patterns for remembering slowly surfaced, and gave us a cushion of calm.

At last. Ready, teacher. I watched Michael plunge in. Wallop! Heavy displacement. Then:

"Sue! Big step. Look to the horizon. Good luck. Go!" I was in and on my way under without a backward glance.

We'd practised all the skills in shallow water, of course, but what I found now was another realm altogether. Vast, silent, warm, multi-coloured, teeming with movement, eerie but not scary. I couldn't believe it. I was actually comfortable! A Piscean in her natural habitat, perhaps.

Lino very slowly took us down to nine metres, letting us all take our own time to adjust. I could almost hear him: "Equalise early, equalise often. Don't touch a thing. Slow, slow, very slow. Watch your buddy."

My 'buddy' took on a new persona. His usually curly hair tried to bolt for the surface, straining up off his scalp like electrified reeds. Before my distorted vision, his body elongated to a ribbon, his deep tan bleached out altogether. I had to fight hard to quell the giggles threatening behind my mouthpiece.

Michael and I were used to placing our lives into each other's keeping. We'd been doing it for months. But the idea assumed extra dimensions down there as we were examined on how to help our 'buddy' if he ran out of air, and vice versa. We both had to remove our mouthpieces and breathe from the same supply. One had to blowout while the other took in the air, both holding to a two-breath rhythm. We also had to find the back-up air source from our buddy's tank, and make a controlled ascent together, plugged in to the same tank. The danger was so visible. One false move, one lapse in concentration, and both my jewels and my husband would be up for grabs.

As we each successfully completed a prescribed skill, Lino formed his thumb and forefinger into an 'O', code for *Yes, you got it!* He shook our hands. He raised his clenched fist, triumphant, Mighty Mouse style. The ritual was always the same, and we never tired of it. I felt childishly proud each time.

We had time to explore once the skills tests were over. We followed Lino very closely, hand-in-hand as we'd been taught. He looked elegant and at ease, moving carefully, respectfully. I remembered what he'd told us at the outset:

"We are privileged to visit underwater. We should look after it. Imagine sitting in your living room and seeing a giant hand coming in the window and groping around. That is how it is for the creatures under water. Respect their place."

We glided past thousands of fish, every size, every colour, spotted, striped, zigzagged and marbled. We saw fluorescent snails, shells of lilac and yellow, huge fronds of raspberry-pink coral, winding caverns and lacy cliffs.

And we saw moments of sheer majesty. A large turtle went about its lawful business just a few metres away, moving with astonishing daintiness. We all stopped still, awed at such unexpected grace. 1 wanted to salute.

Lino then showed us how to investigate interesting shapes in the sand or on the coral, picking them up carefully and putting them back in precisely the same orientation we'd found them. He got very agitated if anyone scuffed sand with their flippers, or backed into coral. We knew some coral is so delicate it will die if it's touched, but we hadn't understood what an art it is not to touch it at all.

At his signal to surface, we straggled up in an untidy line. I was cold and exhausted, but, like everyone, bursting for speech. Back on the boat, we yelled, we squealed, slapped backs, hugged, kissed and damn near cried.

Lino beamed. "Good, huh?"

"Good? Get lost, that was superb!" The American fellow spoke for us all.

Second time down, those turquoise fathoms were no less impressive. I cringed to think I had been ready to forgo them out of abject cowardice.

On the way back to *Alderman,* Michael said with a quiet grin, "I don't think mascara works too well in this game." A little later I surveyed myself in the ship's mirror, and saw the most unappetising vision. My skin had turned cardiac purple, my hair was like fuse-wire, and great globs of mascara were lodged all over my face. But, 1 couldn't care. I'd knocked off Dives One and Two!

Dives Three and Four came days later, because we insisted the weather had to be perfect for the last stage.

After Dive Three, topsides again, I saw that Lino was not a relaxed man.

"Did you see it?" he demanded.

"Yes," said Michael.

"What?" I asked quickly. I didn't like Lino's tone.

Both had seen the flick of something enormous at each end of a big chunk of reef. Lino had been closest.

"If it is a trevalli," he said, "then it's the most gigantic I've ever seen. No, it has to be a tiger shark."

Ho, lucky day! My whole system went into spasm. I was miles out at sea, far from my dependent children, stuck in a flimsy boat with two crazy men who fully expected the next dive to take place in the same spot where a whopping great tiger shark was lurking with obvious intent. That shark, I knew instinctively, was male as well.

Once again, faced with no choice, we didn't make one. But stepping into the water that time was one of the hardest hurdles of my adult life. I clung to the boat's anchor line, fighting a resurgence of all the fears I thought I'd squashed. My breath sounded inordinately loud.

Lino urged me on. He taught us to navigate our way to and from a known spot on the sea floor. We had to take off all our gear, then put it on again. We cleared our masks over and over, and we practised getting back to the surface as if we were out of air. All the while, I was spooked, and couldn't help doing 360 degree lookabouts at every opportunity. Where was that woman-eater? Would I be capable of action if I saw him anyway?

Michael swished about me taking photos, then finally we dived together to the bottom at eighteen metres. I actually forgot my plight then, and did something approximating a dance. Eighteen metres! Pain drilled through my ears; I hadn't equalised properly on the way down. I was aching with fatigue and getting very cold. But I stayed long enough to shake my 'buddy' by the hand.

He was exuberant! During our brief frolic, he threatened to kiss me. There are times when a woman knows she should play hard to get, and this had to be one of them. I signalled he must wait. But he's a persistent devil. When we were resting at nine metres, he got me. He whipped off his mask, and kissed me squarely on the cheek. I was aghast; that's about the most *verboten* prank in the rule book.

The shark never showed itself, but I don't think anyone was disappointed. We dawdled up to the surface after forty minutes under, light-headed with the sheer beauty and scale of what we'd been shown.

"You did good, you did great!" Lino cheered as we floundered on to the boat.

An hour or so later, we staggered aboard *Alderman*, satisfied to the marrow. Our friends fêted us in the approved manner; the children fussed as if their ageing parents had just scaled something galactic. Well, I thought we had.

Michael can tell you what happened when Andrew scaled something less than galactic:

According to the log we had travelled 2,974 nautical miles through just about every kind of violence the sea can turn on, all without serious injury to anyone.

Andrew broke his arm falling out of a tree.

It was a Christmas tree according to the local staff, festooned with long, hard, flat seed pods the size and shape of cutlasses. They were Andrew's downfall. He went high, selecting the weapon most suitable for separating pirates from their limbs, then came down faster than he went up, bouncing off branches on the way.

I was in the boatshed at the time, sorting out our mail and talking to Sophie, a delightfully mischievous Fijian woman with a penchant for giving cheek where cheek is due. I heard a call for *Alderman* on her RT and at her nod, answered it.

"Mr Brown, your buoy has slipped-" I frowned across the water, looking hard at *Alderman*, snug at anchor. "-out of a tree. He's hurt himself."

"What?" I stared at the mike.

When the disorientation stopped I sped to the back of the resort, finding Andrew pale and still on the ground, surrounded by staff, friends, and bits of tree. Sue was putting her first aid skills to work, splinting close to the wrist. She looked calm and assured, but I knew she would be shaky afterwards.

Andrew at Musket Cove. After endless gales at sea, he broke his arm falling out of a tree. That defies all reason.

Sam stayed at the resort with a friend. Andrew, Sue and I took a small plane to Nadi, then a taxi through to Lautoka Hospital.

Queue number one got us a note to join queue number two at X-ray. The only person behind the counter there was a sour Indian in dirty T-shirt, jeans and jandals. I was not about to nit-pick the dress standard of a receptionist. But it turned out he was also the radiographer, surly at the counter, callously indifferent to pain at his machine. He yanked Andrew's arm about as if training for arm wrestling. That got us to queue three, to an overworked Chinese doctor. He studied the film.

"I'll need an operation, won't I?" Andrew suggested.

"No." The doctor managed a smile through his fatigue.

"I'll have to fly home then, won't I?" Andrew tried. He could have named every Air Force craft capable of a mercy dash.

"No. It is a greenstick fracture of the ulna. You will need plaster for two weeks, that is all. You are very lucky."

"Ah." Andrew was only put out for a moment. "It was probably the martial arts breakfall I did when I hit the ground."

That sort of luck meant going straight to the bottom of the priority list: queue four, on a casualty ward bed. An elderly Fijian pastor came first, prayed over Andrew, then wobbled away on his walking stick. Then, hours later, a Fijian doctor came to apply the plaster.

He was something special. He too was in T-shirt, jeans and foot- flaps. And yet he was one of those healers who reassure by their expression and movements: deft, knowing and compassionate.

Which reminded me of the treatment given to Andrew's friend Ian in the village of Naidi. Ian strained his foot and it swelled up alarmingly on top of his instep. One of the village's healing sub-clan trotted up, inspected the foot and began to massage his own foot with great intensity and care. Then he transferred the movement to Ian's foot. The Europeans were just getting used to the idea when the healer put his foot on Ian's foot, then put all his weight on it. Within minutes the swelling was significantly down and Ian was walking around.

By the time we brought Andrew out of the hospital we were ready for medical care ourselves.

At any other time, if Andrew had asked for a night in an expensive hotel we would have laughed. But there were no flights back to Musket Cove and little choice in hotels. We were a push-over. And once in we went crazy. Room service for everything, including a bottle of brandy that didn't stand a chance. Water from real taps, television, shower. And sheets on a bed so wide that you could roll over and still be there.

The next day, Andrew was out and about round Musket Cove, mostly free of pain. He stood forlornly in front of the pool, sponging up sympathy, holding his plaster out for written messages and for the camera. Tough break.

Then there was Sam's no good, horrible, very bad day. It ended in him also being denied the pool. While his friends were human projectiles, bombing the water, he sat at a table nearby writing a letter of apology. It was, he told us miserably, the worst day of his life. And we had to agree.

Technically the offence is known as 'Demanding money with menaces'.

His decline and fall began right after breakfast. No one, but no one, would let him do anything he wanted. Can I fly on the parachute? No. Can I buy lunch on shore today? No. Can you come swimming with me? No, too soon. But he did extract a promise of $1.50 to go hydroplaning. He took our only land bag, with camera still in it, but then abandoned it somewhere ashore when he realised he had forgotten the $1.50. So he promised payment at the boatshed and bummed the ride.

There followed a gap of two hours when we didn't hear from him.

Sometime later he borrowed a surf-board and paddled it 400 metres to *Alderman* to get the money to repay his debt. About 30 metres out he started calling out to show off. I might have been impressed by the feat if I hadn't heard some disturbing stories in the meantime.

"Sam, get over here. I want a word with you."

His eyes went wide. He looked about him wildly, which I thought was an overreaction to my words.

"Sam! Now."

"I can't! I'm sinking!"

He had forgotten to put the bung in. The surfboard's sharp end pointed down even as I watched, then the whole thing rolled over. There was a fast rescue and after I secured it I went back for Sam who was in a lifejacket. It took fifteen minutes to haul the surfboard out and drain it. Then Sam and I went below for meaningful dialogue.

"Right, you know how we've been talking about trust and telling the truth?"

"Yes." His brow was furrowed with puzzlement.

"This is one of those times."

"You mean about the money?"

"I sure do."

His face cleared. He was only too glad to tell me. In fact he was quite indignant at how he had been treated and wanted justice. It was quite simple: the office staff had promised him money for running a message down to Sophie at the boatshed and then refused to pay him. I questioned him closely and he was adamant. Money mentioned, no money forthcoming.

Refused to pay? Even if we were only talking a few cents that was taking advantage of a child. I went ashore. I made accusations. I lowered my voice and made humble enquiries. I came back. Sam saw the steam coming out of my nostrils and realised that once again his world was turning in a different direction from that of adults.

"Sam, let me get this right. They didn't offer to pay, you asked for pay."

"Yes, but they said Sophie would pay."

"No, they said maybe Sophie would pay you. They were laughing. It was a joke."

"Yes, no, but-"

"And did you go and get two big boys to go in and demand the money or else?"

209

"Yes, but-"

"And when that didn't work, you then went down to Sophie at the boatshed, holding a stick!"

Sam's face filled with fright. "But I didn't ... It wasn't for that!"

"And then when Sophie said she didn't owe you any money, you raised the stick."

"No! Yes, but it was for fun! I was pretending!"

"But when Sophie said, 'Little boy are you serious?' you said YES!"

Sam gave a heart-lurching cry of pure terror. "But I meant the money! Not to hurt her. I meant about the money!"

Then he howled with sheer anguish.

I gaped at him a moment, appalled. It was no act. I scooped him up in my arms. He buried his face in my shoulder and shook with sobs as hot tears fell. When the sobs settled, the discussion changed to figuring out where he went wrong, how many times, and what he could do about it now he was in it up to his neck.

So, that afternoon he sat by the pool, writing what was both an apology and an explanation:

Sam writing his letter of apology.

Dear Sophie. I'm sorry I raised my stick up at you. I will not do it again. You see when you said are you serious I thought you meant about the money not the stick. From Sam.

Letter in hand, hand-in-hand, Sam with head bowed in remorse, we trod the long, long path to the boatshed. There, he waited the endless seconds till Sophie was free of adults, bit his lower lip and handed the letter up to her.

When she read it she melted right down to her sandals.

"Oh, my darling!" she breathed. Then she got down to her knees and gave him the warmest hug a seven-year-old boy could possibly want.

32

The next day, Lino cancelled all diving engagements and flew out. The radio had announced the death of the President of Fiji, Ratu Sir Penaia Ganilau. All those from his home village in Taveuni were honour-bound to return there for his funeral. For many, such travel would mean going into debt.

Lino was back the next morning. Sir Penaia was very much alive and the police were investigating the hoax.

"Things are very tense," he said. "It was done because Penaia is a moderate, he is for staying in the Commonwealth. Others don't care. And they don't care about the Indians. We did not bring them here. It is not our problem, it's British problem."

Along with news of the hoax, the local radio reported that leases were about to rise significantly. Indigenous Fijians own ninety-six per cent of the land. We thought of Alusio and Moses and the rest of Vatusogosogo village, already struggling to pay for living on the land they worked.

In New Zealand, a charity dinner with coup leader Sitiveni Rabuka as guest of honour was cancelled. No one wanted to attend.

The days counted down. The knowledge that it was all coming to an end weighed more and more heavily.

This was the third time the fleet had come together since New Zealand. The family-like atmosphere affected us more and more and we dreaded the time when we would have to say goodbye. Movement between vessels was constant. Children flowed from one to another almost as if the yachts were a village.

Which is probably why a mean strain of influenza galloped so quickly through the fleet. A woman and baby were flown to hospital. Sue was flattened for three days. She was so rarely sick that the boys worried and kept going forward to hug her, Sam drawing his finger gently round the perimeter of her face. For a moment he would look awed, as if the idea of his mother being sick was foreign to his understanding of the universe. Then he would leave her with a pat on the head.

With a week to go, Sinclair and Carol George and Davey Vincent flew in from New Zealand. Sinclair and Davey would crew on the return passage, Carol would fly back. It was a fine reunion.

And the Dead Poets Society lived again. Davey played guitar and sang, his music carrying across the boats. Sue and I sang our 'Johnny Sands' song. Davey worked up a guitar accompaniment for *The Tune* because somewhere along the way I had decided I loved it so much I wanted an audience for it. I'd play it in the talent quest after all. The seagull skirl gave the tune a feel of vast open spaces and loneliness. And it sounded much better on industrial strength Jim Beam. I still didn't know it's origin or real name.

Early that evening the southern New Zealand reunion doubled in size. A dinghy came alongside with Anna and Chris and three children from *Karaka*. We had been moored close by them in Lyttelton in the preparation times. To meet them again now, the only family we knew who had also sold their home and sailed away, was very special. Long after the sea swallowed the sun, the adults celebrated in the cockpit and the children romped below.

After a while there was a lot of giggling and Sam came up.

"Mum, where can I find some undies?"

"What for?"

"I need them for a game."

The giggling intensified below. It had that hushed I'm-doing-something-deliciously-naughty ring to it.

"Sounds like a good game."

"Yes. It's a bit of a dare game. Everyone's got to take off a bit of clothing."

Right then, someone below started howling and Sue went to investigate. All the squirming bodies were heaped in total darkness in various mild states of undress in the for'd cabin and someone had stuck an elbow in a face. It wasn't X-rated, but the cabin was taking a beating so the game got the adult thumbs down.

Sinclair George with Michael. He put his life on the line, ignoring medical advice not to join our passage from Fiji to New Zealand. After a first alarm, we admired him for it. He was into life.

There was, however, an X-rated regatta contest. To the entrants it was a wet T-shirt contest, to the critics it was a meat rack, to the sea snake that inspected then swam away it was of no interest. But Andrew was impressed.

"I enjoyed it. The funny thing was those T- shirts didn't really hide anything." What a surprise.

There was also an X-rated yacht in the live figurehead parade. The crew of *Port and Starboard* built a two-and-a-half metre phallus of empty beer cans, an internally cantilevered arrangement that alternated between states of interest and indifference. Given the sensitivity of Fijians to public indecency it's surprising they didn't get a tap on the shoulder from a long uniformed arm.

Some yachts had prepared their figureheads months earlier. There was a jousting knight complete with cardboard horse on *Gallant Cavalier*, a Pink Panther riding a motorbike on *Andromeda*, and the resort put a local yacht *Hobo* in the contest. It had a huge banner proclaiming, 'One nation Fiji', but amongst the forty Fijians on board there was only one Indian. *Ram* won the contest, with a windsurfer and rider in full flight high in the forward rigging.

We were late to the talent quest, missing our curtain call because of child and dinghy logistics. So we stood clutching instruments and feeling foolish, me because of the school recorder, Sue because she had never held a microphone, let alone performed in front of an audience like that. It was one thing for her to hear that there would be hundreds watching, it was another to see them in the flesh - yachties, resort guests, Fijians and Indians, spread out under the coconut palms.

And they were being well entertained. There was an all-male cancan, a superb Italian Elvis Presley, a poem about a boy who teased a lion and ended up tickling its tonsils with his head. The girls from one yacht brought on keyboard, sax and sound system and their performance drew immediate offers of marriage from the audience.

Alderman's name came over the loudspeakers again.

"That's Sam's father," a voice called out, generously allowing the audience to understand where I fitted in.

We did well. For 'Johnny Sands', Sue handled the microphone as if she'd been born crooning. For *The Tune*, Davey didn't miss a beat on the guitar and all my seagull skids and fancy bits squeezed out of the school recorder the right way. None of us hated the applause.

A few days later, many of the yachts were preparing to head north to Vanuatu. We began our own preparations for the passage to New Zealand. There was a final meeting of the fleet, a barbecue. Sinclair, Carol and Davey went ashore, but I stayed on *Alderman* with Sue who was still fighting the fleet 'flu.

About eleven that night, a dinghy came out of the dark, cut its motor, and a pair of hands gripped the rail. It was Brendan from *Mystery Girl*.

"I brought you something," he said and handed up a bag containing a bottle of something and a packet. I didn't know what to say. Their friendship had meant so much to us on this trip and a gift like this... I looked at the packet, which contained a T-shirt. He was grinning. "I just felt I had to give it to you."

"Thanks, Brendan. I don't know what to say."

"You silly bugger. That's your prize. *Alderman* won the talent quest!"

Next morning *Mystery Girl* was gone on the wind, and so were thirty other vessels that we'd come to recognise at a glance, whose crews and skippers we had come to know. The four of us had said most of our goodbyes already, the last few we made by radio.

As a friend had said many months ago, those people were into life. Saying goodbye to them was like a small death.

We took on water and more supplies and dropped Carol off at Nadi. We cleared from Lautoka, discovering in the process that the rumour was true: there really are hazard markers fully submerged at high tide.

That last night we were all very quiet. Davey and Sinclair moved about below and on the deck, stowing gear, arranging their spaces, preparing themselves for their first ocean passage. Sinclair went forward and sat on the bowsprit rail for a long time, looking at the night. Sue and I went for a last row and held hands under warm stars.

In the morning we turned the bowsprit towards New Zealand.

PART FOUR

33

This time, we could have turned back. There was a choice.

The gale fell on us even before we got to the outer reef, just two hours sail from Musket Cove. But we knew from the forecast that it wouldn't be much more than a local effect, a southeast trade cantering round the bottom of Viti Levu. Most of all, we were emotionally committed. I told everyone I would go with the majority decision, a last concession to democracy.

"Keep going," Sinclair said with a determined look on his face. Why so determined, we would find out later.

There was a mutter of agreement. Even the boys, who looked wistfully back at Musket Cove, didn't argue. It was time. Besides, we four had become resigned to

A perfect start back to New Zealand. It didn't last.

gales. We nosed through the passage gingerly in poor water visibility, then we were into the swell and seas and driving rain with deep-reefed main.

There wasn't one of us who didn't look back. The islands were hazy round the edges and rather than sink into the sea, they dissolved into grey.

Motion sickness moved in again, carried aboard by the grey-blue heaving lumps. Sinclair volunteered for more than his share of watches, staying on the helm hour after hour, cheerfully reminding us that he had never been seasick in his life.

I was starting to admit to myself that I was feeling ill when I hooked a mahimahi. I stared bleakly at the golden beast threshing the water out the back and considered losing that particular ambition. But I'd had it too long. I made myself work the line, keeping my eyes on the far horizon, knowing that I would beat the fish but my inner ear would beat me. By the time I had it struggling on deck, I was on hands and knees. Sinclair was steering and Sue was the only one left capable of free will. She came forward with the monkey's fist, gritted her teeth and knocked the fish senseless. Eventually we had some fine meals from it; Davey has a way with the fillets, combining beer, batter and crumbs. Even those of us who had to make an effort to eat applauded his cooking.

Sue is not escaping domestic violence. She's racing to get the 'monkey's fist' – a knotted club – to finish off the mahimahi.

We were right about the local weather effect. It was a short-lived blow. As we flopped out full sail around midnight, Sue and I and the boys told ourselves that we'd had the regulation gale and could now settle down to enjoy a fine passage.

Fools that we were.

But for that night we enjoyed the phosphorescence, the rich floodlight moon and the searing flash of a meteorite.

Twenty-four hours out we had a noon-to-noon run of 152 miles, half of it on deep-reefed main and a small triangle of furler. Andrew took another watch, this time with irreverent assurance. In his log entry, next to *Sea: calm* he drew a graphic picture of me throwing up.

As a final twist of the motion-sickness knife, I developed a headache that laid me out under blankets of pain. When my watch came up, Sue used her first aid voice to tell me to stay put. She did the sked with Kerikeri, I gave in and fell into a deep sleep. When I woke I was already half way to health. That was my pattern for seasickness - recovery late on the second day or on the third. Everyone's pattern was different.

Sinclair was increasingly tense, which puzzled us. He'd had time to get over any ocean-passage nerves and the weather was fine. He was preoccupied, occasionally snapping at the boys, but managed to cover whatever was bothering him with flashes of his wit. He had that rare ability to find humour in anything.

He was often inventive with the boys. Once, he collected cardboard, paper clips, sticky tape and lead sinkers in the cockpit and announced a competition for the best construction. He told the boys, "Points will be awarded for quality of construction and the number of rosters done for me." Sam wasn't too keen on rosters, so he tried a five-dollar bribe. Sinclair recorded it all on video including each boy's explanatory speech.

On day three, the wind rose slightly, the sea became confused.

There was no telltale swell, but I was apprehensive. *Alderman* moved awkwardly again and the discomfort level rose.

The same afternoon, we heard a whistling sound that swiftly became a deafening roar as a jet buzzed us a couple of mast heights up. Those in the cockpit nearly made an involuntary plumbing adjustment. Sue burst up into the cockpit, having heard the sound of a monster wave striking without feeling any movement.

The jet circled, obviously intending to do it again. A corporate jet, probably a Lear. I flipped the VHF on to channel 16 and asked it to identify itself. A very French accent came back.

"We are reconnaissance aircraft from New Caledonia on the way to Fiji. Who are you?"

I was tempted to identify myself as Sphincter Control but answered correctly, adding that he seemed a long way south. The French cowboy repeated simply that he was on the way to Fiji and wished us a good day sailing. Perhaps he thought we were out here on a day trip. He headed northwest, which was going to make him miss Fiji by a long sea mile.

It's clear who does all the work. Sam supervising. Michael resting.

We passed a Korean fishing boat, plunging bows heavily amongst its nets. It didn't respond to calls on the VHF. The only acknowledgement was a raised arm from one of the crew.

The boys adapted more quickly than ever to the passage routine.

This time they were helped by our last-minute retail mission in Lautoka, getting them a pile of comics, one each for each day. We wrapped them individually, labelling with name and date to be opened. And we got them electronic games with beeping sounds that tunnelled under our skins inducing our own beeping sounds of distress. Andrew added peeping to beeping by setting the alarm on his watch, then losing the watch. The sound was omni-directional, so the infernal device took a week to find.

On the fourth day, when everyone else had made peace with their stomachs, Sinclair threw up. He promptly blamed last night's stew, flying in the face of tradition: never antagonise the cook when you're five days from land. But Sinclair wasn't himself. And he became even more tense. He seemed to draw into himself. The nausea continued. He stopped eating and rested constantly when not on watch. He became uncharacteristically grumpy but summoned his wit to bat questions into the slips. It was an effort for him.

"Can I get you anything?" I asked.

"You wouldn't have a cyanide capsule, would you?"

We began to suspect his diabetes. I had not checked that before we started,

222

because as far as I knew it wasn't a serious condition and Sinclair was a proven coastal sailor. Now, he was well enough to make it to his watch, so I didn't press him.

On the fifth day, Sue did. She was in charge of health and first aid and the diabetes angle was worrying her.

"I don't know if it's seasickness or exhaustion or diabetes," he admitted.

She checked that she knew where to find his insulin and needles and that she could carry out the injections. Then a suspicion came to her.

"Were you warned against coming?"

"Yes."

"By a doc?"

"Yes." He looked up sheepishly. "In fact he doesn't expect to see me again."

"Jesus! Sinclair!"

Sue came steaming up to the cockpit. She was particularly alarmed that we were exactly halfway through the passage, four to five days from land whichever way we went. There was some discussion about the worst scenario, a rescue from New Zealand. And of course we were too far away for anything but a ship-to-ship pick-up. I talked to Sinclair but there was nothing more to be learned.

At first I too was annoyed at not being put in the picture. But, the more I thought about it the more my feeling changed to admiration.

Back in New Zealand there's a TV ad that shows a crewman halfway up a mast in driving rain, at night, in a gale. He's right on the edge in defiance of death and yelling out his exhilaration. The sponsors describe that crewman as having 'the attitude'. Which is what Sinclair had in defying the suspended death sentence pronounced by the medical profession. I thought about how I might react if the white-coated establishment kept telling me how I could lengthen my life by thinning its quality.

Some things are more important than courtesies.

Sinclair stopped taking fluids. Sue rehearsed a conversation with Radio Kerikeri, but held off because he remained lucid.

Kerikeri's John Cullen told us to expect a southwesterly front of 30 knots at mid-afternoon. At precisely three in the afternoon it turned up with exactly the predicted strength and I relayed his accuracy back to him at the next sked.

"It's not a gale," I pointed out helpfully to Sue.

"Hah!" she snorted, expecting no quarter from the sea.

The discomfort level went up with the waves. Andrew and Sam snapped and snarled at each other's heels. They fought with Caracas pod cutlasses with such sour temper that I ordered them to throw the weapons overboard. Andrew started a campaign to fly home to Christchurch from Northland.

Three hundred and forty miles to go.

Another blow. But by now we had lost our fear of regular gales.

In a wild orange dawn, the sou'wester went up to forty knots, gusting to fifty. The wind seemed to tear the clouds like fabric and once again the spume took to the air. We had faith in the strength of the rig now, and kept up the deep-reefed main. Even so, we began to lose our westing. To allow for prevailing winds we were supposed to dogleg west between Fiji and New Zealand. We had only managed to put a little west in the bank so we were in danger of being overdrawn.

Sue lurched to the bowsprit for another gale-welcome - assertively informing the sea that it is actually a female dog. She may be onto a whole new psychology here, on how to deal with stress and stressor in one action.

In spite of the battering, Sinclair started to pull through. He began to drink hot sweet tea. He got stuck into glucose tablets, his energy levels rose, the smile we knew very gradually reappeared. We never did make the call for help.

Sue, who Lester once described as the Iron Lady, succumbed to exhaustion. But all she would agree to was staying in her berth a little longer when resting. And even that was hard for her. After nearly 4,000 miles I understood better how difficult it was for her to have the boys at sea. To me their safety was a matter of a series of rules and orders, a small segment of the overall running of *Alderman*. To Sue, the boys were like an extension of herself, concern for their discomfort or fear was something she couldn't switch on and off at will.

We took more photos of the waves breaking over the deck, but without real hope that they would work. A still photo always flattens a gale into a mill pond. Produce a still photo as proof of suffering and landlubbers will think you've been hallucinating.

Somewhere in that gale, Sue and I took a hot shower. The motion was so violent that it was a two-person operation. One of us sat or crouched on the floor, bracing and soaping, while the other directed the water system. Damned hard work, but well worth it.

On the second to last day, the winds kept pedalling from the southwest, but wound back to a more comfortable pace.

The mood on board jumped a couple of notches. Davey sang.

The boys switched to civilised mode and played congenially. Sinclair, having successfully given fate the fingers, was quietly but thoroughly pleased with himself. Sue found him on watch with headphones on his ears, jigging to Joe Cocker. Later, a capricious wave made her stumble and she dropped his box of tapes, smashing nearly every plastic case. But Sinclair's sense of well-being could not be dented and he shrugged and said cheerfully, "It happens."

Sam asked me to show him how to plot our position on the chart.

I nearly said no, because it involved showing him how to interpolate a scale, but he pleaded with me. I relented. And when I came back he had done it to within two millimetres, probably just the error involved in pushing the roller ruler around the chart. I said little, because his head was already hard to get through the companionway. But he must have seen the look on my face.

"That was very very good wasn't it?" he said. Modesty did not yet rank amongst his accomplishments.

It was safe to go forward on deck now, so we investigated a clanking sound. A wave had smashed a plank on the bowsprit – 25mm hardwood. That would have been some wave.

We could almost taste land.

Davey and Sinclair accused me of being a sailing purist and offered to pay for the diesel if we could go faster. I turned down the offer. And I denied the charge, citing our use of the head (marine toilet) as evidence. Purists are fanatics who use buckets as a matter of principle.

Heading into the last night, I listened to the forecast with incredulity. Yet another sou'west front was on the way. We came up hard on the wind to try to stay west of Opua. If the new blow came in too hard or with too much of a southerly component, we would have to forget Opua and bear away to Auckland. That would mean another night at sea and we were in no mood for that.

But the forecast was wrong, the blow didn't happen at all. The seas flattened, the breeze flipped over to the west. We would make Opua by late afternoon.

In near-perfect conditions the land of the long white cloud came up to meet us.

Aotearoa. That part of the coast was new to us, but just knowing it was New Zealand affected us all.

Davey and Sinclair showered early, Davey in high humour, asking if we could rustle up cream for his nappy rash. Both were in good clothes with hair washed and brushed even before we reached Cape Brett. They would be flying back from Opua to Christchurch.

"Great trip," Sinclair said, grinning cheekily.

Sam said he could see a huge yellow 'M' on the horizon and went around moaning that he could see hamburgers floating in the air in front of him.

Andrew took up his favourite position in the bowsprit and acted out fantasies with hand movements whose meaning was beyond us. Then he capered back along the deck.

I took his place at the bowsprit. Soon I found Sue beside me and we gazed towards our homeland rising out of the horizon. After a while Sue spoke, and what she said came as no surprise.

"No more passages."

The endless gales with children in her charge had got to her. She was deeply fatigued, her face drawn, eyes sunk in sockets. I knew what more was coming and she knew I knew.

"You can get crew here, to go down to Lyttelton, can't you?"

I nodded. "Yep."

"I'm going to fly home with the boys."

We motored on towards Opua with an arm around each other. I had no arguments. The boys would want to stay with her, and Sue had nothing left to prove to anyone.

The quarantine flag joined the spreaders and then we were into the Bay of Islands, in the north of New Zealand.

34

I didn't get a crew, because I didn't really try. In fact I made just one phone call, to Alex Cuthbert in Christchurch, who had arranged to join us on the final leg. But his life had changed while we were away and he couldn't come.

I put the phone down, both thankful and nervous.

I had been toying with the idea of going solo down the east coast of New Zealand. If I didn't take a natural opportunity like this, I might never get another.

Something happened to convince me I was right – proving that I had become a superstitious sailor, influenced by signs and portents. I discovered the true title of *The Tune*. It's real name is 'Lonesome Boatman'. It took a while to stop laughing and banging my fist into the palm of my hand.

It was the sign I needed.

Sue and the boys gave up trying to argue me out of it. They stayed long enough to help with the provisioning, and with collecting more detailed charts – on my own I was more likely to run for shelter in a hurry.

Then we parted at Whangarei Airport. After half a year living and learning at such close quarters, that was very difficult. I wonder what the airline staff thought of the two adults and two boys who tried to occupy the same space at the same time for ten minutes in an almost empty terminal.

When they landed in Christchurch, Sue and the boys stayed with my brother Ralph. Dave McDonald brought around a long-range radio so she could listen in to my skeds with the Duffs. But being land-based she wouldn't be able to transmit.

I had to wait forty-eight hours for the right forecast. Then I was out around Cape Brett and heading towards East Cape into a dying southerly. I had been tied up to a wharf for too long and had to go through the motion sickness cycle again. That was harder on my own than I'd expected.

But much worse than any seasickness was the need for sleep. For 4,000 miles we had been so breeze-blown that the wind steering was all we'd needed. So I made a fundamental mistake in the planning. I didn't ask myself what would happen, solo, if there was not enough wind to push the steering vane. If I'd thought it out, I would have bought or borrowed an autopilot.

It was a cruel reversal of fortune that the wind chose to die for three-quarters of my solo trip. I had to stay on the tiller hour after hour, continually nodding off, correcting direction. I had rigged stretch cords to the tiller to allow me to leave it for a few seconds at a time, but even with the finest adjustment it was no better than locking the wheel of a car straight and expecting it to stay on the road.

I took a long curved swing towards East Cape, keeping shelter holes handy, but the same windless weather mocked me all the way, the sluggish air often only a couple of knots shy of enough to use the vane.

Around the cape itself there was plenty of wind. Twenty-five knots, dead astern. I somehow found the energy to pole out the genoa, lifting speed, making as much progress as I could. I left steering to the wind vane, setting the alarm clock for twenty-minute sleeps. Even that wasn't safe; I woke up once to find that I was heading back north.

And the coastal shipping was concentrated around the cape. Another heart-thumping waking, I found a tanker slipping by a couple of hundred metres off. Every year, yachts vanish at sea. There are enough stories of near misses to indicate that many are run down by ships on automatic pilot, whose crew never know that it's happened.

From then on I took just ten-minute naps. *Canterbury Express* passed, bound for Auckland from Lyttelton. *Taiko* went the other way. I had a quick chat with them, but it was only a passing distraction. Dolphins helped in the early hours. I played 'Lonesome Boatman' as they plaited long ribbons of phosphorescence behind them.

I got personal with *Alderman,* talking to her constantly. I also got back to calling the engine Frankie and the wind steer Johnny and I got chatty in the log, jotting down opinions as well as facts.

Life revolved around the skeds. I had never been out of the sight of other humans for so long. On Kerikeri's sked, John moved me up to the front of the call list so I could minimise the time I had to spend below. At night I anticipated the contact with Ian and Glenys Duff so strongly it was like a countdown that started two hours earlier.

As the Wairarapa coast drew closer I became more apprehensive. The thought of being hit by another similar storm made me desperate to be in better shape to handle it. So I pulled into Gisborne, tied up alongside the local dredge and slept for twelve hours. No more than that. I wrote in the log just before leaving:

Away south. Forecast NW dying, some southerly but outlook NE. Slow-moving front forecast for Cook Strait... best to go now. A bit chancy but I'm counting on it dying with a whimper.

I had just pulled in the lines and engaged Frankie when a man appeared on the dredge, holding a bag the size of a couple of large cushions.

"Catch!" he called, but we were still just close enough for him to pass it across. It was full of Hawke's Bay oranges and grapefruit straight off the trees. I called out my thanks, my spirits lifted by the gesture. I looked back at him several times on the way out of the harbour. Either exhaustion or being alone was making me more emotional. And, in spite of the rest, I was making petty but stupid mistakes in judgement. Hitting my head on the boom, dropping the coffee, trying to do a sked on the wrong frequency. I took extra care to get out of the Gisborne shallows safely.

"We've got a surprise for you," Ian said on the night sked. *"Just a moment."*

After a pause, another voice came through.

"Hello, darling! Glad to hear you've had a rest, over."

I had never heard Sue's voice on long range before. It was distorted almost beyond recognition. But it had to be her. A wave of emotion fell over me, bringing tears.

"Hello. It's so good to hear your voice, over!"

"Likewise. I'm out at the Duff's place because it's our anniversary today. You've been married thirteen years, over."

"Who to?" I said, which surely sets a record for knuckles-on-the-deck stupidity. Long-range radio on four megacycles has an audience spread over more than a million square miles.

"Hah! Where are my flowers then?"

Windflowers. They should have been in the answer, but my synapses were damp.

They were still damp when it came to a decision about the Wairarapa coast. Kerikeri forecast northerly, Wellington gave me southeast. Southeast. If that was correct, the Wairarapa would become a lee shore. And the westerly front approaching Cook Strait had shown no signs of weakening. I allowed my abject fear of that coast to drive me to the shallows near Napier for another overnight rest. In the morning I checked again with Ian. No more southeast outlook, the westerly front was still around, but almost stationary.

"I'm on my way," I said. "It might not get better." He agreed.

The Wairarapa coast was absolutely calm.

No wind, no seas, not even any ripples, just the longest and lowest of swells from the Southern Ocean. I kept in tight to the coast, in case the nor'wester came howling over the hills. But there were no telltale clouds. The colour of the cliffs reflected in the water. I kept looking about me, not quite believing the contrast with the way it had treated us five months earlier.

I motored, stark naked, steering with my foot, basking in the warmth and dipping into the bag of oranges and grapefruit. Recipe: *Cut a Hawke's Bay orange in half, hold it over the side and over a glass and squeeze. Drop the squeezed fruit and watch it bob away. Repeat the action with a grapefruit. Strain the contents of the glass with your fingers. Drink deep.*

That night, I dreamed as I nodded over the tiller: there were people at the bottom of my garden, people I had seen before. They were building themselves a house from odds and ends lying in the garden. Every time I looked at it the house got more and more impressive and every time I saw the people I liked them better. They had a spark to them, and strength and creativity. I thought of charging them rent, but didn't. One day I was embarrassed to find myself in their house without asking permission. But then everything began to look familiar and I suddenly realised I didn't need to knock after all.

There had to be a gale of course. It waited, sniggering, in Cook Strait and the bastard rushed me off Cape Palliser.

Maybe that one was self-inflicted. Unknown to me, Radio Wellington had been monitoring my progress south. An hour before the Strait, when the gale looked inevitable, the duty operator called me up. Did I know about a bolt-hole called White Rock, about five miles up the coast from Palliser? I didn't. He pointed out that it was the best available, but hardly ideal. The nor'westers tended to funnel over the hill at that point.

That was enough for me. I turned it down. I'd seen nor'west gales funnelling down valleys. You don't see water, just a white maelstrom. So I came south of Palliser, well east, set Johnny, and dropped or rolled up every bit of sail except the stays'l and set the running back stays.

Having turned down a bolt-hole didn't stop me complaining to John in Kerikeri, who had predicted something less strenuous than a gale.

"I've got fifty knots nor'west here John, over."

"Oh, yes," John said cheerfully. "Well that's Cook Strait for you. They have their own private parties down there."

It's not unknown to throw up at a party. I'd had calm weather for many days now, so I had to go through it all again. The headaches turned up at the worst possible time, the blankets of pain were suffocating when I needed to be at my best. I started to fantasize going into the workshop and putting my head in the vice to balance up the pressure. Which would be better? Sideways? Or fore and aft? I was losing my grip and that led me to another mistake. I looked for a strong pain-killer, chose something I didn't know, and took too many.

In an hour I was really ill.

When the wind gusted higher than fifty knots I knew I should be bare-poling. The stays'l would have to come down. But it was enough trouble just having a piss, which involved kneeling on the cockpit floor with my chest on the seat. I decided that the stays'l could bloody well blowout - I couldn't do anything about it.

So fourteen tons of heavy-dispacement steel bolted across Cook Strait at ten knots under a piece of cloth that's hardly the size of a bedsheet. It didn't blow out. I lay in a stupor on the leeward seat, focusing on just one thing - the energy needed to get up and look around every ten minutes.

Opposite the Kaikoura Mountains the nor'wester and the pain both started to ease. I changed course directly for Lyttelton and called Kerikeri to thank them for everything they had done. I said I would be OK keeping in touch with the Duffs, but John insisted on keeping an ear on me right through.

There's nothing more in *Alderman's* log.

It took all of the following day, a Sunday, to reach Lyttelton Heads. In the early evening there was no other traffic about, except for one lone yacht motoring towards me. Sinclair and Carol's boat *Sea Lark*.

My heart climbed into my throat when I saw that Sue and the boys were on board, waving frantically. They circled and came round the stern while I took down sail. I wanted to jump the space and gather them up in my arms. Sue held up a banner with an echo of Lino: 'Welcome home, You did good, you did great.' Sinclair and Carol grinned from their cockpit. And back at the wharf our friends and family were there as they had been 170 days and 5,000 miles ago.

Sue, Andrew and Sam. The banner says, Welcome Home.
Then, half an hour later, the best of family reunions - which went,
in poet/songwriter Leonard Cohen's famous words,
'a thousand kisses deep'.

35

None of the four of us is the same person that started out at the beginning. The original advice was right when it said that the sea life changes you. That was especially right about the boys. When we compare the before and after photographs there's only a resemblance.

Andrew's ambition now is to join the Air Force. He also wants to be a road-cycling champion. He's made up a curriculum vitae and intends dropping it into local shopkeepers until one of them gives him a job so he can buy a racing bike. Under 'Reliability' his CV says *I feel I am a reliable person and very capable*.

He is. He can use us as referees.

He never did find out if Ellen got his letter. There's another girl now, but he can't bring himself to declare his feelings. His knees go wobbly when he thinks about it. Adrian Mole no longer has all the answers.

Both boys are happy to be back at school. The first signs are that they have not lost academically by their time away. Their purpose seems stronger in whatever they do. Maybe it's just because they're older, it's hard to tell, but I don't think so. Both of them won a school swimming race today.

Sam is going through an angry-young-man phase at the moment. That concerns us, because we remember the pressure we put him under. I like to think there's no connection but I can't be sure. He has learned a little humility, but only with adults and usually only as a matter of convenience. He orders his friends about imperiously and they take it. On the other hand, he's come back thirsty for knowledge and loves to be quizzed. He asks specifically for general knowledge questions and both boys lap up the daily over-the-cereals discussion of a newspaper article.

But then the same boys who adapted to the perils of the sea now want to be driven to school which is barely more than 100 metres away from the gate. And both have their noses back on the television screen when we let them; that monster which a famous New Zealand expatriate rightly called 'the cretiniser'.

The family teamwork is not as tight and reliable as it was in times of danger, a casualty of so much safety and security. But then we know it would take very little to tweak it back to full strength.

Andrew had his own no good, horrible, very bad day this week and Sam withdrew two dollars from his minuscule bank account to buy him a sherbet.

It's said that if couples go cruising together, the bond will either completely dissolve or strengthen immeasurably. Sue and I haven't noticed anything coming unglued. Like the boys, we've both returned independently more confident. Sue plans to put a talent of hers to work re-designing houses. I'll join her on the logistics side. I'm also going to develop what I started before I left: media consultancy and teaching public speaking and media skills.

We're asked these questions more than any other:

If you knew, way back at the start, what you were letting yourself in for, would you have left port?

"Yes," I say.

"Yes," Sue says.

Are you aiming for another voyage?

"I'm thinking about it," I say.

"No. No more passages," Sue says. "And as for looking after children in a storm at sea, never again." She smiles. "But I would be willing to go to the destinations on kerosene sails at 35,000 feet and cheer *Alderman* as she comes in."

Was it all worth it?

Ahah! For that question, Sue and I imagine going back in time, to when we went for the walk that began it all. We stop under the same street lamp and look at each other.

Was it worth it?

"Snap," we both say.

As for *Alderman*, no one asks her anything. She's sitting down at the marina on the full tide, stirring a little, waiting for her next adventure.

GLOSSARY OF NAUTICAL TERMS

abeam	Out to the side of the vessel.
aft	Towards the rear.
bear away	Turn the vessel away from the direction the wind is coming from.
bilges	The lowest internal part of the boat – collects leaking water, diesel or oil. And smells.
blocks	Pulleys.
bollard	Wood or metal post for securing mooring lines.
bombie	Coral 'head'. For wrecking yachts.
boom	Horizontal pole at the bottom of the mainsail.
bosun's chair	Seat used to haul terrified crew up the mast.
bowline	One of the most useful of marine knots.
bowsprit	An extension to the vessel forward of the bow, usually to hold stays. Very long on *Alderman*.
brig	Prison on a vessel.
broach	Turn side on to the waves. A guarantee of sea-sickness. Dangerous in big seas.
centreboard	A flat plate, sometimes literally a board, that drops below the keel reducing sideways drift.
cleat	Fastening for a rope.
coaming	A barrier to keep the water out from the deck or cockpit.
companionway	Steps leading from one level to another.
cockpit	Seating area around the steering wheel. In rough seas, a cold-water spa.
Coruba seat	Seat up over the stern, supposedly for drinking rum. Not much chance of that on passage.
CQR	Type of anchor.
dead reckoning	Fixing an estimated position ahead, based on present conditions.
deep-reef	To reef down to the smallest area of sail.
doghouse	Raised portion of a ship's deck. Usually added to improve headroom below or as shelter.
doldrums	An area with no wind. A rare condition on this journey!
downwind	The direction the wind is going.
fender	Pads put over the side to soften impact with another object.
for'd	Forward towards the bow.
forestay	Forward stay (see stay).

furler	Sail that rolls up round the stay.
futtocks	Platform high up the mast.
gaff	Pole with large hook for hauling fish aboard.
galley	Kitchen.
genoa	Biggest forward sail except for spinnaker.
gimballed	Mounted on pivots to stay upright while the vessel rolls.
GPS	Global Positioning System. Fixes position using signals from satellites.
gybe	Allow the mainsail to be caught by wind from astern and flipped across to the other side.
gybe preventer	Device that prevents an unintentional and possibly disastrous gybe.
halyard	Rope and/or wire that hauls up a sail.
hard on wind	Sails in tight, the vessel pointing as close as possible to where the wind is coming from.
hatch	Cover over opening to deck. On *Alderman,* made of clear perspex to light the interior.
head	Toilet.
hove-to	At a halt with storm sails set for drifting sideways in a controlled manner. Tiller or wheel is usually lashed.
jack stay	Line lying along deck for attaching safety harnesses.
leading lights	Two lights on land in different places. When in line with them the vessel is in a safe channel.
lee or leeward	On the downwind side of the vessel.
lifeline (rail)	Lines around edge of deck to stop people falling overboard.
log	Two meanings: 1. Book for recording important day-to-day events on board. 2. Instrument that measures speed.
main	Mainsail.
masthead	Top of the mast.
miles	Always means nautical miles. 1 Nm = 1.25 land miles.
monkey's fist	Heavy weight for throwing a line across the water.
offshore	Ocean passage as opposed to a coastal trip.
on the wind	Pointing the vessel as close as possible to where the wind is coming from.
painter	Rope on the bow of a dinghy for tying up.
pick	A type of anchor.
pooped	Filled up by a wave breaking over the stern.
port	On the left when facing the bow.
quarter	Out somewhere between the side and behind the vessel.
ratlines	Rope (or wire) ladder from deck up mast.

reach	Sailing with the wind coming from the side, or from the side and behind. It's the fastest point of sail.
reef down	Pull sail partly down, reducing area exposed to the wind.
RT	Radio telephone.
rubbing strip	External rib on both sides of the hull to protect from collisions.
sea cock	Valve that opens or closes at hull, e.g. for toilet or basin.
seas	Irregular waves (see swell).
sheet	Rope (not sail).
sked	Another way of saying schedule, usually referring to the time for a two-way radio contact.
snub	Place rope into the top end of an anchor chain, putting 'give' into the line.
spreaders	Cross pieces on the mast to hold the stays out.
spreader lights	For illuminating the deck.
SSB	Long range radio.
starboard	On the right when facing the bow. Starb'd for short.
staunchion	Short vertical pole to hold up lifelines.
stay	Wire that holds up the mast.
stays'l (staysail)	Small sail just forward of the mast.
storm drogue	Acts like a small parachute in the water, slowing the vessel down.
swell	Regular undulating waves (see seas).
tack	Describes which side of the vessel is presented to the wind.
tiller	Steering arm attached to the rudder.
topping lift	A rope that holds up the end of the boom.
transom	Far back end wall of vessel.
trim tab	Mini rudder on the back of the main rudder.
troll	Fish by towing a hook behind a vessel. Considered cheating by fishing purists.
upwind	Towards where the wind is coming from.
VHF	Short range radio (about fifty miles).
watch	Rostered time on duty at the helm.
way point	In navigation, a place on the anticipated track of the vessel.
weather cloth	Cloth round the stern protecting the cockpit from wind and waves.
westing	Angling west to take advantage of anticipated westerly winds.
winch	Turning drum that winds up a rope.
wind steer	Automatic steering system driven from a small wind vane.
windward	Out to the side of the vessel that is presented to the wind.

Many thanks

It took more than the log and the family's memory to write down what happened. It was so valuable to be able to compare notes with friends like Aileen and Dave McDonald, Dave (Davey) Vincent, Lester Parkes and Sinclair George, who were with us on different passages. Then there was all the advice, help and support they gave the four of us at the beginning when we knew next to nothing. To all of them, we are more grateful than we can express.

Thank you to Geoff Stone, who not only sold us the wonderful craft *Alderman,* but was always willing to give advice when asked. This greenhorn did lots of asking.

And how can we possibly express enough gratitude to all the wonderful cruising sailors we met? Not only did you give us ten thousand sailing lessons just by talking, you gave us friendship and showed us a way of life that's full beyond compare. We can't even begin to list your names, but the chances are that if we exchanged more than greetings you're here. Of course these pages contain only fragments of you - Sue and I know they can't do you justice – but we truly hope you'll enjoy them anyway.

As an obsessed yachtie once said to me in Lyttelton, "I like cruising people. They're into life."

Printed in Great Britain
by Amazon.co.uk, Ltd.,
Marston Gate.